W9-BUP-778

CHURCHILL'S
SHADOW RAIDERS

CHURCHILL'S
SHADOW RAIDERS

THE RACE TO DEVELOP RADAR,
WWII'S INVISIBLE SECRET WEAPON

Damien Lewis

CITADEL PRESS
Kensington Publishing Corp.
www.kensingtonbooks.com

CITADEL PRESS BOOKS are published by

Kensington Publishing Corp.
119 West 40th Street
New York, NY 10018

First published in Great Britain by Quercus Editions Ltd., an Hachette UK company,
under the title *SAS Shadow Raiders*.

All Kensington titles, imprints, and distributed lines are available at special quantity
discounts for bulk purchases for sales promotions, premiums, fund-raising, educational,
or institutional use. Special book excerpts or customized printings can also be created to
fit specific needs. For details, write or phone the office of the Kensington sales manager:
Kensington Publishing Corp., 119 West 40th Street, New York, NY 10018, attn: Sales
Department; phone 1-800-221-2647.

ISBN-13: 978-0-8065-4063-4
ISBN-10: 0-8065-4063-X

First Citadel hardcover printing: May 2020

10 9 8 7 6 5 4 3 2 1

Printed in the United States of America

Library of Congress Control Number: 2019951386

Electronic edition:

ISBN-13: 978-0-8065-4065-8 (e-book)
ISBN-10: 0-8065-4-65-6 (e-book)

For Paul, Sophie, Lorna & Samantha
With heartfelt thanks

Invictus

Out of the night that covers me,
Black as the pit from pole to pole,
I thank whatever gods may be
For my unconquerable soul.

In the fell clutch of circumstance
I have not winced nor cried aloud.
Under the bludgeonings of chance
My head is bloody, but unbowed.

Beyond this place of wrath and tears
Looms but the Horror of the shade,
And yet the menace of the years
Finds and shall find me unafraid.

It matters not how strait the gate,
How charged with punishments the scroll,
I am the master of my fate,
I am the captain of my soul.

William Ernest Henley

'It is not the critic who counts; not the man who points out how the strong man stumbles, or where the doer of deeds could have done them better. The credit belongs to the man who is actually in the arena, whose face is marred by dust and sweat and blood; who strives valiantly; who errs, who comes short again and again, because there is no effort without error and shortcoming; but who does actually strive to do the deeds; who knows great enthusiasms, the great devotions; who spends himself in a worthy cause; who at the best knows in the end the triumph of high achievement, and who at the worst, if he fails, at least fails while daring greatly, so that his place shall never be with those cold and timid souls who neither know victory nor defeat.'

Theodore Roosevelt, 23 April 1910, Sorbonne, France

Contents

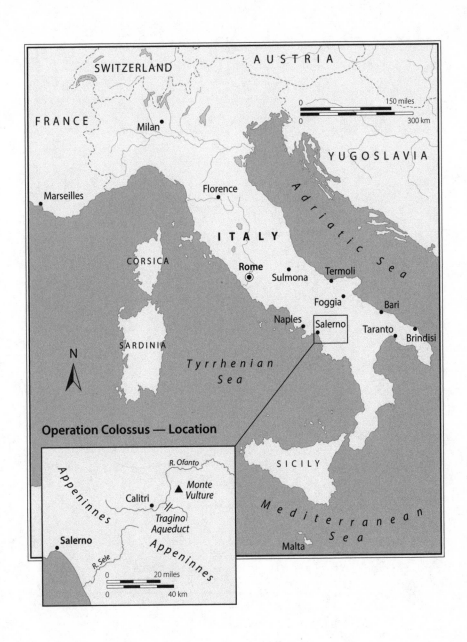

Operation Colossus — Location

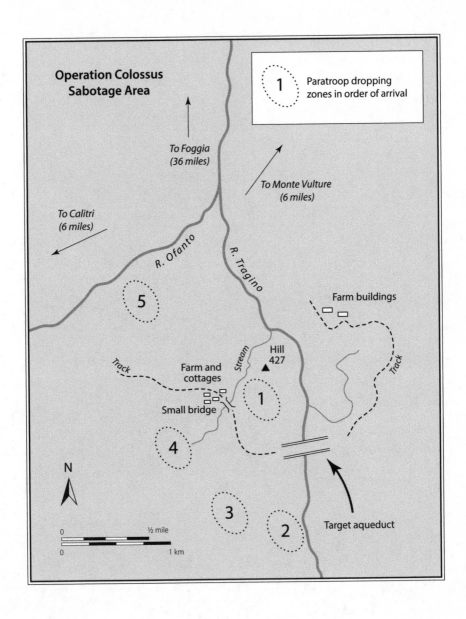

Operation Colossus Sabotage Area

1 Paratroop dropping zones in order of arrival

To Foggia
(36 miles)

To Monte Vulture
(6 miles)

To Calitri
(6 miles)

R. Ofanto

R. Tragino

5

Farm buildings

Track

Stream

Hill
427

Farm and
cottages

Track

1

Small bridge

4

N

0   ½ mile
0   1 km

3

2

Target aqueduct

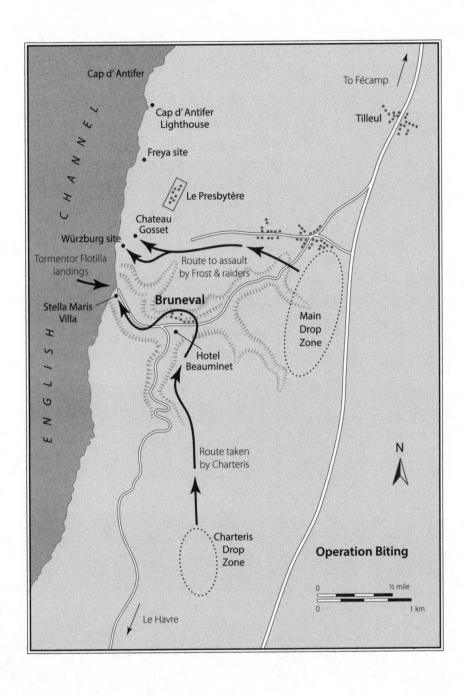

Cap d' Antifer

CHANNEL

Cap d' Antifer
Lighthouse

Freya site

Le Presbytère

Chateau
Gosset

Würzburg site

Tormentor Flotilla
landings

Stella Maris
Villa

ENGLISH

To Fécamp

Tilleul

Route to assault
by Frost & raiders

Bruneval

Main
Drop
Zone

Hotel
Beauminet

Route taken
by Charteris

Charteris
Drop
Zone

Le Havre

N

Operation Biting

0   ½ mile
0   1 km

Author's Note

There are sadly few survivors from the Second World War operations depicted in these pages. Throughout the period researching and writing this book I have endeavoured to be in contact with as many as possible, plus surviving family members of those who have passed away. If there are further witnesses to the stories told here who are inclined to come forward, please do get in touch, as I will endeavour to include further recollections of the operations portrayed in this book in future editions.

The time spent by Allied servicemen and women as Special Service volunteers was often traumatic and wreathed in layers of secrecy, and many chose to take their stories to their graves. Memories tend to differ and apparently none more so than those concerning operations behind enemy lines. The written accounts that do exist can tend to differ in their detail and timescale, and locations and chronologies are sometimes contradictory. I have endeavoured to provide an accurate sense of place, timescale and narrative to the story as depicted in these pages.

Where various accounts of a mission appear to be particularly confused, the methodology I have used to reconstruct where, when and how events took place is the 'most likely' scenario. If two or more testimonies or sources point to a particular time or place or sequence of events, I have opted to use that account as most likely.

The above notwithstanding, any mistakes herein are entirely of my own making, and I would be happy to correct any in future editions. Likewise, while I have endeavoured to locate the copyright holders of the photos, sketches and other images and material used in this book, this has not always been straightforward or easy. Again, I would be happy to correct any mistakes in future editions.

I have chosen the title *SAS Shadow Raiders* for this book, because that is the unit from which the first operation, and that which followed, sprang. Of course, other units – the nascent Parachute Regiment, the RAF, Royal Navy and Britain's scientists – played key roles, and that is not to detract from their contribution to this vital and little-told piece of wartime history.

One final note: 'radar' is an American-derived term, one that came into usage towards the end of the Second World War. For much of the war the British used the term 'RDF' – short for Radio Direction Finding, the Germans the term *Dezimeter Telegraphie* (DF). Radar was a useful, palindromic word that tripped more easily off the tongue. It stood for – and stands for – *RA*dio *D*etection *A*nd *R*anging. It fell into common usage, and is the term I have used throughout this book.

Preface

In the summer of 2018 I was invited to speak at the Malvern Festival of Military History. After the event, I was approached by an individual from the Malvern Radar and Technology History Society (MRATHS), perhaps not a name that trips too easily off the tongue. Mike Burstow proved personable and hugely enthused by his subject, and particularly about the Radar War, which played such a pivotal role in the Second World War.

He suggested it was something I probably would not know much about, as it had been so little publicized, at least in the popular media, but which constituted an utterly gripping tale of scientific genius, skulduggery, derring-do, bluff and deception. As it happened, I'd long been fascinated by the Bruneval Raid, or Operation Biting as it was codenamed at the time – a smash-and-grab mission by a few score men to seize a piece of war-winning Nazi technology, the Wehrmacht's mysterious 'paraboloid' radar.

My interest in the story quickened when Mike explained that his charity, MRATHS, had rescued for posterity the entire archive – or what remained of it from the Second World War – of Britain's foremost radar research establishment, known as the Telecommunications Research Establishment, or TRE for short. TRE had been at the very heart of defeating Nazi Germany's radar and other vital technologies, and boffins from TRE had played some daredevil roles – including on D-Day, when they landed at Omaha and Gold beaches. A TRE scientist had even formed a part of the assault party deployed in February 1942, on Op Biting, to snatch the enemy's prized radar.

Mike offered me access to that archive, one that even at the time of writing is still being catalogued and assessed. It consists of tens of thousands of documents, photographs and examples of the technology itself, most of which had been languishing in abandoned buildings, about to be destroyed, when a handful of former military technology boffins, including Mike and the archivist, Hugh Williams, discovered it all and realized the need to save it for posterity.

They'd formed MRATHS, rescued the material, and the rest as they say is history. Via their archive, and the kind attentions and guiding hand of Mike and his team, I was drawn ever deeper into the Bruneval raid and the wider Radar War. The riveting story that unfolds in these pages is the result. But in researching this, I came across something equally spectacular, equally untold.

Being an airborne raid, Operation Biting is generally seen as the first battle honour for Britain's Parachute Regiment. But the forerunner to Biting, the first ever airborne raid by Allied forces, provides a powerful prelude to the mission to snatch Nazi Germany's radar. For the first years of the war, our fledgling airborne forces had to fight tooth and nail for recruits, resources and airframes, and to get assigned missions. Assailed on all sides by naysayers, doubters and detractors, they would not have succeeded without Winston Churchill's dogged backing.

The first ever Allied airborne mission, codenamed Colossus, was launched in February 1941 and was described in official records as a 'disaster'. Not a man returned from the operation: all went 'into the bag'. An extraordinary undertaking by anyone's reckoning, a few dozen very brave men had been dispatched into the heart of Europe on a raid of breathtaking proportions. But my research – thankfully, much documentation on Colossus has survived in the various archives – suggests that it was far from being the disaster portrayed. Indeed, Colossus was the foundation stone from which Biting was launched.

What struck me as fascinating about Colossus is that it was undertaken by a unit known as the Special Air Service, almost a year before David Stirling 'founded' the SAS in the North African desert, in the winter of 1941. Moreover, when Stirling came up with his idea for a desert raiding force, he was advised by Colonel Dudley Clarke, one of the founding fathers of Britain's special forces, to take on the mantle and legacy of those who had gone before, by naming his new outfit, after them, the Special Air Service.

In the days after Dunkirk, Clarke had founded the Commandos – units charged to take the fight to the victorious enemy at Britain's darkest hour. With Churchill's visionary backing, just weeks after Dunkirk the first boatloads of Clarke's Commandos raided the coast of Nazi-occupied France. All Clarke's recruits were volunteers and he referred to them as the 'Special Service'. When, at Churchill's urging, Clarke raised a battalion of airborne Commandos, he inserted the word 'Air' into that name, so at a stroke they became the 'Special Air Service.'

These, then, were the men who undertook Operation Colossus. These early Special Air Service recruits, and the training they pioneered, plus the incredible operation they undertook, represent the precursor to the SAS proper; an extraordinary 'origins story' for how The Regiment came into being. Discovering this rich chapter of untold SAS history, one that reaches back into the summer of 1940, when recruitment and training for Clarke's SAS first began, has been hugely exciting. It extends the history of the SAS regiment back into the earliest chapters of the war proper, after Nazi Germany's lightning advance through Western Europe had put an abrupt end to the so-called Phoney War.

In one way, that this prequel to the SAS story has remained untold for so long is remarkable. But actually, regimental history is not always the strong point of special forces units – and especially not those which, as happened with the SAS and SBS, were summarily disbanded at war's end (and not reformed until the 1950s). Reclaiming this legacy, the SAS origins story, has been a huge privilege and one that I have been thrilled to pursue as I have.

In that spirit, let me take you to a fleet of ageing Whitley bombers clawing through the dark skies over Nazi-occupied Europe, in February 1941.

Damien Lewis
Dorset, May 2019

Chapter 1

The six men were wedged into the aircraft's narrow hold like the proverbial sardines in a tin. No one ever had parachuting in mind when designing the Armstrong Whitworth Whitley, a medium night-bomber nicknamed the 'Flying Barn Door', due to the square, hard-edged – some might argue downright ugly – appearance of the warplane, with its large, angular wings.

Aerodynamic the Whitley was not. Obsolete by the start of the war, by now – 10 February 1941 – the aircraft was increasingly being withdrawn from frontline service. Oddly, airborne operations somehow fell into that category – non-frontline duties – even when, like now, these troops were preparing to parachute some six hundred miles *behind* enemy lines.

Being one of the earliest airborne recruits, Major Trevor Alan Gordon Pritchard – a long-serving volunteer with 11 Special Air Service – was resigned to the several hours of cramped, freezing conditions that lay ahead, riding the Flying Barn Door. A rare bonus were the inflatable Li-Los – rubber mattresses – with which his men had been issued, to insulate themselves from the cold metal of the fuselage, as they sat nose-to-tail, their backs pressed against one side, their boots jammed against the other.

From the initials of his first three names – Trevor Alan Gordon – the men had coined the nickname 'Tag' for their commander, but it was never one they'd use to his face. Several of Pritchard's officers were on first-name terms with their men, in keeping with the informal, egalitarian nature of their unit. But Pritchard, a ten-year Army veteran and a tough-as-old-boots regular, was only ever going to be addressed as 'Sir' by those under his command.

The product of a typically robust British public-school education, Pritchard had been commissioned into the Royal Welch Fusiliers – an infantry regiment with two-and-a-half centuries of history behind it – but had hungered for more action. In the summer of 1940 Winston Churchill had called for the formation of 'troops of the hunter class', to foment 'a reign of terror down the enemy coast'. Pritchard had answered Churchill's call, signing up as one of the earliest volunteers. Tonight's mission was all about making Churchill's urgings a reality, striking further and harder than had ever been done before.

Tag Pritchard was square-faced, with prominent eyebrows and a solid, level gaze. There was a no-nonsense look about him. An Army heavyweight boxing champion, those who had tried to go twelve rounds in the ring with him had learned to their cost that he didn't take prisoners. In uniform, he was known as a quiet, somewhat gruff leader; a man of few words, but when he spoke others tended to listen. Out of uniform, he had the one surprising quirk: he was never to be seen without a monocle – a single eye-glass – attached to a long black ribbon. Never one to cuss, Pritchard was known to be fiercely loyal. He was a leader who commanded respect, not one who sought out friendship or affirmation.

Via his earphones, Pritchard listened in on the chat, as the pilot of his Whitley, Wing Commander J. B. 'Willie' Tait, chatted to his crew. While the aircraft was hardly state-of-the-art, Pritchard could have no greater confidence in those flying her.

Tait had already won a Distinguished Flying Cross (DFC) for the long-range bombing sorties he'd executed over Berlin, rising to command 51 Squadron RAF, the unit tasked to deliver Pritchard and his raiders to target.

The sun was setting over the island of Malta – Britain's besieged Mediterranean outpost, lying fifty miles off the coast of southern Italy – as Tait and his crew prepared to get airborne, running through their flight-checks with the calm thoroughness that Pritchard had come to expect. On tonight's mission Tait would earn for himself a Distinguished Service Order (DSO), and by war's end he'd have won that decoration three times over, plus the DFC twice, making him one of the RAF's most decorated pilots.

But all of that lay sometime in the future. Tonight, Tait was leading a flight of eight Whitleys packed full of would-be parachutists – plus their loads of weaponry and explosives – into the untested and the unknown. Their mission was fittingly code-named Operation Colossus, after the ancient mythical god that bestrode the world: it was to be the first ever British airborne raid, no Allied parachutists having ever flown into combat before. As firsts went, Colossus was one hell of an ambitious and daring undertaking, especially when launched from aircraft such as these.

Due to a design quirk, the Whitley flew with a pronounced nose-down attitude, making the hold pitch at a bizarre angle, like the deck of some storm-tossed ship. With no viable side-door, the only means for the men to exit was via a dark, narrow hole sunk into the floor of the fuselage. Under normal conditions, that hole would have contained a ventral gun-turret, one from which one of the Whitley's crew could unleash fire. But in winter 1940/41, desperate times called for desperate measures. With no other planes available to raise Britain's fledgling airborne forces, the Whitley's gun-turret had been removed and replaced with a round dustbin-like jump tube.

Leaping through it was not without its dangers, so much so that those who were forced to train on the Whitley had come to refer to the aircraft as the 'Flying Coffin'. Jumping with too much enthusiasm risked smashing one's head against the far side of the hole, nicknamed – with typical fatalism – the 'Whitley kiss'. Conversely, leaping with too little vigour risked the paratrooper getting jammed in the hole, complete with all his airborne and combat paraphernalia. The Whitley was known as 'The Elephant' by those who were forced to jump from her, the hole via which they exited earning a very obvious associated nickname.

But as Wing Commander Tait brought the Whitley's twin Rolls-Royce Merlin engines up to speed, readying the aircraft for take-off, Pritchard felt a certain sense of confidence. He was com-manding a force of thirty-six men, some of the British Army's finest, deemed 'capable of the greatest bodily and mental strain'. Of the thousands who had stepped forward to answer Churchill's call, less than 5 per cent had made it through to the Commandos and associated outfits, including No. 11 Special Air Service.

From that elite group, Major Pritchard had had the luxury of hand-picking his team. He'd done so in a manner designed to foster the independence and self-reliance for which such outfits were becoming famed: he'd selected five junior officers, each of whom was allowed to pick his best operators in turn. All had to be volunteers.

In early January 1941 the 450 men of 11 SAS had been called on parade. An operation was being planned with 'the intention of penetrating deep into enemy territory', they were told. It was 'top-secret' and they were honour-bound 'not to speak a word of it to anyone'. The chances of coming out alive were slim, and any captured might well be shot as spies. Those who wished to volunteer were asked to take one step forwards. Every officer and man did just that, as if in one smooth movement. It spoke volumes about 11 SAS and the incredible esprit de corps that had been fostered.

A period of intensive training had followed, as from those several hundred volunteers Pritchard's cadre of raiders – codenamed X Troop – had taken shape and been formed. Despite the icy conditions, the average day began with pre-dawn PT, daily runs, and fifteen-mile fast marches under full loads of kit. Nights were occupied with shooting practice using the kind of weapons the raiders would take into action: the Colt automatic – 'Browning' – handgun, plus the iconic 'Tommy Gun', the favoured weapon for Allied special forces.

Although it was a twenty-year-old design, the American-made Thompson sub-machinegun was famed for its reliability and its pure grunt and punch. Synonymous with gangsters and the mafia, it had earned various nicknames – 'The Annihilator', the 'Chicago Piano', the 'Chopper' and the 'Trench Sweeper'. Fitted with a 30-round stick magazine, or a 50-round drum, it spewed out its heavy, .45 calibre rounds at over 800 per minute. It wasn't lightweight and it wasn't particularly accurate at over 150 yards, but at close quarters it was lethal.

Specialists drew up a diet to maximize stamina and build up reserves of energy. Bespoke rations were manufactured for the first Allied airborne raiders to take into battle. They included slabs of 'pemmican', a concentrated mixture of meat fat and protein, which could be boiled in water to make a thick, sludgy 'porridge'. Pioneered as a food for Polar explorers, each raider was to carry two pounds of pemmican per day, the standard cold-climate ration.

Once the X Troopers had exhausted the opportunities at their para-training school, they were shipped north to the Scottish Highlands. There, the Lovat Scouts had put them through a course of Irregular Warfare, based at a country house a few miles from Fort William, on the rugged western coast. Formed during the Boer War in South Africa, the Lovat Scouts had drawn recruits from the gamekeepers of the Highland Estates. Experts in fieldcraft, survival and mountain warfare, their first commander, American Major Frederick Burnham, had described the Scouts as 'half-wolf, half-jackrabbit'.

Their official motto was 'Je suis prest' – an archaic spelling of the French for 'I am ready'. The unofficial motto coined by Burnham was: 'He who shoots and runs away, lives to shoot another day.' The British Army's first ever snipers – or 'sharp-shooters' as they were then called – Lovat Scouts had served in the First World War with distinction. The Scottish Highlands were not too dissimilar to the kind of terrain that Pritchard's SAS were about to deploy to, and they were there to learn how to fight and survive in such an environment.

On meeting their first Lovat Scout instructor, a grey-haired and gnarled figure, he had announced enigmatically that they'd just 'go for a wee walk together'. Many of the younger SAS men had scoffed. 'Don't worry, Dad,' one of the upstarts quipped, 'we'll wait for you at the top.' When they finally reached the summit of Ben Nevis, that 'father figure' was waiting for them, quietly puffing away on his pipe.

'What kept ye?' he enquired. Then he told them to do it all over again, only quicker this time.

Self-reliance was as crucial as toughness and aggression, for the kind of mission that was coming. The raiders were taught to be happy with only themselves for company in the mountains. 'Fight and survive alone, if you are separated from your mates,' was the order of the day. They were taught to track and kill a wild animal. 'If you can stalk a deer, you can hunt a man,' one veteran Scout told them.

The training was unrelenting. A 'day off' involved just a 'wee run' to the summit of Ben Nevis. Finally, two middle-aged Scotsmen arrived at the camp. One was short and portly, the other tall and beanpole-like and both were dressed in smart suits. They looked like . . . accountants. What on earth were they doing there, the X Troopers wondered?

The two mystery figures introduced themselves as William Fairbairn and Eric Sykes. Appearances can be misleading: they were both former policemen from the tough streets of Shanghai, then an Anglo-American colony. Fairbairn and Sykes taught the skills they'd learned at close quarters in China's largest city: knife-fighting, hand-to-hand combat, and how to wrest a pistol from an assailant before he even had a chance to fire.

They taught to kill using fair means or foul; via the back of the hand; via a matchbox even. Their weapons – knives, pistols – were kept concealed beneath a jacket until the last possible moment, so the enemy had no idea what was coming. 'Remember, gentlemen, go for the ears, eyes or testicles,' was one of their oft-repeated refrains.

The men of X Troop returned to their airborne school feeling invincible. There they learned how to execute night-drops, parachuting under cover of darkness. Training was unrelenting, and one man was to pay the ultimate price. On 22 January Sergeant

Dennis found himself drifting in strong winds towards an ice-covered lake, lying to one side of the landing zone. Despite efforts to avoid it, he cracked into the ice, plunged into freezing water and mud, becoming stuck fast. In spite of being a strong swimmer, he was unable to free himself and drowned before help could reach him.

Operation Colossus had claimed its first victim, and before they'd even got boots on the ground. Shaking off the dark shadow cast by Sergeant Dennis's death, the X Troopers were charged to put on a show for the top brass, to demonstrate just what Britain's airborne forces might be capable of. They were to drop over Salisbury Plain and seize an 'enemy-held position' – in reality a quaint Wiltshire village manned by regular infantry.

Landing barely yards from the observers, the paratroopers were in no mood to waste time, let alone their newly acquired Lovat Scout and Fairbairn-Sykes training. They commandeered a vehicle at knifepoint, which just happened to be a top VIP's limousine, forcing the chauffeur to drive them to the village. Using that as their Trojan Horse, plus a truck in which to hide under a tarpaulin, they surprised the defenders and liberated the village in short order.

The limousine happened to belong to Prince Olaf, the Crown Prince of Norway, who was in Britain to lead the Norwegian Government in exile, acting as a rallying point for the Norwegian resistance. Watching the demonstration along with a score of field marshals and top generals, Prince Olaf had been delighted at the theft of his vehicle, buying the raiders a celebratory round of pints in the village pub.

A few select and trusted journalists had been invited to the demonstration, although they would not be permitted to report on it for some months. One would write: 'Our parachute men are, as might be supposed, of considerable resource, initiative and daring. Some of the men who came down near me were busy "inducing" the driver of Prince Olaf of Norway's car at bayonet point to take them across the country. The men certainly looked pretty tough.'

Just how 'tough' and 'daring' they were was about to be tested in the hostile skies and over the snow-bound mountains of Italy, then the heartland of Fascist Europe. For the mission, two of the eight Whitleys were slated to carry no parachutists. Instead, their bomb racks would be loaded with 7,000 pounds of munitions. They were to fly diversionary raids, hitting targets adjacent to the paratroopers' landing zone. That way, if the fleet of aircraft was heard passing overhead, the enemy should conclude it was simply a bombing raid.

Whitleys had flown bombing missions over Italy before, so the ruse had form. On the night of 11/12 June 1940, just hours after Italy had sided with Nazi Germany, declaring war on Britain, the RAF had mounted Operation Haddock, a fleet of Whitleys bombing the northern cities of Turin and Genoa, via a refuelling stop in the Channel Islands, which at that point still lay in British hands.

As the Whitleys prepared for take-off from their Malta airstrip, Wing Commander Tait testing his engines' thrust against the aircraft's brakes, Major Pritchard tried to make himself as comfortable as possible, straightening his para-smock (then called a 'jumping jacket'), and adjusting the lie of the parachute at his back, but at five-foot-ten and with the broad physique of a rugby player and boxer, it was never going to be easy.

When Pritchard, a real lion of a man, had volunteered for

airborne operations, some had suggested he was too bulky for parachuting. He had gone on to prove them wrong. As with all his men, he would leap through the Whitley's narrow tube unburdened by most of the paraphernalia of war. All he had strapped to his person was a pistol, a Commando knife, a water bottle, and a small backpack containing basic rations. Everything else that he and his men needed for the raid – Bren guns, Tommy guns, grenades, high explosives – was packed into containers held in the Whitley's bomb-racks, to be released by parachute.

There were certain other top-secret devices secreted on Pritchard's person, but they were invisible to even the closest scrutiny. A few days prior to leaving the UK, the raiders' battle tunics had been taken away, so that covert items could be hidden among them. Each man had 50,000 lire – a veritable king's ransom in Italy – sewn into either the collar or the waistband of his tunic, plus the officers were given a fistful of gold sovereigns, so they could buy their passage through any territory no matter what the local currency.

In the seam above the left breast pocket was sewn a tiny, flexible hacksaw blade, and in the lining of the sleeves were hidden two silk escape maps, each a foot square – one showing the northern part of Italy, the other the southern half. Each had a metal collar stud, which, when the white paint was scraped off the underside, would reveal a tiny, but usable, compass.

As the Whitleys began to move, taxiing towards the runway, Pritchard took a firmer grip of his core of inner calm, reflecting upon the naming of their mission: *Operation Colossus*. It was peculiarly appropriate: tonight's raid was, by anyone's reckoning, a colossal undertaking.

He and his men had already journeyed over 1,600 miles, when moving from the UK to their forward operating base, here in Malta. That flight had seemed never-ending, taking all of a long February night to complete, and for the most part they had been moving through enemy airspace – Nazi-occupied France, plus Mussolini's Fascist Italy, which was allied to Nazi Germany, forming the Axis powers, along with Japan.

Menaced by anti-aircraft fire over the French coast, the men had wondered how the German gunners had managed to see the Whitleys in the thick darkness. Did they possess some special means to probe the night sky; a cunning piece of technology that enabled them to pierce the clouds up to their 15,000-foot cruise altitude? Hitler's Germany was known to have mastered fearsome new machines of war, the *blitzkrieg* – 'lightning-war' – tactics of his Stuka dive-bombers and armour being but one such manifestation.

The parachutists' fear had proved momentary – a passing terror – as vicious bursts of flak had thundered in the sky all around, the flashes of the explosions pulsing through the fuselage eerily, throwing the hunched figures into stark relief. The worst thing about being locked into the Whitley's hold was the lack of vision: designed as a bomber, there were few windows or port-holes. To many it was horribly, sickeningly claustrophobic.

Like being confined to a coffin.

Those in the flight cabin could see the licks of flak – flaming snowballs bursting in the night sky to either side and to the front of the aircraft. But then the Whitleys had broken through the barrage of enemy fire, droning onwards across hundreds of miles of enemy airspace. At one stage one of the bombers had been hunted by a Luftwaffe night-fighter, but with its four Browning machine-guns set in the rear turret, the Whitley had managed to beat off its pursuer.

Yet upon arrival at Malta – a hunk of sun-blasted rock surrounded by azure seas – further peril had lain in wait. Britain's island fortress was under siege from the air. Bombs had crashed down among the ranks of Whitleys, the explosions sending jagged shards of shrapnel tearing into the airframes. Fortunately, due to its robust construction, the Whitley was able to take some serious punishment and still remain operational, and the ground crews had managed to repair the worst of the damage.

But air-raid warnings had kept interrupting the frenetic preparations, as the men had raced to get the aircraft airworthy and loaded for the coming mission. 'The risk of damage to Whitley aircraft by hostile action was considerable,' recorded the official report on Colossus, stamped 'MOST SECRET'. Take-off from Malta would have to be made 'at the earliest possible moment'.

X Troop, Pritchard reflected ruefully, was a peculiarly apposite name for his raiding party. But what exactly did the 'X' stand for? X as in 'hush-hush' – beyond top secret? Or 'X' as in 'ex' – a force of men written off as expendables, dispatched into the unknown to attempt something that had never been tried before and was perhaps undoable? Had they been written off, before they'd even got started?

Pritchard couldn't be certain, but he had his suspicions. They'd had a strangely emotional – one might almost say foreboding – send-off, and from none other than the Chief of Combined Operations, the newly formed command that supposedly brought together Army, Air Force and Navy for such special missions, though in reality the three services seemed famously prone to bickering over 'turf' and who was in control.

Admiral Sir Roger Keyes had a legendary reputation, earned during the First World War and his leadership of what had become known as the 'Zeebrugge Raid'. On 23 April 1918, Keyes had masterminded the daring attack on the Belgian harbour of Zeebrugge, scuttling two obsolete ships, HMS *Intrepid* and *Iphigenia*, their hulls filled with concrete, in the narrowest section of the Bruges Canal, part of a German Navy U-boat base, and ramming it with a pair of submarines, each of which was packed with five tonnes of explosives.

Though suffering over five hundred casualties – all the men were volunteers – the raid was hailed as a British victory, and no fewer than eight Victoria Crosses were awarded to those who'd taken part. More recently, on 7 May 1940, dressed in the full uniform of the Admiral of the Fleet, medals included, Keyes had addressed the House of Commons, invoking Horatio Nelson in urging Britain's leaders to dig deep and find the will to fight.

'One hundred and forty years ago, Nelson said, "I am of the opinion that the boldest measures are the safest," and that still holds good today', Keyes had declared combatively.

Two days later Chamberlain's government had fallen, bringing Winston Churchill to power. In his dash and daring and with his unconventional mindset, Keyes was a kindred spirit to Churchill. Like-minded souls, both were convinced that even at Britain's darkest hour, attack was still the best form of defence. Britain needed to hit back at a seemingly omnipotent foe, striking wherever she might be vulnerable. Churchill was a long-time admirer of Keyes, and he was the obvious choice as his commander for special operations.

For Keyes, then aged in his late sixties, Operation Colossus was intensely personal. It represented the culmination of all that he – and Churchill – had hungered for. 'This operation is an ideal one in which to employ a part of the specially-trained parachute force,' he declared. 'Its successful conclusion will have far-reaching effects upon the course of the war, and its effect upon enemy morale will be incalculable.'

Prior to X Troop's departure, Keyes had shaken hands with every man, speaking to each in turn. A die-hard believer in the use of airborne forces to thrust deep into enemy territory, he had appeared unusually sombre and grave. He'd paused the longest at two figures. One, unsurprisingly, was Major Pritchard, the rock around which his raiders might tether their occasionally storm-tossed ships. The other was a last-minute addition to X Troop and a real man of mystery, not to mention a comparatively grizzled and aged warrior.

A forty-something veteran of the First World War, Flight Lieutenant Ralph Lucky was fluent in several languages, including Italian. Hailing from Bisley, a quaint village of Cotswold stone houses in Gloucestershire, he'd spent the inter-war years in the Middle East, though no one knew doing quite what, and he was married to an Egyptian. Few doubted that he hailed from some sneaky-beaky outfit, most likely the Special Operations Executive (SOE) – more commonly known as 'The Ministry For Ungentlemanly Warfare'.

At Churchill's behest, SOE had been founded to do what HMG could not be seen to be doing, and was charged to break every civilized norm and all known rules of war. The global conflict was a 'total war', as far as Churchill saw it, and it would need to be fought no holds barred. SOE agents would need to head deep into enemy lands to raise guerrilla armies, fomenting the spirit of resistance. SOE had a hidden hand in Operation Colossus, and many suspected that 'Flight Lieutenant Lucky' was the SOE's man on the mission.

One of the X Troopers had a particular reason to resent Flight Lieutenant Lucky's last-minute addition to their number. Lance Corporal Harry 'Lucky' Pexton – buck-toothed, tousle-haired – had earned his nickname the hard way, by keeping a smile on his face no matter what. A twenty-three-year-old painter and decorator from Grimsby, Pexton's attitude to his first jump summed up his spirit. Having made a fine landing, he'd turned to his mates and quipped: 'As I stood at that hole waiting to jump, I knew in a flash that by joining this mob I'd made the greatest mistake in my life.'

During training with the Lovat Scouts in Scotland, Lucky Pexton had suffered the misfortune of spraining an ankle near the summit of Ben Nevis. No one was allowed to help him down again. He was told he'd have to crawl back to camp if need be. Pexton knew the military drivers in the area were forbidden from giving lifts to any troops. 'To hell with that!' he told himself. Cheekily, he'd flagged down a passing truck and managed to cadge a ride back to camp.

Lucky Pexton resented another 'Lucky' joining their elite number, and especially if that man's 'name' had been earned the easy way, as a cloak-and-dagger cover. 'I'm the lucky one,' he insisted. 'If "Lucky" is that man's real name then I'm a Dutchman. Who could possibly have a name like that?' It was funny how the tables had been turned: always-cheerful and always-lucky Pexton getting fuming mad, because a usurper had stolen his nickname.

By contrast to Flight Lieutenant Lucky's mature years, most of the raiders were in their early twenties or younger. The 'baby', Trooper Alan Ross, was just nineteen and ever since he could remember he'd been 'Army mad', being a voracious reader of war books. As soon as Britain had declared war on Germany, he'd resigned from his trainee salesman's job and volunteered for Special Service, his keenness trumping his obvious youth.

In July 1940, a batch of raw recruits had had to make their first jump. 'It's as easy as falling out of bed,' the instructor had enthused. As the pilot had throttled back his engines, it was Trooper Ross who'd taken pole position, legs dangling into the void. At the word 'Go!' he'd slipped through the Whitley's hole with barely a moment's hesitation. The instructor had turned to the others. 'See. Dead easy. The youngest of you lot, too, isn't he?' After that, none could refuse to follow Trooper Ross's lead, five further jumpers floating to earth in miraculous-seeming safety.

But not all would find parachuting so easy. During one training flight a Trooper Evans's name was called. He was about to take his parachute but hesitated for an instant. In that moment, another trainee, Corporal Douglas Jones, had stepped forward and grabbed the 'chute meant for Evans. When the time came to jump, Corporal Jones had made a perfect landing, but glancing up to check on the man next in line, he'd seen a figure plummeting to earth, his parachute balling up a like a load of damp washing.

Trooper Evans had landed barely a hundred yards away, being killed on impact. It was a hugely sobering moment for Jones, and all in 11 SAS. In airborne operations, death might only ever be a hair's breadth away.

As he spoke to each of the X Troopers in turn, Admiral Keyes had paused at the distinctive figure of Flight Lieutenant Lucky, conversing almost as if the two were old friends. It had made the rest wonder just who was this mystery figure that had been foisted onto their mission. Once he was done with Lucky, Keyes had stepped back to address the troop, stressing how there were 'no better, fitter or braver men' in the entire British Army, and how theirs was 'a very important job', fulfilling a 'very vital role'.

'We shall be waiting to hear how you have got on,' Keyes continued. Then he'd added, almost as if in afterthought: 'I decided that I just couldn't let you go without coming here to say goodbye . . .' It had left some with a strangely unsettled feeling, as if 'goodbye' carried a terrible finality, boding little prospect of return. Then Keyes had lowered his voice still further. 'A pity,' he'd murmured. 'A damn pity.'

Seemingly pulling himself together, Admiral Keyes told the raiders how proud he was of them, before drawing himself to attention, erect as a flagstaff, and saluting them all.

Only those standing closest to Keyes had heard those final comments, but still the word had spread. It had left many, Pritchard included, with the distinct impression that the Chief of Combined Operations didn't expect to see many of them again. He might have every confidence in their pulling off the attack, but it looked as if he felt the prospects of them getting out again were pitifully slim, and in the high emotion of the moment had been unable to hide it.

As the Whitleys' engines roared for take-off, the aircraft straining to get airborne, Pritchard forced such disturbing thoughts to the back of his mind. He had other things to worry about right now. In one of the nearby warplanes one of his men had been taken suddenly ill. He was running a high temperature. Though rare, there was malaria in Malta. The man could be seriously sick, and Pritchard couldn't allow for any lame ducks on this mission.

Indeed, his orders were crystal clear: any man incapacitated or injured on operations was to be left behind. That was the esprit de corps that had been fostered during the weeks of ferocious training in the Scottish Highlands: nothing could be allowed to interfere with the prosecution of the attack, the success of the mission.

Moments before the Whitleys began to move, the sick man was ordered off his aircraft. A dark figure tumbled from the fuselage and dashed to get clear. They were one man down – thirty-five, as opposed to thirty-six – and before the fleet of warplanes had even taken to the skies. It was somehow distinctly ominous.

So strict had been the security over Colossus that no one apart from Pritchard and one fellow officer, Lieutenant Anthony Deane-Drummond, had known the true nature of the mission, until just an hour or so before mounting up the aircraft. Pritchard had needed to know, for obvious reasons. Lieutenant Deane-Drummond had needed to know, for he had flown out as the advance party, tasked with organizing the Malta side of operations, prior to the main force's arrival.

Not least of Deane-Drummond's responsibilities had been to liaise with the commander of HMS *Triumph*, the submarine that was charged to slip into Italian waters several days hence, to perform a covert pick-up of the raiding party and sail them back to friendly shores. Deane-Drummond – all of twenty-three years in age – had been granted access to the most sensitive of information, and after Major Pritchard, his was one of the most arduous and demanding roles on Colossus. He'd been chosen due to his solid military pedigree, though it was more by dint of luck than design that he'd earned it.

At age nine, Deane-Drummond's father – something of a

philanderer – had divorced his mother, remarrying twice thereafter. The young Deane-Drummond had been raised by his mother in a rented home, the Old Vicarage, in the Cotswold village of Little Barrington, begging a hand-me-down Purdey shotgun and horses off a wealthy aunt. Viewed by his mother as not particularly bright or physically robust, she'd sent her son to Marlborough College, for it was 'nice and high up and had lots of fresh air', and should serve to harden him up. Fortunately, his absent father was still willing to pay the school fees.

Marlborough College – motto, 'God gives the increase' (Latin: *Deus Dat Incrementum*) – was founded to educate wealthy sons of the English clergy, and it was one of the toughest of such establishments at the time. At first feeling utterly lost, Deane-Drummond was rescued by his tutor, one A. R. Peppin. Master Peppin not only fostered in his young charge a love of ancient history and maths, he imparted a sage piece of advice: 'Put your heart and soul – as well as brains – into anything you do . . .'

It was a lesson that Deane-Drummond had never forgotten. Bucking his mother's predictions, he'd graduated to the Royal Military Academy, Woolwich, and after that the Royal Signals. In the summer of 1937, finding himself with time to kill, Deane-Drummond had decided to learn to fly, something he'd always yearned to do. He'd taken up gliding and, remembering Master Peppin's urgings, he'd gone on to become a foremost gliding champion. But first had come the outbreak of war.

Deployed to France as part of the British Expeditionary Force (BEF), Deane-Drummond had suffered the ignominy of defeat and the evacuation from Dunkirk. While the miracle of the little ships had been presented in the British press as a great victory, in truth, he lamented, 'the superb but tiny British Army had been flung off the continent.' The stories in the media rankled and he hungered to hit back.

The opportunity had come when the call went out for Special Service Volunteers. Deane-Drummond's skill at flying made him an ideal recruit for airborne forces, and in July 1940 he'd joined 11 SAS. His first parachute jump had been from a Bristol Bombay – an ageing troop transport, if anything even more obsolete than the Whitley. The Bombay had a side-door that could be lifted off its hinges. Deane-Drummond's parachute cord – the static line which caused it to open shortly after jumping – had been lashed to one of those hinges.

He'd duly leapt from the aircraft's open door, the double half-hitch around the hinge holding good, and he'd floated to earth unharmed. Some six months later he'd flown out to Malta on a Sunderland seaplane, several days ahead of the main party of raiders, charged with ensuring that all went smoothly, for a forty-eight-hour transit was envisaged. If the Whitleys stayed on the ground any longer, they were likely to get bombed to smithereens.

That rapid turn-around had been achieved, and it was only as the men were about to board the Whitleys that Pritchard had finally told them what lay ahead, and even then it wasn't the whole story. None of his men seemed to resent the tight secrecy; the fact that they had been kept in the dark.

It had been up to the Inter-Services Security Board (ISSB) – part of Churchill's War Cabinet tasked with coordinating deception operations – to come up with a feasible cover story for Colossus. In a January 1941 'SECRET' document, ISSB had announced: 'The cover decided upon for dissemination amongst the troops [is] the destruction of a bridge carrying an important railway and road at an unidentified point in ABYSSINIA ...'

To give body to the ISSB's lies, maps of East Africa (Abyssinia is part of modern-day Ethiopia) had been pinned up in the operations room, and photos of East African railway bridges left lying around the place. But mostly, the men of X Troop hadn't wanted to know the destination of the coming raid, for fear they might inadvertently give the game away to the enemy.

Just before the men had boarded the Whitleys at Malta, Pritchard had judged the time was right to reveal the truth. He gave his men the bare bones of the operation. They were not flying south to Abyssinia, which was then held by the Italians, he explained. Instead, they were heading north into the very heart of Fascist Europe – making for a mountainous area of Italy situated 150 miles to the south of Rome.

Their target was not a rail bridge. It was an aqueduct lying in the shadows of Monte Vulture, a 4,350-foot extinct volcano. It piped fresh drinking water to three of Italy's key ports, serving several million people. If they could blow it up, it would cause all kinds of problems, for those harbours dispatched Italy's men and arms to battle. If they could be paralysed, it might transform the fortunes of the war in North Africa.

Upon realizing they were to strike at Italy itself, not some far-flung outpost of empire, a ragged cheer went up from the men. While not revealing the full details of their escape plan, Pritchard explained that a long and arduous trek lay ahead, if and when they'd destroyed their target. He was proud that they had been chosen for such a momentous mission, he declared, Britain's first ever strike by airborne forces.

He'd rounded things off with typical bluntness, declaring: 'You are pioneers – or guinea pigs . . . You can choose whatever word you prefer.' That warning given, Pritchard had taken

Deane-Drummond and the rest of his officers to one side, to brief them on the escape route and their intended rendezvous with HMS *Triumph*. Then, as a velvet-hued dusk had descended over the airstrip, the raiders had mounted up the Whitleys and they had lifted off from Malta, clawing their way into the darkening skies.

Few aboard those warplanes were in danger of losing their nerve. Even the lone figure who had bailed out at the very last minute was adamant that he had wanted to continue. But to paraphrase Churchill, people often act heroically because they don't appreciate the dangers that lie ahead. Others see those dangers and are afraid them, but do what they do in spite of their fears. No man can be braver than that.

Bravery there was in abundance, but fear still stalked the holds of those Whitleys. They climbed to cruise altitude, the eight aircraft taking up a holding pattern to the north of Malta, awaiting nightfall to better hide their thrust deep into enemy airspace. As they circled over the shadowed sea, trepidation seized hold of some, roiling in their guts. Often, it was the least-expected individuals who were seemingly at risk of 'crapping out' – of refusing to continue with the mission.

But every man present tonight was a volunteer, and each had been free to go back to his unit at any time, had he chosen to do so. Likewise, that was the only form of 'discipline' required among such self-reliant, independent-spirited warriors: the threat of being thrown out of their exalted brotherhood was more than enough to keep most in line.

As Churchill had averred, men such as the Special Service Volunteers would push on with their mission, stepping into the unknown, *in spite of their fear*. Indeed, none of the X Troopers would have been there – preparing to mount the first ever Allied airborne raid – if it hadn't been for the dogged perseverance of Britain's wartime leader. They owed their very existence to him.

Whatever the next few hours might bring, it was at Churchill's urging that they were heading into the darkness and the unknown.

Chapter 2

Eight months earlier, on 4 June 1940, even as the last of the little ships had steamed away from Dunkirk, Churchill had delivered a momentous speech to parliament, hailing the rescuing of so many 'out of the jaws of death and shame, to their native land and to the tasks that lie immediately ahead'. But he'd added a trenchant reminder: 'We must be very careful not to assign to this deliverance the attributes of a victory. Wars are not won by evacuation.'

Eloquent. Pithy. A timely call to action, it reflected absolutely Churchill's mindset.

One man with whom those words resonated most powerfully was Lieutenant-Colonel Dudley Wrangel Clarke, one of the most intrepid, if enigmatic and little-known figures of the war. Travelling home from the War Office that evening, Clarke had racked his brains for inspiration, considering what other nations had done when besieged by a seemingly omnipotent foe. There had to be lessons from history, if only he could alight upon them.

In a sense, Clarke was uniquely placed to do so. Known as a maverick free-thinker, he'd first come to notice when foremost British commander General Archibald Wavell had recognized his 'unorthodox outlook on soldiering' and his 'ingenuity and somewhat impish sense of humour'. Clarke's most infamous exploit during the war would be when he was arrested in Madrid, the capital of supposedly neutral Spain, dressed – very convincingly – as a woman, on some cloak-and-dagger business.

Clarke had spent his infant years growing up in South Africa at the time of the Boer War, his family braving the 1899 Siege of Ladysmith (a city in north-eastern South Africa) by Boer forces. A quarter of a million British troops had been tied down by the Boer Commandos, loosely organized bands of highly mobile horsemen numbering no more than 50,000 in strength. Having no regular army, the Boers would form ad hoc militias, electing their own officers, each fighter carrying whatever weaponry and kit he could muster.

Dressed in regular khaki farming clothes – jacket, trousers and slouch-hat (a wide-brimmed felt hat) – and sporting hunting rifles, they rode into battle astride their own steeds. Most had spent their lives in the saddle working the land, and they were expert hunters and survivalists. Largely equipped and fed by what they could win from the enemy – in this case, British troops – Boer Commando bands were held together by the prowess and charisma of their leaders.

To Clarke, they were the antithesis of modern European armies, and the stories of their thrilling exploits were burned into his mind. As Clarke reflected upon such memories, it occurred to him that the Boer Commandos could be 'reborn' in Britain, to aim 'mosquito stings upon the ponderous bulk of a German Army'. Hurriedly, he noted down the main concepts of 'Commando' operations. Mobility was the key – the ability to strike swiftly, then withdraw just as quickly, in hit-and-run attacks.

The British had their mastery of the sea, of course, and having seized practically all of Western Europe the Germany military was strung out along thousands of miles of potentially vulnerable coastline. There seemed no reason why the Commando concept shouldn't be adopted by British troops – small bands, stripped to the minimum of kit, following a charismatic leader, striking from the night-dark sea and melting away just as quickly. Before retiring to bed, Clarke summed up his musing on a single sheet of note paper.

The following morning Clarke, who served as the assistant to General John Dill, the Chief of the Imperial General Staff (CIGS), heard Dill declare, somewhat gloomily: 'We shall have to find a way of helping the Army to exercise its offensive spirit once again.' Clarke had jumped right in, outlining his concept for a British Commando. General Dill asked him for a short paper presenting his ideas, to help sell it to Churchill, with whom he would speak right away.

Churchill, of course, had direct experience of the Boer War. In October 1899, he'd headed out to South Africa, serving as a foreign correspondent for the *London Morning Post*, then one of the foremost newspapers of the day. He was travelling on an armoured train when it was ambushed by the Boer Commandos. As shells and bullets had pinged all around, Churchill had helped organize the train's defences, but while others had made their getaway he was captured.

Carted off to prison in the Boer capital, Pretoria, his daring escape became the stuff of legend. Scaling the prison fence, he hid by day, moving only during the hours of darkness, stealing food and drinking from streams. Enraged, the Boers had launched a massive man-hunt, posters offering a reward for Churchill, 'dead or alive'. Still he'd managed to cross hundreds of miles of enemy territory and escape. Later, Churchill returned to the Boer conflict, both as a reporter and a combatant, and its memory was etched deep in his mind, as was the dash and daring of his adversaries.

The day after penning his proposal, Clarke was told by General Dill: 'Your Commando scheme is approved . . . Try to get a raid across the Channel at the earliest possible moment.' He'd won Churchill's backing. Clarke was ordered to hand over all duties immediately, so he could set up a 'raiding headquarters' right away. It was to be given the innocuous-sounding cover-name 'Section MO9', short for Military Office 9.

To further obfuscate MO9's true purpose, Dudley Clarke took the unusual step of recruiting several redoubtable women to staff his HQ. The foremost, Constance Rumbold, was the daughter of Sir Horace Rumbold, who'd served as Britain's ambassador to Berlin in the 1930s, during which time he'd repeatedly warned of Hitler's aggressive ambitions.

Constance Rumbold offered up the family home on Grosvenor Crescent, in London's plush Belgravia district, as a covert meeting place for MO9 business. She founded a bogus charity, and all MO9 officers were charged to report to Grosvenor Crescent in plain clothes, telling the butler they were there on 'charity business'. It might have seemed a little melodramatic, but London in 1940 was jam-packed with refugees from across Nazi-occupied Europe, and everyone was mindful of how 'loose talk costs lives'.

Against much 'sage' advice, Clarke recruited David Niven, the debonair Hollywood actor, as his second-in-command, believing him to have just the right combination of flair, without being too constrained by the rigidity of professional soldiering. Having joined MO9's exalted number, Niven promptly got himself arrested under suspicion of being a German spy. It was a Sunday, and Niven had spent the day out of London, visiting friends. After dinner he was motoring back to town, when the air-raid warnings had sounded, road-blocks being erected to guard against enemy landings.

Niven had pulled over and changed into uniform, so he could proceed relatively unmolested. Unfortunately, two eagle-eyed Home Guard officers had spied him doing so, overpowering Niven before his change of clothing was complete. Clarke had duly taken a call from Scotland Yard, but had managed to convince them that their prisoner was indeed the famous actor, David Niven, who was now serving in a top-secret arm of the military.

Clarke's HQ, cover and second-in-command sorted, his next challenge was where to source his recruits. Fortunately, in Scotland, a band of eminently suitable soldiers were sitting around with very little to do. Ten so-called Independent Companies had been formed to operate in Scandinavia as mobile forces. Five were busy fighting the Germans in Norway, though their days there were numbered. The five remaining companies had not been dispatched, and they were awash with the dispiriting rumour that they were about to be disbanded.

Clarke headed to their base, where he explained that he was looking for several hundred Special Service Volunteers for raiding operations. Those who stepped forward would make up the first Commando, with a view to more being formed. A raid would have to be mounted in quick order, to prove to Churchill – and the wider world – that the British Army had the wherewithal and the will to buck defeat and to strike back. He was inundated with volunteers.

So important was Clarke's mission that he was answerable only to the Chiefs of Staff and Churchill. Even so, there was precious little equipment with which to do anything. His Commandos resorted to training with RAF Crash Boats, air-sea rescue craft designed to pluck downed pilots out of the drink – hardly suited to amphibious landings.

Even as Clarke's first raid was being planned, objections were raised. Surely, the War Cabinet argued, Clarke didn't intend to formally christen his force the 'Commandos'? The name had all the connotations of the Boer irregulars, with their lack of military orderliness and discipline. The War Cabinet decreed that Clarke's unit change its name. Henceforth, the raiders would be known as Special Service troops, or 'SS' for short. The dark connotations of calling them *that* were all too clear.

'Desperate days demanded desperate remedies,' Clarke himself argued. Finally, General Dill himself was forced to intervene, to 'give Commando an authoritative blessing'. Clarke enjoyed the full backing of Churchill and General Dill, plus his long-time associate, General Archibald Wavell. Wavell, then serving as Commander Middle East and battling the Italians in North Africa, had described his ideal soldier as a mixture of 'cat-burglar, poacher and gunman', and he had long favoured deception, guile and unorthodox operations.

Clarke sought to go one step further with his Commandos. 'We looked for the dash of the Elizabethan pirate, the Chicago gangster, and the Frontier tribesman,' he remarked. Crucially, his Commandos would need to be self-starters and independently minded, so they would press on to their objective no matter what might have befallen their fellows to left or right.

To foster such independence of spirit, Clarke decreed that a daily allowance be given to each volunteer, from which he had to house, feed and transport himself. There would be no barracks, or rations or quotas of military vehicles. Recruits would have to find their own lodgings, eat at hostelries as they saw fit, and make their own way to embarkation points using whatever transport came to hand. It was a revolutionary concept, but the bean counters at the War Office took it all in their stride, coming up with the magical figure of 6s 8d as the individual Commando's proper daily allowance.

In London, Clarke established a central Commando store – a cross between an armoury stuffed with Tommy Guns, and a film studio cram-full of props, including 'all sorts of unorthodox equipment, such as enemy uniforms and equipment, special explosives . . . in addition to every kind of weapon which the Commandos might need'.

Churchill declared that he wanted 5,000 such Commandos, and the call went out for Special Service Volunteers to step forward for hazardous duties. Clarke looked forward to having ten separate Commandos, each of 500 men, one of which would be an exclusively airborne unit, trained for parachute insertions deep into enemy territory. But first, in late June 1940, he needed to execute his inaugural raid, to prove his concept in action.

On the night of 24/25 June 1940 – less than three weeks after Clarke's Commandos had been founded – 120 men of No. 2 Commando set sail in four RAF Crash Boats, carrying thirty raiders apiece. Led by Major Ronnie Tod, the former commander of No. 6 Independent Company and one of Clarke's earliest Scottish recruits, Clarke himself was riding with them, although he was strictly forbidden from going ashore.

Under cover of darkness, the four craft crept towards the French coast, off Le Touquet, in the Pas-de-Calais region. Just twenty days earlier the last of the little ships had fled in the opposite direction, carrying the remnants of a defeated British Army. It was a herculean feat to be striking back again so swiftly. In the ensuing action, three of the craft landed their men successfully, and there were fierce skirmishes ashore, as the raiders targeted a hotel known to billet German troops.

But the June night was short, and barely three hours had been allotted before the boats had to withdraw. Come daybreak they had to be well off the coast. The Crash Boat in which Clarke was riding came under fierce fire from a German bicycle patrol, which had raced along the beach to investigate all the commotion. It was also menaced by a German E-boat, a heavily armed fast-attack craft capable of speeds approaching 50 knots.

Fortunately, they managed to give the E-boat the slip, as did the other Crash Boats, and all made it back safely to British shores. Operation Collar, as the mission was codenamed, was hailed as a success. The Germans had taken casualties, the Commandos had lost not a man, and there had been very few injuries. Ironically, one of those was Dudley Clarke himself, who had had his ear shot almost in half, when under fire from the bicycle patrol. Once it was sewn together again and bandaged it healed well enough.

To a British nation desperate for positive news, Operation Collar proved a real tonic. A communiqué was issued to the press, which was both bullish and refreshingly honest:

Naval and military units yesterday carried out successful reconnaissance of the enemy coastline. Landings were effected at a number of points and contact made with German troops. Casualties were inflicted and some enemy dead fell into our hands. Much useful information was obtained. Our forces suffered no casualties.

Dudley Clarke expressed a 'modest pride' in the achievements of Op Collar: they had landed 120 Commandos on enemy shores, wrought a little damage and got them all back home again. An editorial in *The Times* summed up the mood of the nation. It read: 'The point is that this incident shows the offensive spirit, which is exactly what the public wants . . .' But it was on the far side of the Atlantic that the media really went to town, US newspapers hailing the bulldog spirit of this new breed of piratical British raider.

In time, Hitler himself would berate the Commandos as being 'terror and sabotage troops' who, he claimed, 'acted outside the Geneva convention'. German propaganda would take up this line, calling the Commandos 'murderous thugs and cut-throats' who preferred to kill their enemies rather than to take them prisoner. All the publicity had one major side effect: Dudley Clarke was inundated with volunteers who wished to join the ranks of the daring Special Service Volunteers.

At the outbreak of the war Churchill had been hugely impressed – if not daunted – by German parachute operations, Hitler's *Fallschirmjäger* – paratroopers – seizing Belgium's key defences, in a lightning airborne raid known as the Battle of Fort Eben-Emael. Some fifty DFS230 gliders had landed silently in four waves, enabling German paratroopers to seize four different objectives in Belgium – Fort Eben-Emael, plus three strategically placed bridges.

In that lightning airborne operation, 500 *Fallschirmjäger* – many dropped by parachute – had opened the way for German ground troops to roll into France, using Belgium as the launch-pad for their *blitzkrieg*. Churchill had watched aghast, but typically he had vowed that what the enemy could do, Britain had to do better. 'Let us raise a force of 10,000 parachutists,' he had declared, in one of his subsequent memos.

Following Operation Collar, there was no shortage of volunteers. The challenge was equipping them. The RAF was pitifully short of airframes. All they could offer were a few ageing Whitleys. Regardless, the first paratroopers began airborne training. As Clarke wanted to distinguish them from his seaborne commandos, he decided to insert the word 'Air' into the Special Service name: at a stroke they became the Special Air Service.

And so, unwittingly, a legend was born.

The first unit formed was christened 11 Special Air Service; '11', so as to bluff the enemy that ten other airborne brigades were already in existence. At Ringway, a flat, windblown civilian airstrip just to the south of Manchester, the Central Landing School was founded, Clarke's top-secret airborne training establishment. So little understood was the concept of airborne operations, especially within an Army high-command fearful of a German invasion, that letters turned up at Ringway addressed to the 'Central Laundry School' and 'The Central Sunday School', among other equally laughable misnomers.

Ringway had the advantage that no less a figure than Wing Commander Sir Henry Nigel St Valery Norman, 2nd Baronet, had taken up command there. A graduate of the Royal Military College, Sandhurst, Norman had served in the First World War with artillery and signals units, before spending the inter-war years learning to fly and rising through the ranks of the RAF. More to the point, Norman – like Keyes and Churchill – was a die-hard advocate of airborne forces.

As an added bonus, Lord Egerton of Tatton's Cheshire country estate lay adjacent to Ringway. Another First World War veteran and aviation enthusiast, Maurice Egerton, 4th Baron Egerton, offered up that expanse of open parkland within which the fledgling parachutists could train. With no expertise whatsoever within the British military regarding parachute operations, two former Hollywood stuntmen were brought in to instruct the earliest recruits.

Bearing in mind how pioneering were those early efforts – in truth it was the blind leading the blind – it was an irony not lost upon Clarke that his airborne raiders were to be some of the first to strike again against the enemy. By autumn 1940, Operation Colossus – though it had yet to attain its iconic codename, and was then known simply as 'Project T' – was in the offing. If Operation Collar had proved that Britain still had pluck and punch, Colossus would demonstrate that she could take the fight deep into the enemy's back yard.

But this was an operation that Clarke was sadly to miss. In November 1940 he received an urgent summons from General Wavell, asking him to depart post haste for Cairo. Clarke was to leave his beloved Commandos, charged instead to develop the dark arts of trickery, deception and bluff, to help trounce the Italians in North Africa. It was a task to which he would appear a born master, but he bade farewell to his Commandos with lingering regret.

After a circuitous series of flights, Clarke reached Cairo on 12 December 1940, less than two months before the Operation Colossus raiders were to fly to Malta. Clarke had no staff in Cairo and he worked alone, his office being a converted bathroom in British Army headquarters. His official title was simply Intelligence Officer. His cover was that he was working for MI9, the British 'escape and evasion factory', whose job it was to enable Allied POWs to slip the enemy's clutches.

His real mission – beyond-top-secret; codenamed Operation Abeam – was one he hardly could have attempted without his previous Commando experience. By the turn of the year Clarke had begun to fabricate the supposed existence of a British airborne regiment in North Africa, which in truth did not exist, to play upon Italian fears. Realizing that bending the truth was far better than creating a lie, Clarke 'formed' I Special Air Service, using faked documents, photos and reports, which he made sure would fall into Italian hands.

He had dummy parachutists dropped in the open desert, where they were sure to be spotted by the enemy. He had 'soldiers' wearing SAS uniforms wander around the streets of Cairo, talking all too freely about their carefree, daredevil, cut-throat airborne ways. Of course, the real SAS paratroopers were even then involved in intensive training, in preparation for Operation Colossus, so the deception had real meat behind it.

That summer, Clarke was to make the acquaintance of David Stirling, who was then serving with No. 8 Commando, recently arrived in North Africa. Stirling recognized in Clarke a hugely influential fellow, and he shared with him his ideas for creating a deep-desert raiding party. Clarke sensed an opportunity to further his great deception: if real parachutists could strike at the Italians' rear in North Africa, so much the better. It would give body to his lies.

Clarke counselled Stirling to use the name of an already existing outfit, and to take on their mantle and legacy. As Stirling would remark of the moment: 'The name SAS came mainly from the fact that I was anxious to get the full cooperation of a very ingenious individual . . . Dudley Clarke promised to give me all the help he could, if I would use the name of his bogus brigade of parachutists, which was the Special Air Service – the SAS.' In fact, they were far from 'bogus': they were Clarke's originals, formed out of his earliest Commandos.

David Stirling's first mission, Operation Squatter, was eerily similar to Colossus. In November 1941, sixty-five of his fledgling SAS would parachute deep into the desert, to raid Axis airfields. Largely due to a terrible storm that blew up, Operation Squatter would prove an unmitigated disaster: only twenty-two men made it out alive and not a single enemy aircraft was destroyed. None of Stirling's men should have jumped amidst such unseasonable conditions, but from that disaster the seeds of genius and glory were to be sown.

Before all that could happen, Major Pritchard and his X Troopers would wing their way north under moonlit Italian skies, to launch a raid intended to change the course of the war.

The date for Operation Colossus had been chosen with infinite care. On the night of 10/11 February 1941, the moon would be 98.5 per cent full. Those planning Colossus had stressed the vital importance of hitting what they termed the 'moon window' – the short period within each month when by the light of the moon alone pilots might navigate their way to a remote drop-zone.

'As much moonlight as possible is essential in order to locate the target, which is not easy to find,' a 2 January 1941 Colossus planning report averred. 'Full moon is on 12th February. The operation should therefore take place as early as possible between 9th and 19th February.'

The concept of the moon window had been pioneered by the SOE when inserting lone agents into enemy-occupied France, most often using the Westland Lysander light aircraft, nicknamed the 'Lizzie' by those who flew her. The Lizzie's rugged construction and short take-off-and-landing capabilities meant it could deliver agents to small improvised airstrips. Hitting the moon window was crucial for such missions.

Indeed, originally Colossus had been conceived as a mission for the SOE, and it could hardly have had a stranger or more bizarre beginning. It was a bookish Oxford don and classicist, more comfortable speaking in Latin than his native English, who had first dreamed up the idea. On 27 June 1940, in a handwritten letter on Magdalen College notepaper, Professor Colin Graham Hardie had laid out his extraordinary proposition.

'The following suggestion may be useful, now that we are at war with Italy,' he'd declared, in a flowing, elegant hand etched via fountain pen. 'The water supply of the whole area of S. E. Italy . . . is derived from one aqueduct, the Aqueduct Pugliese. It is all fed from the one river, Sele, which flows into the . . . sea south of Salerno . . .' If the aqueduct could be destroyed, Hardie suggested, 'you will make the Italians have to supply 2–3 million people with water to drink, including two naval bases, Taranto and Brindisi.'

Hardie's proposition was backed by intensely detailed knowledge of the aqueduct. Completed in 1914, it was an extraordinary feat of engineering, running for 213.5 kilometres through Italy's Apennine Mountains, via an ingenious system of channels and bridges, plus 97 kilometres of tunnels. En route, '65 towns are furnished with potable water,' Hardie wrote. 'The principal aqueduct is constructed of masonry (not concrete)' and 'spans a long valley . . . if effectively destroyed it would cut off water supply . . .'

Hardie's intimate knowledge of the Aqueduct Pugliese had come about largely by accident: in the years before the war, he'd served as Director of the British School at Rome. Ironically, bearing in mind Hardie's June 1940 proposal, the School's charter was to promote knowledge of Italy's history and culture among British citizens. Hardie had a deep appreciation of all that, being a renowned Italian scholar with a deep love of the Italian classics. But now, with Italy at war with Britain, he'd turned his fine mind to something entirely different, by proposing what would very likely be the death by thirst of a very large number of Italian souls.

Ungentlemanly warfare this most certainly was, and Hardie's plan received an enthusiastic response from its recipients, the grandmasters of those dark arts. 'It presents a most important target, especially at the present time,' SOE concluded, excitedly. Audacious, unthinkable, ruthless in the extreme – it was exactly the kind of operation that Churchill had envisaged when conceiving of SOE in the first place.

'How wonderful it would be if the Germans could be made to wonder where they were going to be struck next,' Churchill had declared, in early 1940. The same held equally true for the Italians. Indeed, SOE's cover name was the Ministry for Economic Warfare, and its role was to make 'stabbing attacks . . . between the chinks of the enemy's military and economic armour'. Sabotage of every sort was the order of the day, and Hardie's plan fitted the bill absolutely.

Sinister, deniable, covert, the SOE would hide its activities behind a series of shadow identities, including the 'Inter-Services Research Bureau', 'The Firm' and 'The Racket'. 'We have to organize movements in enemy occupied territory comparable to the Sinn Fein movement in Ireland . . .' declared Dr Hugh Dalton, Churchill's first minister at SOE. 'We must use many different methods, including industrial and military sabotage . . . We need absolute secrecy, a certain fanatical enthusiasm, and willingness to work with people of different nationalities.'

Hardie's plan promised all of that and more. Recruited quietly into SOE, as were numerous British academics at the time, Hardie added flesh to his idea. The key question was how best to sabotage the Aqueduct Pugliese. Every conceivable option was considered, including a suggestion 'to float a large quantity of explosives in bags . . . via an inspection manhole, so that the end of the tunnel which the aqueduct enters . . . should be destroyed'.

That option was ruled out, owing to the fact that the tunnels were 'bored in solid rock, and it is not considered that the clearing away of the debris following the explosion would take more than three or four days'. If the Aqueduct Pugliese were to be sabotaged, it had to be put out of action for a month at least, the SOE planners determined. Only that way could the maximum disruption – and death – be wreaked on the enemy.

By winter 1940, Hardie's scheme had acquired official status: it was designated as the 'Water Project: Southern Italy' and categorized 'MOST SECRET'. The ground water at Brindisi, Bari and Taranto – Italy's key naval port – was 'heavily tainted by magnesium and quite unfit for human consumption,' SOE reported. There was no alternative drinking water for several million people, together with large numbers of troops in transit, 'including perhaps Germans'.

SOE planners studied what intelligence they had mustered: it consisted of a handful of obscure architectural and engineering journals, covering the construction of the Aqueduct Pugliese. One, the March 1920 edition of *Il Giornale del Genio Civilie* – the

Milan Journal of Civil Engineering – included photos of some of the aqueduct's key infrastructure, plus basic statistics on its dimensions and means of construction.

As the SOE well appreciated, the Italian War Ministry was alert to the dangers. An October 1940 copy of its *Nazione Militare – Military Review* – had fallen into their hands. It stressed the vulnerability of the aqueduct as a target. 'Special supply arrangements are necessary ... in the event of the valuable Apulian Aqueduct becoming unusable as a result of war damage ... Drinking water is scarce and localised.'

SOE held one major trump card. A British engineer had been engaged to help with the aqueduct's original construction. He advised SOE that there were two key bridges that carried the water across deep valleys. One, a large, arched aqueduct, crossed the River Bradano; the other, a smaller aqueduct sixteen kilometres upstream, spanned the River Tragino via a series of rectangular pillars. If either could be hit, the engineer advised, 'it could not be repaired in under one month,' due to the remote nature of the region.

The Tragino aqueduct was seen as the more viable of the two. That, SOE decided, had to be their target. A 1920s photograph of it, taken from *Il Giornale del Genio Civilie*, was studied closely. The area in question was too mountainous and remote to constitute a 'bombable target'. It could not be hit from the air. Clearly, this called for boots – agents – on the ground.

Crucially, while the Tragino aqueduct itself was made of reinforced concrete, the three piers supporting it were said to be of masonry – i.e. brickwork. 'This is a most important point, since the cutting charge required for reinforced concrete is approximately thirty times as great as that required for masonry.' In other words, the piers should be vulnerable to attack by a small force of men, with whatever explosives they could carry.

Planners set to calculating exactly what weight of charges would be needed to bring down the Tragino aqueduct from end to end. To blow up the three piers would involve packing explosives to either side, so entailing six packages in all. 'Thus the total weight of explosives required for the demolition of the bridge is $6 \times 280 = 1,680$ pounds,' the experts concluded.

Clearly, to carry that weight of war materiel through such rugged terrain would require several dozen men. As the Tragino aqueduct lay smack-bang in the centre of Italy, practically one hundred kilometres from either coastline, a seaborne assault was out of the question. This called for an airborne raiding party, going in under cover of darkness, but could British paratroopers make a landing over such precipitous terrain?

A document entitled 'Some particulars re Water Project' and stamped 'MOST SECRET', recorded the heights of a dozen or more peaks in the region: '4,000' . . . 2,700' . . . 2,400' . . . 3,700'' and Monte Vulture itself, at over 4,300 feet of altitude. Even if a force of parachutists could navigate those peaks and land safely, a road ran adjacent to the viaduct. Even a night-time sabotage effort might be overheard 'if the boring drills are noisy' – those used to cut holes in the piers in which to pack the charges.

By late autumn 1940, Major R. H. Barry, Operations Director at SOE, was beginning to accept that such a mission (now code-named Project T – 'T' for Tragino) was beyond the means of SOE. A thirty-two-year-old veteran of Dunkirk, Major Barry had been recruited into SOE due to his wide military experience. In November 1940, SOE had reiterated that, 'undermining the strength of spirit of enemy forces . . . should be the constant aim of our subversive organisations.' Depriving several million Italians of fresh drinking water would certainly do that and more, but SOE just didn't have the manpower to launch such a daring and fraught undertaking.

Reluctantly, SOE concluded that it had 'no agents in Italy ... and there was no likelihood for many months of being able to undertake clandestine operations [there].' And as far as Project T was concerned, time was not on anyone's side.

In a 'MOST SECRET' letter of December 1940, despatched from the Ministry of Economic Warfare's Berkeley Square head-quarters to Combined Operations, SOE was forced to come clean. 'This Section is not yet in a position to provide either a suitable demolition squad duly equipped or, if such could be found at relatively short notice, to land the party at a convenient place in Italy ... I am sorry that we cannot, for the present, be more helpful ...'

In essence, Project T had been handed lock, stock and barrel to Admiral Sir Roger Keyes, at Combined Operations. SOE's remit was now restricted to inserting a two-man advance party of fluent Italian speakers, to cut the telephone wires at the aqueduct, to prevent the 'early arrival of strong reinforcements [which] would ruin the project'.

Keyes and his planning staff began their preparations. Time was critical, for the fear was that German troops would be drafted in to Italy. Project T was 'urgent, as German Air and Military reinforcements were expected, with the anticipated effect of stiff-ening the Italian morale'. More to the point, the February 1941 moon window was the last available to any strike force, for after that 'the shorter nights would not allow the Whitleys to fly to Malta and back under cover of darkness.'

In their 2 January 1941 'Outline Plan', stage one required 'S.O.E.'s men . . . to lie up till the evening of D.1 [Day One] . . . when they must cut the telephone wires leading to the village and small houses in the neighbourhood . . .' Once the aqueduct was blown, the 'party then makes its way to the coast, either together or in small batches, seizing a lorry or bicycles if possible. On the night of D.8 [Day 8] a submarine will be in the Bay of Salerno with punts, ready to come in on pre-arranged signal. If necessary submarine will call again on D.15 [Day 15].'

To boost the chances of the raiders' escape, planners proposed 'to lay a false trail, in the opposite direction to the one which the fugitives intend to take. A map might be left behind at the scene . . . showing a marked route . . . and a signal for a submarine to go to a R.V. [rendezvous] in the wrong ocean might be sent in clear.' 'In clear' meant not in code, so with the intention that the Italians would intercept it.

The raiders' escape plan was to go the way least expected – heading west, towards the Mediterranean coast, which would involve passing through the rugged Apennine Mountains, which in places rise to over 6,000 feet in altitude. By contrast, the route east towards Italy's Adriatic coast ran mostly across fertile plains and constituted far easier going, and so a false trail should be laid in that direction.

Regardless of such arrangements, the Outline Plan concluded: 'It is considered that the party has a 50-50 chance of escape . . . They should all (excluding the Advance Party) wear uniforms, so as to retain their status as troops.' Acutely aware of how much this was a rush job, Keyes himself noted how 'the inadequacy of the preparation and training is painfully evident.'

No wonder, then, that Keyes had addressed his raiders in

such sombre spirits, prior to their departure from the UK. He knew that it was an even bet that most would end up as POWs, that was if the Italians treated them as bona fide soldiers, as opposed to 'spies', in which case they might well be executed without trial.

On 8 January 1941 Keyes wrote a short letter to the Chiefs of Staff, attaching 'A note on Project "T" for the information of the Prime Minister . . . A picture of the actual bridge is also attached.' That photo was one taken from the Milan Journal of Civil Engineering. Keyes outlined how they intended to 'cut off the water supply to the province . . . for at least one month, by destroying the bridge carrying the Apulian Aqueduct over the stream at TRAGINO,' by dropping 'a demolition party of Special Air Service . . .'

All that Project T now required was Churchill's seal of approval.

So, from the scribblings of an Oxford classics professor, via the offices of SOE and Admiral Keyes, Project T for Tragino arrived upon the desk of the British Prime Minister. Though the document didn't spell it out in such blunt terms, what Churchill was being asked to sign off on was a raid that aimed to make several million Italians perish from thirst, or at the very least flee southern Italy in a mass-exodus of refugees.

But at that moment, Britain was embroiled in the most desperate struggle for survival. The Battle of Britain was but a raw and bloody memory barely weeks old, the Blitz was pounding Britain's cities on a nightly basis, nearly all of Western Europe had fallen under Nazi dominion, and Britain, along with the Colonies, stood alone against the might of Nazi Germany, Italy and Japan.

Desperate times called for desperate measures. On 9 January

1941 Churchill scribbled three short words at the foot of the Project T proposal: 'I approve. WSC.'

Colossus had been green-lit.

Keyes had one last throw of the dice to try to better protect his raiders. On 6 February he petitioned the War Office that a warning be passed to the Italians, via diplomatic channels. In essence, it would put the Italian authorities on notice that if any captured British soldiers were 'shot out of hand or mistreated', there would be serious ramifications.

Chiefs of Staff responded that Keyes' suggestion was 'impracticable . . . If the threat is to have any value . . . this would have to be just before the Operation is undertaken in order that local authorities be warned. This would prejudice secrecy . . .' They added that, 'as the troops will be dressed in uniform, there is no reason to suppose that the Southern Italians are likely to treat them as other than soldiers.'

Keyes – despite his reservations – duly issued his 'Operation Order'. He wrote: 'X Troop, landed by parachute, will blow up the target . . . The nature of the operation is such as may render last minute changes in tactics necessary . . . Initiative, coolness and determination in pressing home the attack are vital to ensure complete success . . .' This was exactly the kind of ethos and esprit de corps that Keyes had nurtured among his raiding forces. He added a final line to his Operation Order: 'The importance of preserving ABSOLUTE SECRECY cannot be too highly emphasised.'

The die was cast.

Chapter 3

At 1210 hours on 11 January 1941, a 'Secret Cypher Message' – basically, an encoded telegram – had been sent from London to Malta, with an urgent request. The Colossus planners needed air-recce photos of the target.

'Vertical photos are required approximate scale 1/25,000 of bridge crossing the stream at Tragino . . . For secrecy reasons photographs should be taken on one run only . . . Map used by pilot should not be marked . . . To cover photographic flight leaflets might be dropped . . .'

A small RAF reconnaissance squadron was based at Malta, flying the US-made Martin Model 167 medium bomber. Seventy-five of these aircraft had fallen into British hands, when the French, poised to sign the 22 June 1940 armistice with Germany, had handed them over to the RAF. The French Air Force had ordered the aircraft shortly before the outbreak of the war and they were rechristened the 'Maryland' under RAF service.

Powered by twin Pratt & Whitney Wasp engines and with a crew of three, the Maryland was capable of pushing 500 kph. A fast and nimble warplane armed with six machineguns, it proved a fine recce aircraft, at least in the early stages of the war. Those based at Malta were forever getting bombed, but somehow the ground-crew managed to keep a handful operational and dashing through the thin blue. In doing so, one pilot, Flight

Lieutenant Adrian 'Warby' Wharburton, had earned a legendary reputation, combining his daring low-level reconnaissance sorties with attacking Italian ports and submarines, and shooting down enemy warplanes.

In autumn 1940, the Italian fleet anchored at Taranto was viewed as a serious threat to British operations in the Mediterranean. Recce photos were urgently required. In early November, Wharburton and crew had executed a daring sortie 'at zero feet', according to his own words, flying a Maryland nicknamed the 'Sardine Tin' due to the number of holes blasted in her fuselage. At Taranto, they surprised five battleships, fourteen cruisers and twenty-seven destroyers, returning with their precious photos, plus a ship's aerial wrapped around their tail wheel.

On 10 November 1940, the British carrier HMS *Illustrious* stole into range of Taranto harbour and launched a flight of obsolete Fairey Swordfish biplanes – appropriately nicknamed 'The Stringbag' – armed with torpedoes. Despite having a top speed of only 143 mph, the Swordfish attack proved remarkably effective: the Italian fleet lost half of its capital ships in one night, and amazingly only two of the nineteen Swordfish that had reached Taranto were shot down. Wharburton's recce photos had been crucial to that success.

Though he was known as a maverick and a rebel, Wharburton was awarded a DFC that December, and more gallantry awards would follow. He'd gained a reputation for 'getting his pictures' no matter what. But even he experienced problems with the Colossus recce mission. It involved flying across large tracts of the Italian landmass, as opposed to a quick dash in and out of a coastal port. The weather proved the foremost challenge. That January and February, Italy's mountainous spine was cloaked in fierce storms and banks of low cloud. For days on end, no flying was possible.

Shortly after sending the telegram requesting air-recce photos, a 'HUSH MOST SECRET' coded message was dispatched from London to Malta, making further demands: 'Request you will make a Submarine with punt available for withdrawing raiding party . . . from West Coast of Italy about third week in February. Submarine will be required to make two visits . . .'

By way of response, HMS *Triumph* – a T-Class diesel-electric submarine – began rehearsals for taking the thirty-six Colossus raiders off the Italian coast, under cover of darkness. It was only by a small miracle that *Triumph* was still operational. In December 1939 she'd hit a mine in the North Sea, which had blown off an 18-foot section of her bows. Somehow, *Triumph*'s skipper had managed to nurse her back to port. *Triumph* had been repaired, but she'd only been back in action a matter of weeks.

In London, General Hastings 'Pug' Ismay, Churchill's chief military adviser – who would go on to describe Britain's then leader as 'the greatest War Prime Minister in our history' – provided a blow-by-blow account of Colossus preparations, including the planned submarine rescue. 'Triumph has already done some practising,' he reported to the Prime Minister, 'using Berthon boats and Special Service troops, at Filfola.'

Filfola – more commonly known as Filfla – is a barren, uninhabited islet lying three miles to the south of Malta; perfect for practising such manoeuvres in absolute secrecy. But once again the trouble was shortages in even the most basic of equipment. The 'Berthon boats' mentioned by Ismay were Berthon Collapsible Lifeboats, developed in the 1850s by the Reverend Edward Lyon Berthon. Their double canvas skin made them lightweight and collapsible, so suitable for storage in cramped vessels, like submarines.

But Berthon boats were hardly ideal for sneaking into a hostile inlet, to collect several dozen raiders, as the rehearsals at Filfla had proved. A 28 January 'Hush Most Secret' message telegraphed from Malta to London, reported: 'During practise with Berthon boats at sea in good conditions . . . 2 out of 3 available boats sank and were lost . . . Punts appear essential, but very little time is left for fitting.'

Punts – flat-bottomed wooden craft – would need to be fitted to the hull of HMS *Triumph*, or another means found to carry them. The planned pick-up point for the Colossus raiders – the estuary of the River Sele, lying some fifty miles due west of the target – was described by mission planners as constituting 'one of the most unhealthy and deserted districts in Italy. Malaria is rife . . . On both sides of the river, swamps stretch parallel with the sea.'

In one sense, that was exactly why the Sele estuary had been chosen as the rescue point for the Colossus raiders: swampy, malarial – no other right-minded individuals were likely to be present. But only flat-bottomed craft like punts stood any chance of slipping in and out of such shallow, marshy waters. The question was, would any be made available in time?

Just twenty-four hours before 'Tag' Pritchard's raiding force was to take to the air over Malta, Wharburton's Maryland roared triumphantly home. The 'recce ace' had secured his photos. Pritchard and Deane-Drummond gathered excitedly as prints were pinned to the wall of the makeshift operations room. They were excellent, the Tragino aqueduct showing up clearly as a slash of black lying to the south-west of the snow-covered mass of Monte Vulture.

Close study of the photos was hugely encouraging. Prior to this moment, raid planners had simply had to presume there were no major defences at the target. Now they had resounding proof. 'The area gives no indication of any defensive measures,' read a 'MOST SECRET' analysis of the recce photos. 'The surroundings are sparsely inhabited, and the likelihood of interruption ... seems more remote than at first thought.

'The area selected for the dropping appeared level and smooth, cultivated land without wall or many obstructions,' the report continued. 'The snow level was approximately 3,000'. The snow areas could be sketched in on a 1/25,000 map for study by the party.'

Typically, Wharburton had gone one better during his daring recce mission: as well as capturing photos of the aqueduct, he'd shot 'a complete strip, from it to the coast'. In other words, his photographs covered the route the Whitley pilots intended to take, as they spirited the raiders to their target.

A 'strip mosaic' – a collage of Wharburton's images stretching from the mouth of the River Sele to the Tragino aqueduct – was created, and the photos 'were studied by the party at a late conference, which lasted 'til midnight.' Enlargements were made of key images, at five inches to the square mile, and handed out to the raiding force commanders, plus the pilots. The weather forecast for the following evening, 10 February, was ideal: for once it would be a cold, dry night with little cloud, which meant lots of moonlight.

Amidst the rush of last-minute preparations, Tag Pritchard and Deane-Drummond managed to meet up with Lieutenant Commander Wilfrid Woods, the captain of HMS *Triumph*. Woods had already earned a fearsome reputation for savaging

Axis vessels in the Mediterranean, and he'd also landed and recovered agents from hostile shores. As they discussed the Sele estuary rendezvous, it was clear that the Colossus raiders could be in no better hands.

Lt-Cmdr Woods's plans for the pick-up were both daring and practicable. He figured he could get the stern of his submarine to within a ship's length of the shoreline, whereupon he'd send out one of the punts that he'd managed to get hold of, 'with as small a crew as possible, towing a . . . line, and to haul it back to ship on receipt of a pre-arranged signal.' Once he'd ferried all of Pritchard's raiders across, he would withdraw, 'towing the punt until well clear of the shore and then scuttling it'.

As the punts would need to be lashed to the submarine's hull, and might be lost during passage, Woods had a back-up plan. It was for 'one hand to swim ashore with enough heaving line . . . to which would be secured an R.A.F. dinghey [sic] with 12 life jackets.' This would be used to ferry the raiders to his vessel. Should bad weather hamper the rescue, Woods proposed floating ashore 'tinned provisions and rum secured to an R.A.F. dinghey'.

If the Whitleys reached the target, and the raiders managed to parachute into it, blow the aqueduct and make it across the mountains to the Sele estuary, neither Pritchard nor Deane-Drummond were in any doubt that Woods would do his utmost to spirit them to safety. Reassuringly, they would have two bites at the cherry: Triumph would pull in to the coast on 16 February, so six days after their parachute drop, and again four days later. But a world of unknowns and uncertainties lay between then and now.

Tag Pritchard – 'no more cheerful and born leader . . . could

51

have been found' – had settled upon a set of verbal recognition signals to be used by his men on the ground. The challenge to be cried out was: 'Heil Hitler!' The answer: 'Viva Duce' – long live The Leader, Mussolini.

Since learning of their true destination, his raiders had adopted a somewhat ribald song as the theme tune for their mission. The first line began: 'Oh! What a surprise for the Duce!' Few of the others are printable. Mussolini styled himself as 'His Excellency Benito Mussolini, Head of Government, Leader of Fascism and Founder of the Empire,' or 'Il Duce' for short. The raiders were singing lustily about the surprise they intended to deliver him, even as the Whitleys clawed their way into the dusk skies.

The fleet of eight warplanes climbed to a 10,000-foot cruise altitude, crossed the toe of Sicily and pressed on towards mainland Italy. In Deane-Drummond's aircraft he felt his eardrums tighten, as they gained height to avoid flak over the Italian mainland. Despite the insulation of his inflatable Li-Lo he was plagued by an intense iciness, the bare metal fuselage seeming to suck the cold from out of the freezing air at such altitude, and to concentrate it inside the plane's dimly lit hold.

There were a few bursts of fire as they thundered over the coastline, white breakers clearly visible to those in the cockpit, glistening silver-blue in the moonlight, but the flak was nothing much to worry about. After they were through it, Deane-Drummond counselled his men to try to catch some sleep, for who knew when they might next get the chance.

He was amazed at how calm his party seemed. Partly, it was down to his very capable second-in-command, Sergeant Arthur Lillian Lawley, at thirty-five one of the real veterans of the unit.

Lawley, a long-serving regular, was an experienced Vickers gunner, the Vickers being a water-cooled .303 calibre British machinegun popular with the troops. He'd soldiered with the South Wales Borderers – a fine infantry regiment with a 280-year history – earning the nickname 'Taff', though he'd actually been born and brought up in London's East End.

Lawley had then spent a short spell as a London bus driver, but had joined up again just as soon as Hitler had sent his troops into Poland. He was blessed with a typical cockney wit with which to boost the men's spirits and extract that last modicum of effort, even when they were dog tired. Fine-featured, handsome, with a quietly confident – almost cocky – gaze, Lawley had been itching for action ever since volunteering. He would be acting as Deane-Drummond's dispatcher – being the last to jump, ushering the others out of the aircraft.

The hole in the Whitley's floor was covered by a pair of plywood doors, with three men positioned to the fore of it and three aft. They'd go out alternately, swinging their legs into the hole and dropping through. The main stores of arms, explosives and other heavy kit were carried in containers held in the Whitley's bomb racks. They would be released after three men had jumped, so in the midst of the 'stick', to help with locating the loads on the ground.

The temptation, even now, was to open the plywood doors, so they could gaze down upon enemy territory, but Deane-Drummond knew that would make it unbearably cold. It was far better to leave it until the very last moment. In other aircraft, other raiders found their own way to pass the hours, as the tension ebbed and flowed through the airframes.

Men killed time by playing cards, but there was barely enough illumination. In one aircraft, twenty-two-year-old Sergeant Johnny 'Big Jock' Walker – as opposed to 'Little Jock' Durie – interspersed the 'Surprise for Il Duce' song by belting out Scottish folk ballads. In another, Corporal Douglas Eric Jones – only recently wed – studied an anthology of poems by torchlight. Fittingly entitled *The Knapsack*, it covered themes ranging from love – perfect for a newlywed – to war and mortality.

Pipe-smoking, debonair and strikingly handsome, Jones had allocated that anthology a permanent place in his rucksack, ever since volunteering for Special Service. A twenty-two-year-old upholsterer by trade, at war's outbreak he'd found himself manning a searchlight on his native Devon coast. It was the sheer monotony of the work that had made him volunteer for hazardous duties, and despite the knowledge that it would mean time away from his sweetheart.

The commander on Jones's aircraft was Captain Christopher Gerald Lea, from Worcestershire, who was one of the tallest among the raiders, being all of six foot three. Hailing from a military family, Captain Lea had volunteered for Special Service, looking forward to 'short, sharp battles, with reasonable comfort in between'. At a cocktail party a few days before departing for Malta, a young woman had remarked of him, admiringly: 'He has the face of a Greek God, and should be holding a lily in his hand.' Only shortly, it was far more likely to be a Tommy Gun.

It was Corporal Jones who, during training, had by chance taken the parachute destined for Trooper Evans – Evans's momentary hesitation meaning he had taken the next in line, plummeting to earth beneath a defective 'chute. It had underlined the arbitrary nature of life and death. As Jones read from *The Knapsack*, he felt particularly moved by the lines of First World War poet Julian Grenfell's *Into Battle*:

> *And when the burning moment breaks,*
> *And all things else are out of mind,*
> *And only joy of battle takes*
> *Him by the throat and makes him blind . . .*

> *The thundering line of battle stands,*
> *And in the air Death moans and sings;*
> *But Day shall clasp him with strong hands,*
> *And night shall fold him in soft wings.*

He read and reread those verses, which spoke to him most powerfully. In those lines there was an exhilaration that he felt palpably in the darkened hold of that warplane. But there was also plain, raw fear of death: that too he felt pulse this way and that among his fellow raiders.

In one aircraft, a young man feared he'd wet himself with fright. That was until he realized with relief that the cold patch he'd felt creeping through his trousers was where a hole had been torn in the fuselage, letting an icy draft in. Thank God, he told himself. His greatest worry had been what his fellow raiders would have thought of him, if he *had* wet his pants.

On Deane-Drummond's aircraft his men dozed in the intense cold, using their rucksacks as makeshift pillows. Lumpy and uncomfortable, each was stuffed full of personal rations – pemmican, hardtack biscuits (dense savoury crackers), chocolate and raisins – calculated to last for six days; enough to get them to the rendezvous with HMS *Triumph*. Stocks of cigarettes were stored in billycans and stuffed in pockets. One man in five had packed a small stove, with a supply of solid-fuel blocks, and every man carried matches. Trouser pockets were lined with soft leather, for holding grenades.

To Deane-Drummond it seemed as if his men had only been asleep for minutes, when he heard the pilot announce that they had reached their rendezvous point, where the eight aircraft would form up over the summit of Monte Vulture. Perhaps it was Wharburton's 'strip mosaic' of photos that had accounted for the pinpoint accuracy of the pilot's navigation. Their intention had been to use the roads and railway lines to trace their way to the target, but Wharburton's shots had proved hugely helpful.

'No difficulty was experienced in identifying the objective and surrounding landmarks,' a report filed by the Whitley's aircrew would record. 'The weather was absolutely perfect and visibility was comparable with early dusk on a fine day. Detail on the ground stood out, and the snow-covered peaks, rocky valleys and clustered mountain towns and villages made a beautiful scene.'

Monte Vulture marked the parting of the ways. From here, two Whitleys would peel off, to execute their diversionary bombing raid, while the remaining aircraft, each carrying half a dozen raiders apiece, would dive towards the valley carrying the Tragino. As the warplanes began their descent, Deane-Drummond heard the cry over his earphones: 'Fifteen minutes to target!'

At his signal, the men were jolted into action. They tore open the plywood jump-doors, an icy blast ripping into the warplane's interior, then turned to clip the static lines of their 'chutes to the anchor bar, which ran along the roof of the hold. Despite their thick battledress, para-smocks, fur-lined jumping helmets and gloves, the men shivered in the intense draught, which howled through the hole like an Arctic storm.

The landscape below was visible now, bathed in a ghostly light. Everything seemed so crystal clear but toytown-like as it whipped past: impossibly convoluted roads, twisting from one spur to another, in an effort to connect isolated villages and farms. Along one toiled a lone vehicle. A bus, or a troop transport? At this height it was hard to tell. But around all, dominating all, towered the mountains.

Snowy peaks glittered beguilingly in the moonlight, like the jumbled slices of some gigantic cake, iced in crisp white. The breathtaking beauty did little to mask the danger. Those gazing down couldn't help but worry if their drop by parachute might deposit them in some knife-cut ravine or hard-edged gorge. The terrain below seemed honeycombed with such obstacles, and beneath the snows hidden perils were sure to lurk.

The Whitleys, with Deane-Drummond's in the lead, were making for Calitri, the nearest large settlement. Soon, individual trees and cattle were clear to see, as the aircraft kept losing altitude. As they came over Calitri at low level, Deane-Drummond handed Sergeant Lawley the headphones, so he could listen in on instructions from the cockpit. The Whitley turned onto a southeast bearing to drop the first stick around 'Hill 427', as the small hillock chosen as their drop-zone had been codenamed.

Moments later, Deane-Drummond spied the Whitley's reargunner emerge from his tail position. 'The pilot can't get to you!' he cried. 'The intercom must have failed!'

'What's he trying to say?' Deane-Drummond yelled back, above the roar of the wind.

'You're due to drop in under a minute. Get cracking!'

With Sergeant Lawley on his feet, the others gathered around the hole. The aircraft dropped lower, sweeping over the glistening expanse of the River Ofanto, into which the Tragino emptied, as the pilot prepared to fly up the very maw of the valley of the *torrente* Tragino at just a few hundred feet of altitude.

The red light set in the ceiling blinked on: *prepare to jump.* There were but precious seconds now before Deane-Drummond and his men would have to hurl themselves into the void. He glanced around at the faces of the others. It all seemed so unreal. Why on earth were they braced at that icy hole, about to dive into the unknown? His men were gazing around at each other, pale-faced and tense and similarly discomfited. Just seconds now . . .

The red light switched to green. 'Green light!' yelled the imperturbable Sergeant Lawley. 'No. 1, GO!'

The first man disappeared, slipping beneath the floor of the hold, to be swallowed into the howling void.

'Two!' Lawley bawled. 'Three!'

Bang on cue the next two leapt.

'Containers!' Lawley cried, punching the release switch that let the containers drop away from the aircraft's wings.

The fourth parachutist – seated opposite Deane-Drummond – went next, then it was his turn. He jumped, plummeting through the speeding Whitley's slipstream, his legs jerked savagely backwards by its force. Moments later there was a crack like a whip in the air above him as his 'chute opened, a sharp jerk on his shoulders as it arrested his descent, and he found himself floating gently a few hundred feet above Italian soil.

The first thing that struck him was the absolute deafening silence, which contrasted so powerfully with the monotonous drone of the aircraft's engines. He gazed around, searching for his 'stick'. Directly below he could see the containers, swinging to-and-fro beneath their chutes, which were colour-coded to mark them out as container-drops. They were so close Deane-Drummond felt as if he could almost reach out and touch them.

Below that, he counted four similar 'chutes to his own, huge upturned saucers seeming iridescent in the silvery light of the moon. Above him, Sergeant Lawley had stepped through the hole, and was floating earthwards beneath his own billowing expanse of canopy. Theirs had all the appearances of being a perfect drop. Now to execute a similarly fine landing.

They had been released low – at no more than five hundred feet – and there were only a few seconds left. Deane-Drummond studied the terrain below his feet. He could make out the aqueduct, looking exactly as it had in Wharburton's recce photos. *Well done that pilot*, he told himself. It was a pinpoint-accurate drop. To either side lay a cluster of cottages and farmsteads: it was Deane-Drummond's role to get those cleared, their inhabitants pacified or otherwise dealt with.

The terrain appeared exactly as he had imagined, only far wilder and more precipitous. He steered for the slope rising just above the aqueduct, bracing himself for the landing. Pulling on the rigging lines with all his might, to slow his descent, he felt his feet thump into the ground and he rolled onto his side, the canopy collapsing gently on top of him. Deane-Drummond figured he'd landed one hundred yards from the aqueduct, no more. It was one of the best touchdowns he had ever made.

He felt for his quick-release catch, punched it so as to free himself from the parachute harness, struggled free of its folds and clambered to his feet. He could see the containers lying just a few feet away, with already a pair of shadowy figures crouched over them. They were supposed to have marker lights blinking away, to guide the parachutists. None seemed to be working, so it was hugely fortunate they had landed so close.

Having drawn his pistol, Deane Drummond stole towards the containers. As he approached, he heard a cry of challenge: 'Heil Hitler!'

'Viva Duce!' he yelled in reply.

The challenger was Sergeant Lawley, and in his hands he held a Tommy Gun.

'You okay, Sergeant?' Deane-Drummond asked.

'Yes, sir.'

'Good.' He gestured at the Tommy Guns. 'I'll have one of those.' Lawley handed over one of the distinctive submachine guns. 'That's a lot better,' Deane-Drummond announced, cradling the weapon in his arms.

To the east towered the dark bulk of Monte Vulture, and they were almost in its shadow . . . A vulture, awaiting its prey. Shaking off a distinct sense of unease, Deane Drummond gathered his men, dividing them into two parties: one to clear the homesteads above the target, the other to clear those below, and all inhabitants to be brought to him at the muster point – the aqueduct itself.

'Any of you heard or seen any of the other Whitleys?' he asked.

None had.

He gestured at the nearest buildings. 'Right, make sure you bring out every living soul . . . If there are Italian soldiers and they resist, use your weapons. We can't afford to lose a single man.'

As his men set off, Deane-Drummond stole towards the aqueduct itself. It looked utterly deserted. He reached the nearest pier, the rush of water overhead sounding deafening in the still, eerie quiet. It felt unearthly. Unnerving. The scene appeared so beguilingly peaceful, as if they had landed in some Scottish glen. The main difference was the peaks to left and right, which were so much wilder, plus there was little heather or pine forest. All the slopes seemed to be ploughed-up, no matter how steep, in preparation for planting some crop or other.

He strained eyes and ears for any sign of the other parachutists. There was not a sniff of movement or the drone of an aircraft anywhere. He and his men had been scheduled to drop at 2130. They'd done so at 2142, so just twelve minutes late. Not bad, having navigated five hundred miles of hostile airspace.

The other Whitleys had been slated to follow in quick succession, but not a hint of them was there anywhere. Somehow, in the descent from Monte Vulture, his aircraft seemed to have lost the others. Deane-Drummond felt an odd sensation in the pit of his stomach. If all the other Whitleys had missed the target, were he and his men to be the only ones to make it?

The windows of the nearby homesteads eyed him balefully, several glimmering with lantern light. Doubtless, the roar of the Whitley had woken the occupants. On the far side of the aqueduct a track led over a rise, to a further set of buildings. Beyond that lay a road and railway, which led in turn to Calitri, perched on the far hillside, lights twinkling away. There, the enemy seemed wide awake. They too must have heard the throb of the passing warplane, as it swept low over their rooftops.

Some, certainly, would have spied the parachutists, slipping through the moonlit heavens like ghosts. It must have been obvious they were making for the aqueduct. In which case, in which of those buildings near and far were hostile forces readying themselves to investigate? He couldn't be certain. What he did know was that right now there were only six British raiders on the ground, constituting precious little firepower to repulse any enemy.

As he waited, the stillness and quiet was torn apart by the crump of distant explosions. It had the distinctive signature of an air-raid. No doubt it was the two Whitleys in action, making their diversionary attacks. But where on earth were the missing aircraft and the raiders they carried? He cursed to himself silently. Were they all lost? Were he and his men 'on their own'?

Deane-Drummond felt himself cough with the cold, loud into the silence. If his party alone had made it, Colossus was finished before it had even got started. None of his men had the skill or expertise, let alone the explosives, to blow the aqueduct. They were combat troops, here to fight.

In one of the missing Whitleys rode Captain Gerald Francis Daly, of the Royal Engineers, with a force of fellow sappers – demolitions experts – and much of the explosives. It was Daly and his team who had the training and the wherewithal to deal the target a knockout blow. Quiet, studious, pipe-smoking – a lover of fast cars and fine clothes – Daly's chief role was to blow the Tragino aqueduct to smithereens, but he was nowhere to be seen.

All of a sudden the silence was broken by a loud crashing amidst the undergrowth and thorn scrub in the valley below. Deane-Drummond stiffened, readying his weapon to open fire. It was enemy troops no doubt, for he'd neither seen nor heard any other parachute drops. In the moonlit valley of the river Tragino, it looked as if he and his men would be forced to make a last stand.

*

Some fifty miles to the north of Deane-Drummond's position, Whitley 'E for Edward', the lead diversionary aircraft, had just dumped its payload over Foggia railyard, a vital hub in Italy's war-logistics network. In the cockpit rode Wing Commander Sir Nigel Norman, the Air Commander of Colossus, who was determined to witness how well the parachutists had fared. Indeed, although he was a First World War veteran, he regretted very much that he wasn't sufficiently parachute-trained to jump with the men.

From his vantage point in the Whitley's cockpit he was an enthusiastic eyewitness to the first ever combat drop of Allied paratroopers: 'It was easy to see the parachutes floating down. It was a moment one will never forget, but even more I shall remember the . . . wonderful spirit of the men we dropped, their bearing and the way they got into the aircraft . . . singing a song, with special words of their own not particularly suited to the B.B.C.'

Over Foggia, his lone Whitley had likewise done spectacularly well. It had 'bombed the railway station and yard, setting fire to a fuel train, the trucks of which exploded and caused large fires'. One train that 'attempted to leave the station was machine gunned, and M.G. fire was also directed onto the area amid the burning train, to prevent it being put out . . . Smoke from the station was very black and reached over 2,000 ft . . .'

But the second aircraft of his flight suffered markedly different fortunes. Whitley 'S for Sugar', flown by Pilot Officer Jack Wotherspoon, had stuck close to Wing Commander Norman's tail until shortly before the bombing run. Then, all of a sudden the Whitley's port engine had seized up. The aircraft had lurched violently, the crew fearing it would go into a sickening spin, but somehow Wotherspoon had managed to wrestle back control.

After plummeting five hundred feet, Wotherspoon was able to stabilize the aircraft enough to make a ponderous about turn. Jettisoning the Whitley's bombs, he decided to set a course for Malta and try to make it home on the one engine. But some minutes later that too began to cough and splutter alarmingly. It had lost coolant and was fast overheating. The stricken warplane didn't have much life left in her, of that Wotherspoon was certain.

Ordering his crew to prepare to bale out, it was then that he made a fateful decision. Studying the map on his lap, he chose a spot on the western coast upon which to attempt a crash-landing. It was the flat, soft, sandy terrain of the Sele River estuary, the very same point where HMS *Triumph* was scheduled to rendez-vous with the Colossus raiders, six days hence.

Wotherspoon ordered a message sent to Malta headquarters in Syko code, informing them of his intentions. He and those of his crew who opted to stick with the stricken warplane and brave the crash-landing would attempt to hide in the Sele River estuary, in case a British vessel could be sent to rescue them. They'd remain there for five days, awaiting pick-up.

Syko code employed an ingenious mechanism that transposed the letters of a Morse signal into other characters of the alphabet, using a formula that differed for each day of the month. It was difficult to use and often baffled the RAF operators, as much as it did the enemy, but it was also far from impossible to break, hence its use mostly in emergencies.

HQ Malta concluded of S for Sugar's mayday call, which was transmitted twice: 'Compromise of this signal is possible.' In other words, Italian listening stations might have picked up the call and deciphered it, so learning exactly where the stricken British warplane intended to put down.

As matters transpired, most of Wotherspoon's crew decided to take their chances bailing out by parachute. He duly crash-landed at the Sele estuary, S for Sugar ploughing a noisy and muddy furrow through the soft sand and silt, before coming to a smoking halt just short of the water.

Unbeknown to him, his mayday call and crash-landing would have untold consequences for the Colossus mission as a whole.

Chapter 4

Utterly oblivious to such airborne dramas, Deane-Drummond had his Tommy Gun trained on the thick patch of scrub lying below him in the moon-washed valley. A figure emerged, puffing and panting with exertion. Deane-Drummond eased off the pressure on the trigger. The man who had parted the branches and come stomping into the open, only to gaze up at the aqueduct in momentary amazement, was 'old Tag himself'.

It turned out that Pritchard's aircraft had dropped his party a mile or so downstream, on the banks of the River Ofanto. They'd landed on the pebbles, realizing that their pilot had released them over the wrong stretch of water. During his descent, Pritchard had spied the target, looking exactly like he'd expected from Wharburton's recce photos. But he'd also seen the odd shadowy figure moving around it. Were they his own men, or the enemy? And if hostile forces were at the aqueduct, would he and his party have to fight to secure it?

He'd got his answer upon bursting out of the woodland and spying one of his own men, Tommy Gun at the ready. He strode over, and Deane-Drummond gave him a rapid briefing on the situation. The aqueduct was unoccupied, and his men were at that very moment rounding up the locals. The obvious question, bearing in mind the enemy recognised this as a key strategic target, was why had it been left unguarded? Or were there enemy soldiers nearby, taking shelter in the warmth of the locals' houses?

Sergeant 'Taff' Lawley was just then approaching the first building, seeking answers. He had a man on either shoulder and they moved silently, crouching low wherever the moon cast them into bright light and shadow. A door opened, and a dog barked. The three raiders dropped onto the freezing, muddy earth and lay there unmoving. Moments later dog and man disappeared, and Lawley led his team forward at a dash.

Reaching the door from which man and animal had appeared, Lawley ordered one to remain outside to provide cover, and in case anyone emerged from the other buildings. That sorted, he stepped back and booted the front door open. They dashed inside, guns at the ready. Before them lay a stone-flagged room, lit by the dim flame of a paraffin lantern. From around a wooden table several figures stared at them in wide-eyed amazement.

There was an elderly man, a younger male, a woman and some children. The shock of the two British soldiers' sudden appearance seemed to have robbed them of the powers of speech. Lawley tried some calming gestures and a few words in English, designed to reassure. But his pronouncements were met by a torrent of panicked Italian, not a word of which he understood. To break the impasse, he stepped forward and offered a hand for the elder of the family to shake. At seeing this, some of the fear drained from the man's eyes. Reassuring them that no one was about to be shot, Lawley ushered the family outside, the figures pausing only to grab some warm clothing.

That done, he moved to the second house in the hamlet. The same procedure was repeated, only this time he discovered a man in the uniform of an Italian soldier seated at the family table. As

Lawley stepped forward to shake hands with the elder, the soldier made a sudden dive for a weapon leaning against one wall. Lawley was faster, kicking the gun away and menacing the Italian with the muzzle of his Tommy Gun.

'One more trick out of you, and I'll blow your guts out,' he growled.

The enemy soldier might not have understood the words, but the barrel pointing at his stomach coupled with the expression on Lawley's face spoke volumes. Lawley gestured with the gun again. 'I'll use it if I have to.'

The Italian soldier nodded his understanding. All the fight had gone out of him. Lawley and his men searched the remainder of the buildings, rounding up some two dozen villagers in all, plus the one soldier. It seemed as if the aqueduct had only had a single guard allocated to it. Locking the dogs in an outhouse, Lawley formed the captives up and marched them towards the rendezvous point at the aqueduct.

Even as they started to move, the heavens began to reverberate with the drone of approaching aircraft. The first became visible, small in the distance, but growing in size and losing height all the time. Behind it another appeared, until three Whitleys could be seen swooping in towards the drop-zone. Everyone paused to watch – British soldiers and Italian prisoners alike.

The lead aircraft roared overhead, trailing a string of parachutes behind it. It was a beautiful, almost magical sight, like droplets from the moon suspended in the heavens. All gazed skywards transfixed. Parachute operations were all but unknown at the time, so it appeared to the locals as little short of a miracle.

Despite the strange men with guns who were now keeping them company, the children pointed and waved excitedly, crying:

'*Angeli! Angeli!*' Their parents and grandparents crossed themselves, invoking divine protection. Later, the new arrivals would share some of their chocolate rations with the children, but for now they floated to earth with far less angelic intentions in mind.

Captain Lea's aircraft was one of the first in, Corporal Jones – the poetry reader – jumping with him. As luck would have it, Jones plummeted into the midst of an icy river, momentarily going completely under. When he surfaced, he was lucky not to be trapped beneath his parachute, and by the time he'd struggled to shore he was exhausted and fighting for breath.

He hauled himself out, hit the release catch jettisoning his 'chute, watching it dragged off in the swift-flowing waters. He was soaking wet and chilled to the bone, plus coughing-up river water. Still he forced his frozen limbs to move. If he didn't get going, he would surely freeze to death.

After Captain Lea's party came one led by Lieutenant George Paterson, known as 'the Big Canadian', to distinguish him from his fellow raider, a tough, wiry Canadian nicknamed 'Killer' Jowett. At six foot three Paterson was an easy-going giant, a tough backwoodsman hailing from the city of Kelowna, in British Columbia, lying on the shores of the vast Okanagan Lake. A laid-back individual, Paterson didn't like to stand on ceremony or for any of his men to call him Sir. It was all first-name terms in his party.

By contrast, Lieutenant Geoff 'Killer' Jowett, from Montreal, was a small, wiry dynamo of a man renowned for his unbreakable stamina and fiery spirit, hence the nickname. Jowett, like Paterson, didn't like his men to salute or stand to attention much. He just expected them to give their all in the fight against the Nazi – or Fascist – enemy. As Killer Jowett had leapt with gusto from the belly of their warplane, another man from the 'Colonies', Australian Corporal J. Grice, had jumped alongside him.

In one Whitley there was a momentary emergency: Sergeant Percy Clements, a former Leicestershire miner, got jammed in the jump hole. The aircraft was forced to fly around to make a fresh approach, before his comrades managed to free him. In two of those planes the containers were frozen solid in the bomb racks and failed to drop. Another man, none other than Harry 'Lucky' Pexton, having endured the 'long, cold flight' in a 'coffin for many hours', landed in an olive tree. He managed to cut himself free and reach the ground without injury. Lucky indeed.

Mostly, the drops of the parachutists went remarkably well, which was an amazing achievement considering the boulders, gullies and ravines that littered the landscape. When all had mustered at the aqueduct, only one man was found to have injured himself. Lance-Corporal Harry Boulter, from Knutsford, in Cheshire – whose parent unit was the South Staffordshires – had landed on the bank of the Tragino River, crashing into a large boulder.

When Boulter had tried to get to his feet, he realized his ankle was broken. Still, he set about trying to drag his way up towards the aqueduct. Some of his fellow X Troopers helped him to a grassy slope, which offered easier going, whereupon they had to remind themselves of their orders: they had to leave him to make his own way.

By 2245 the skies above the Tragino were clear, and no other aircraft were to be seen. The 51 Squadron pilots would report: 'Very little sign of local activity . . . The lights of a car were seen approaching the bridge . . . the car apparently stopped, for the lights went out. No other vehicles were observed . . . Our own troops were seen moving on the ground. Several times they flashed up their torches . . . to show they had landed successfully.'

From the air at least, all seemed well at the target. Only, it wasn't . . . Five aircraft had released their loads – men and materiel – relatively successfully. But one Whitley, 'J for Juliet', was missing. In many ways, J for Juliet was the very last warplane the operation could afford to have gone astray. Packed full of explosives and carrying Captain Daly's sappers, it was the means by which the target was supposed to be destroyed. But J for Juliet was nowhere to be seen.

At the aqueduct, Tag Pritchard paused to take stock. A lesser man might well have baulked at such a predicament. Prior to leaving the UK, Pritchard had pored over the Operational Instruction, marked 'MOST SECRET AND PERSONAL', committing it to memory. It stated: 'The minimum strength with which the operation is to be carried out is four (4) aircraft . . . each aircraft will carry eight "X" troops. If the operational strength . . . falls below this level, the operation will be cancelled.'

In other words, it required thirty-two raiders to carry out the mission. Five aircraft had dropped their men, but on doing a head-count Pritchard realized he had only twenty-six X Troopers, himself included, on the ground. He was already well short of the 'minimum strength' prescribed in his orders, and one of his twenty-six was injured.

Unbeknown to Pritchard, four men had mysteriously failed to make the jump – one officer and three other ranks. They were presently aboard the Whitleys, heading back to Malta. Worse still, as the official Colossus report would record, 'not much more than a third of the charge of 2240 lbs. of explosives was dropped.' Admiral Keyes' planners had increased the amount required to

71

blow the aqueduct from the 1,680 pounds that SOE had originally calculated, to 2240 pounds. But Pritchard had little more than a third of that available on the ground. The rest was frozen in the Whitleys' bomb racks, or on Captain Daly's missing aircraft.

Regardless, they had come too far to fail now, as far as Pritchard was concerned. First priority was to get his defences set. He didn't doubt enemy forces would be along shortly, seeking to investigate what he and his men were up to. He gathered his officers.

'At the moment we've got the aqueduct to ourselves,' he announced. 'But ... we won't be left unmolested for long.' He figured the parachute drop had to have been spotted, and that 'enemy troops are probably racing here at this moment.'

Pritchard dispatched Deane-Drummond and his men to guard the track leading to the target. Captain Lea's group was split in two, each party charged to hold one end of the aqueduct. Lieutenant 'Killer' Jowett's force, meanwhile, were sent further downstream, to where the Tragino emptied into the Ofanto, to form a semi-circle of troops blocking any incursion that way.

Defences set, Pritchard turned to speak to Lieutenant George Paterson, 'the Big Canadian'. 'A word if you please. You're aware Captain Daly isn't here?'

'Yes, sir.'

'Goodness knows where he is, but he hasn't turned up.' As Paterson was the next most senior sapper after Daly, the demolition would now have to fall to him, Pritchard explained. 'I'm afraid you'll have to mastermind the job yourself.' Paterson was to inspect the aqueduct and work out how to demolish it as he saw fit.

'Okay, sir,' Paterson replied, seeming remarkably unperturbed.

Pritchard turned to the next task in hand – gathering together whatever explosives they did have. He'd been forced to leave the heavy, forty-pound crates where they'd fallen, so he and his men could move quickly. It occurred to him that the able-bodied locals could make themselves very useful right now, helping manhandle the explosives the mile or so up the valley.

Fortunately, Pritchard had Trooper Nastri, his Cockney-Italian 'shadow' with him, so he would be able to make himself understood. In the final analysis, the SOE's proposal to insert two agents ahead of the raiders, to 'cut the telephone wires', had been ruled out. If they were caught, the mission would be blown wide open. Instead, two Italians living in Britain had been drafted in to X Troop, as the SOE's men on the mission.

Trooper Nicol Nastri was a small, wiry-looking man, and had lived much of his life in the East End of London. As with many 'enemy aliens' then resident in Britain, at war's outbreak Nastri had faced either internment, or being recruited into the Pioneer Corps, wherein such nationals were tasked with manual labour, such as digging defences, handling stores and laying prefabricated roads.

Nastri had little interest in becoming one of the 'King's Own Loyal Enemy Aliens', as the Pioneer Corps jokingly referred to themselves. Instead, he'd volunteered for SOE. Dark-haired and distinctly Italian of looks, Nastri faced great risk on a mission such as Colossus, for he was parachuting back into his home country. His job was to stick to Pritchard 'like a limpet', but if captured he could be shot as a traitor or spy.

It was immensely brave of Nastri to have volunteered for such a mission, and on doing so his one request had been that his father, who worked as a chef at London's National Sporting Club, be returned his radio set, on which he loved listening to the BBC.

As an 'enemy alien' it had been confiscated at the outbreak of the war.

'Considering what his son is doing, this seems only fair,' wrote a senior officer, of Nastri's request. 'I wonder if you could pull the right strings to get it done. Nastri does not know what he is going to do any more than the others . . .' In an effort to better protect him, Nastri had been issued with Army papers identifying him as Trooper 'John Tristan' – most English-sounding, but actually 'Tristan' was very nearly an anagram of his actual surname, Nastri.

If anything, the second Italian on Colossus was at even greater risk. Attached to X Troop at the last minute, in case Nastri was killed or captured, Fortunato Picchi – suave, balding, distinctly portly - was a forty-something banqueting manager from London's famous Savoy Hotel. Fiercely anti-Fascist, he'd only managed the one parachute jump before deploying to Malta, so it was something of a double miracle that he'd made it down safely.

Picchi's Army papers identified him as 'No. 3846154, Trooper Pierre Dupont' – a Frenchman, in case his thickly accented English needed explaining away. His SOE report praised his attitude and spirit: 'Is prepared to shine in all England's trials and has no desire to be treated in any way different from an English soldier.' Deane-Drummond would echo such sentiments, describing Picchi as 'the most surprising of our party – and certainly not the least courageous . . . He was fanatical, both in his hatred of the Fascists and his love of Italy . . . no one would have recognised him as the hero he proved to be.'

At Ringway, the two Italian trainees had joined what were euphemistically known as 'The Specials' – secret agents, plus members of the Resistance from across occupied Europe, including Czechs, Poles, Norwegians, French, Yugoslavs and Dutch. They were trained for insertion back into their home countries, to raise guerrilla forces for war. They learned to master parachuting into water and into deep snow, carrying with them pairs of skis. Some 10,000 were trained at Ringway, including scores of women.

Both Picchi and Nastri were to more than prove their worth on Colossus, as Pritchard began outlining exactly what he intended with the explosives. The local men had been locked in an out-house, to keep them from causing any trouble. But Pritchard wanted them released, and ferrying boxes of explosives to the aqueduct. 'Put them to work!' he exhorted Nastri and Picchi.

The two interpreters did just that, the locals responding to their Italian instructions with remarkable enthusiasm. They seemed overjoyed to have something practical to do, rather than mooning about as captives. Nothing ever happened in this part of Italy, they explained, and this would give them something interesting to talk about for the remainder of their lives!

With a Tommy Gun resting across his knees, Pritchard squatted down to observe the work, his back to one of the aqueduct's piers. He saw figures toiling up the slope under heavy loads, his men joking with the Italian 'porters' as best they could. It was amazing how happy the locals seemed to be to collaborate in an operation designed to blow up their own aqueduct. Or maybe they didn't understand what was really going on here.

Lieutenant Paterson stood off to one side, examining the piers. The central one lay in the midst of the fast-flowing Tragino, so no chance that could be blown. But with chisel in hand, the Big Canadian began to knock chunks out of one of the side piers, the sound of his hammering echoing across the valley. Pritchard gazed at the lights of Calitri: for how much longer could they make such a disturbance, without the enemy venturing forth to investigate?

That question was about to be answered. A lone figure appeared on the track, pedalling hell-for-leather in the direction of the Tragino. Deane-Drummond wasted no time in pouncing upon the man and dispossessing him of his bicycle. It turned out he was the local station master, who'd come to investigate the strange goings on. Parties of Carabinieri – armed Italian police – were known to patrol the area, the frightened man exclaimed, and he'd wondered if that's who the strangers were.

Deane-Drummond sent around word that all should redouble their vigilance. That done, the station master was put to work, helping the villagers lug the crates of explosives uphill. Deane-Drummond had discovered that the track he was guarding led to a bridge, one that had been built so construction traffic could get to the site of the aqueduct. Wide-enough to take a large truck, it struck him as constituting an excellent secondary target. It would prevent any vehicles reaching the aqueduct to repair it – that was if they managed to blow it at all.

Certainly, Lieutenant Paterson was having his doubts ... As the Big Canadian had feared upon viewing Wharburton's recce photos, the piers of the aqueduct weren't made of brickwork at all. The mission briefings had got it all wrong. He'd knocked enough render away to be certain: they were made of reinforced concrete. He now faced the challenge of trying to sabotage a target that would take thirty times more explosive power than they'd allowed for, and with only a third of what should have been to hand.

In the mission orders, it was abundantly clear what was

expected of the raiders: 'After being dropped, "X" Troop will destroy the bridge by blowing up each of the three piers simultaneously.' Indeed, they'd practised such demolitions work on a mock-up of the target, back at their base in the UK. But they'd done so working on the assumption that the intelligence on the target was correct, and that the piers were made of brickwork.

Having discovered the bitter truth, Paterson made his way towards his commander, whose well-oiled Tommy Gun glistened softly in the moonlight. The Big Canadian was unusually grim-faced as he began to address Pritchard.

'Afraid the aqueduct is one hell of a sight stronger than we thought . . .'

'What's your trouble, Paterson?'

The Big Canadian explained how they didn't stand a chance of blowing all three piers. So far, Pritchard figured around 700 pounds of 'guncotton' – the nitrocellulose-based explosive they were using as a blasting agent – had been brought in. Their only hope was to concentrate all their charges on the one pier alone, Paterson reasoned, in the hope they might sever it. But there were no guarantees.

'Carry on,' Pritchard told him. 'I'll stand by your judgement.' What other option did he have?

Paterson chose the westernmost pier as the one to attack. One thing did lift his spirits a little: a few more cases of explosives had been found, and he had around 800 pounds in all. He ordered the men to stack the crates of guncotton all around the base of the pier, tamping the charges with earth and rocks, so as to direct the explosive force inwards. Meanwhile, Paterson got Corporal Douglas Jones, the poet-raider, to place an assault ladder (which had also been parachuted in) against the pier, so they could scale its height. Jones slung a wire around the top, attaching a string of 'necklace charges' directly beneath the waterway.

Just as Paterson was about to declare that the whole devilish concoction was ready, a distant drone became audible above the noise of dozens of men – British soldiers and Italian civilians – at work. The noise came and went, as the mystery plane slipped behind snow-capped heights. Was this an enemy search aircraft, sent out to spy upon the Tragino valley? Or was it maybe an inbound warplane, about to strafe and bomb them, undoing all the good work they hoped they had achieved?

The drone grew to a roar, and the aircraft had the distinctive engine note of a heavily laden bomber. It seemed to be making directly for their position, but whether it was German or Italian, or indeed British, no one could tell. All work ceased as eyes scanned the heavens. The aircraft came and went in a flash, passing to the south of their position and slipping behind a mountain top. Most figured it to have been a Whitley. But how? Surely, all the flights had long since turned for Malta?

The warplane had set the dogs barking, and the howling was taken up all across the valley, as curs in isolated farmsteads responded far and wide. The raiders figured the townsfolk would be able to hear the barking from Calitri itself, perched at 1,500 feet on the far hillside. A place that size would have telephones, and its inhabitants would be more than capable of raising the alarm.

Paterson began to hurry now. Taking the detonators, which were packed in tins lined with cotton-wool, he inserted them into the charges and paid out the fuses. Once that was done, he sent an order not to bring up any more explosives. Deane-Drummond stopped the last porters, requisitioning the two crates of guncotton. He figured there was more than enough here to demolish what he had come to see as 'his' bridge. With the help of Lance-Corporal Robert 'Bob' Watson, a Royal Engineer and an early volunteer for airborne operations, Deane-Drummond wedged the crates under one end. At thirty-one years of age Watson, a Geordie and a bricklayer before the war, was one of the oldest of the raiders, but he remained a born adventurer at heart. Watson got the detonators and fuse in place while Trooper Ross, the baby of the unit, prepared to light it. When all was ready, Deane-Drummond sent a runner to Pritchard, to warn him that they would blow this bridge just as soon as the main charge went bang.

'Not a minute before I give the word,' he cautioned. Nothing could be allowed to endanger the main job.

He was blowing the bridge mostly to frustrate any repairs of the aqueduct, but also 'for the fun of the thing', he admitted. He checked his watch: 0015 hours on 11 February 1941. What a way to usher in the new day.

In a rush now, Deane-Drummond hustled the Italian 'porters' back to the outbuilding they'd been incarcerated in earlier. Before shutting and bolting the door, he got Picchi to warn them in no uncertain terms that sentries were being posted outside. Should any try so much as a peep through door or window, those sentries had orders to 'shoot to kill'.

At 0029 hours all was ready. Pritchard fired the warning charge – a one-pound slab of guncotton – reverberations from the explosion echoing back and forth across the mountains, like a sharp clap of thunder. The raiders now had sixty seconds in which to take cover. As they ran for the nearest spur of land, two figures, Pritchard and Paterson, turned back to the main charge.

They eyed each other. 'Okay, then?' Pritchard queried.

'Okay,' the Big Canadian confirmed. 'Remember, just as soon as I've ignited it we've got sixty seconds.'

With that, Paterson bent over the fuse and set fire to it. As it began to hiss and spark, both men turned and ran. They made for a nearby outcrop of rock, throwing themselves behind it. There they waited, Pritchard counting down the seconds via the luminous dial of his watch. A minute passed. No explosion. More seconds ticked by. Still nothing.

It was from the direction of Deane-Drummond's bridge that the first detonation was heard. '"Whoomf!" Our bridge went up in a cloud of flying concrete . . .' Deane-Drummond observed. Not expecting there to be so much debris, he, Lance-Corporal Watson and Trooper Ross were showered with chunks of masonry and fragments of iron. Some of the blasted remains cascaded down onto the nearby farmstead.

A woman came running out, baby clutched in her arms, wailing hysterically. Deane-Drummond and his men hurried to check if any damage had been done. No one was injured, but the villagers seemed beside themselves with worry, convinced that their homesteads were about to be blown sky-high. The 'mad aliens from the sky', as Picchi had heard the locals describe the raiders, would leave no building unscathed, they feared.

Back at the aqueduct there was still no sign of any action. Paterson clambered to his feet, warily. 'Better go see what's gone wrong,' he ventured.

Pritchard joined him. They crept forward 'in considerable tenseness . . . to examine the presumably faulty fuse,' placing their rubber-soled boots as gently as they could on the ground, as if the slightest tremor might trigger the pile of guncotton. They'd covered no more than twelve yards when all of a sudden the night was torn asunder. There was what Pritchard described as 'the father and mother' of all explosions, the terrain before them dissolving into a whirlwind of 'flash, concussion and shower of debris'.

Hurling themselves flat, Pritchard and Paterson covered their heads with their hands, as rocks and shattered concrete tore all around. Blast after blast tore apart the quiet, as one seemed to trigger another, until all merged into one fearful peal of thunder, such as none had ever heard before. The sharp, blinding flashes of the explosions cut through the night, pulsing like lightning across the valley, blazing out over ploughed fields and snowbound slopes, while the blasts rolled around the mountaintops like volleys of cannon fire.

From behind the spur where they had taken cover, the X Troopers raised their heads, cautiously, to see the aqueduct enveloped in a thick plume of dust and smoke, which rose, pillar-like, into the air. They saw two figures, Pritchard and Paterson, pick themselves up from the dirt and dash forwards to check what damage may have been done.

Now was the moment of truth – when they would discover if all their efforts had borne fruit, or if all had been for nought.

In a neighbouring valley a good few miles away, five figures came to a halt. Captain Daly and his sappers paused to listen. After making the rendezvous point over Monte Vulture, somehow their aircraft, J for Juliet, had lost its way. They'd ended up being dropped at 2345 – so two hours late – and in the wrong place. 'We were unfortunately "tipped out" in the wrong gorge,' Daly would report of their predicament. They'd had no choice but to lift their heavy packs, making for the neighbouring valley, where the target must lie.

Captain Daly, hailing from a military family, was barely five-and-a-half feet tall, but what he lacked in height he more than made up for in soldiering ability. He was another veteran of Dunkirk, and was known to be 'as tough as a little acorn'. He'd volunteered for Special Service when a visiting recruiting major had joked: 'I'm looking for small chaps who can get through a hole easily.' He'd meant a Whitley's hole, of course, as Daly had soon discovered.

Daly and his men were halfway up their side of the ridge, when the noise of a massive explosion echoed across from the far side. As they stood still and listened, the reverberations dying away into a ringing silence, they figured it could only be one thing: the charges being detonated at the aqueduct. It seemed as if the main body of raiders had acted without their specialist team of sappers, plus all the weight of explosives they were carrying.

Daly glanced at the others. 'Good man, that Paterson,' he remarked simply, of the Big Canadian.

All agreed that there was little point in blindly pressing on. Having checked his map, Daly confirmed that the rendezvous point with the submarine lay in the opposite direction. All it made any sense to do was to retrace their steps, starting the long trudge westwards. 'We altered our course for the coast,' Daly would report, 'and the pre-arranged rendezvous at the mouth of the river SEALI [sic].'

They did just that, wondering all the while how successful the saboteurs may have been.

Chapter 5

Spattered in mud and debris, Pritchard and Paterson came to a halt some ten yards from where the explosives had been piled against the western pier. The scene had so utterly changed, it rendered them momentarily speechless. 'Half the aqueduct was down,' Pritchard observed, the target pier having completely disintegrated, while a second lay at a crazy angle, and the waterway itself was rent with huge cracks, from which water cascaded in a deafening roar.

Ruptured at both ends, torrents poured from either side of the aqueduct, forming two foaming waterfalls, from where the twin deluges converged, draining into the Tragino itself to form one raging torrent that tore down the hillside and surged into the valley beyond. For long seconds they stared at the devastation in undisguised glee. Clearly, the Italian version of reinforced concrete wasn't quite as 'reinforced' as they made it in the UK.

Finally, Tag Pritchard broke the silence – or rather, yelled above the wild roar of the water. 'Come on! We've no time to lose!'

They dashed back to the others, the expressions on their dirty, mud-spattered faces alone telling the incredible story. They were bombarded with questions, as X Troopers demanded to know just how successful the sabotage had proved. Pritchard held up a hand for quiet.

'Listen to the sound of that,' he announced.

The men did. Silence settled over them, but it was underscored by the sound of gurgling, rushing water – thousands of cubic feet of the life-giving stuff, gushing away uselessly into the valley below. The engineering feat that was the Apulian Aqueduct – all 213.5 kilometres of it, tracing its twisting course through the Apennine Mountains – had been well and truly ruptured.

The raiders gave vent to their feeling, volleys of cheers ringing out across the hills. Against all odds, in spite of the faulty intelligence and the failed drops, they'd delivered their surprise to Il Duce all right. Now they had to ensure that he didn't deliver a surprise to them in turn, for a long and treacherous escape march lay before them, and they were sure to be hunted all the way.

One man had been forced to watch the sabotage from a distance – Lance-Corporal Harry Boulter, with his injured ankle. He'd lain in his grassy field, back propped against a rock, for a good two hours. Once he'd heard the explosions and the cheers, he forgot for a moment his predicament and his pain.

He smiled to himself. 'Bloody marvellous.' He kept repeating that phrase, over and over again.

Tag Pritchard gathered his men. He told them how proud he was of them all, and the 'splendid job' they'd wrought. He'd love to see 'old Mussolini's face' when he learned of the success of the raid. But there was no time for that now. Instead, they faced a sixty-mile trek to the coast. He told them they had a 'sporting chance' of making it, if they moved only at night, resting up in cover during daylight.

Pritchard cautioned that what lay ahead would test them to the very limits. It was uncharted mountainous terrain. Much of the time they would be thousands of feet above sea level, and it would be desolate and bitterly cold. But they were the 'best trained bunch' in the British Army, and with luck they would make it. As they needed to travel light, they were to dismantle most of their Tommy Guns, and bury them in the mud. If they stumbled into any trouble they might have need of the firepower, but speed was more a priority.

They were to split into three groups. One was to be led by Killer Jowett and Flight Lieutenant Lucky – if that was indeed his real name. Another would be commanded by Captain Lea and Lieutenant Paterson, the Big Canadian and architect of so much of the destruction that night. The third would consist of Pritchard and Deane-Drummond and a dozen-odd men.

'There isn't much more to say but good luck to you all,' Pritchard concluded, gruffly.

That only left a swift farewell to Lance Corporal Boulter, who knew very well that he would be left behind. Pritchard gave the wounded man some painkillers and instructions on how to use them, and having apologized for having to abandon him, wished the man luck. The worst that could happen was that Boulter would be taken prisoner and be out of the war for a while.

Pritchard was about to depart, when he turned back to the wounded man. If the Italians did seize him, he warned, they were bound to try to make him talk. He reminded Boulter they were relying on him not to breathe a word about how many raiders there were, or where they might be heading.

'I've not let you down yet, sir, and I'm not likely to now,' Boulter told him.

'Good man.'

With that they shook hands and Pritchard hurried on his way.

The rest of the raiders came, one by one, to wish Boulter farewell. They pressed chocolate and cigarettes upon him, but mostly he asked for a Tommy Gun and as much ammo as they could spare. He'd be able to make far more use of it than they would, burying it in the mud. *They* had the worst of it, he joked. *They* had a bloody long march over the mountains ahead of them. *He* could rest up, cradle his weapon and await the dawn.

It was 0100 hours by the time the twenty-five raiders were ready to move out. With barely another word Tag Pritchard led the way west towards the first, distant ridge line. Within minutes thick, gloopy mud was sucking at their boots. It glimmered darkly in the moonlight, stretching to the heights above. The men heard Pritchard bark out a curse. He was known never to swear. The conditions underfoot were getting even to him.

A lone figure darted back for a moment. It was Deane-Drummond, dashing across to Boulter. He'd already said his goodbyes along with the rest, but he returned momentarily to shake the wounded man's hand. There was nothing else he could think of to say. With that he turned and ran to rejoin the ranks of troops, moving in single file, ever higher into the mountains.

Boulter watched them go. He traced their line of march, like files of ants, black against the snowy whiteness, until the last figure was no more. He felt cold now. He was in pain. His injured foot had swollen so much he decided to cut off his boot. Then he wrapped the foot in his leather para-helmet, packing the inside with snow to reduce the swelling, after which he managed to hobble to a nearby hut.

It was empty. He crawled inside, scrabbled up some straw, lay down and fell into an exhausted sleep.

Even as Boulter drifted into a cold, uncertain slumber, so a 'Most Secret' coded message was winging its way from

Malta to London. It was 0245 hours on 11 February, and Wing Commander Norman had only recently touched down. He was overjoyed to announce the initial success of the mission.

Operation Colossus night 10/11 Feb. Six aircraft dropped X Troop and stores in vicinity of objective in ideal conditions ... Two additional Whitleys created diversion. Petrol train set on fire FOGGIA station. One returned to base. Second aircraft missing. Crew thought to have abandoned aircraft after engine trouble. No A.A. or ... opposition. No E.A. encountered.

All things considered, Colossus appeared to have gone astoundingly well. The raiders had been dropped as planned, there had been few enemy air defences – 'AA': anti-aircraft fire; 'EA': enemy aircraft – and little opposition encountered on the ground, as far as anyone could tell.

In London, mission planners hailed the herculean efforts of the RAF aircrew, who had succeeded in finding their way hundreds of miles from Malta and back again, to execute mostly pinpoint-accurate drops, and with such limited navigational resources as the Whitleys possessed. Now they just had to wait for confirmation of the success of the raid on the ground.

Typically, Wharburton was itching to get airborne again, and to secure recce photos to confirm absolutely just what a surprise the X Troopers had delivered to Il Duce. Just as soon as it was light, he would make his first attempt. And just as soon as those photos could be analysed, everyone, right up to the level of Churchill, could be acquainted with the good news.

*

As luck would have it, the winter of 1940/41 was one of the worst in living memory in Italy. For weeks on end snow and sleet had hammered into the mountains, the temperature plummeting. Tiny streams had swollen into raging torrents. The X Troopers, fleeing west over the moon-washed heights, had all of that to face and more.

They forded the worst of the rivers in single file, each grasping the pack of the man in front. During one such crossing, 'Big Jock' Walker – all six-foot-two of Scottish beef and sinew – had to reach out and rescue a fellow raider, who was in danger of being swept away, dragging him back into line.

Below the snowline, they were forced to trudge through ploughed fields ankle-deep in mud. Pritchard described the terrain underfoot as 'the most glutinous stuff imaginable'. On the steeper slopes, men fought to gain a hold using Commando knives, the butts of their few remaining Tommy Guns, or even their bare hands. For every foot of height gained, it was just as easy to slide right back again.

Once they hit the snowline, other dangers beckoned. The numbing cold penetrated everything. Even though they kept permanently on the move, the X Troopers could not keep warm. Snow-filled holes lay in wait. Some, as large as quarries, were easy enough to avoid. Others, the size of small trucks, were undetectable until a Trooper plunged in, and had to be hauled out by a chain of men linking arms.

Tag Pritchard – tireless, buoyed up by the success of the mission – drove his party on, the pace unrelenting. Even so, the high spirits natural to such men after scoring such an unprecedented success gradually began to abate. Bit by bit, the silence of agonized exhaustion settled upon the frozen, mud-caked figures.

Pritchard aimed to make a high ridge, and to stick to that for as long as possible, but unseen fissures littered their path. There was no time to make lengthy detours. On the icy downslopes, he and his men slithered and careered wildly, trying their best to avoid trees and boulders. Then they faced the seemingly impossible climb out again. Time and again such features blocked their way. Time and again, they were 'much hampered by heavy equipment and rubber boots on muddy ground'.

At one point there was a sharp crack like a pistol shot, and the entire flank of the hillside above them began to move. A sea of snow, mud and boulders cascaded toward Pritchard and his men, but downhill lay only a precipice several hundred feet deep. The men were forced to stand their ground against the tide of detritus, as the evil-seeming avalanche surged around them, before crashing into the void beyond.

Come first light, it was a small miracle that none of Pritchard's party had been seriously injured or killed. The two other escape parties – three, if Captain Daly and his four sappers were included – had suffered equally appalling conditions and privations. Amazingly, not a man among them had yet been lost to death or injury. But with dawn, other priorities took over: avoiding the eyes and ears of the enemy.

As the light strengthened, Pritchard and his men spied a ravine with a thick patch of scrub at one end. Down the guts of that gorge ran a thin, icy stream: life-giving water. Pritchard consulted Deane-Drummond. Both agreed it was a perfect hideaway. They scrambled down. Once in shelter, those carrying the stoves broke them out and got busy. Hot tea laced with sugar helped warm bodies and revive spirits. But the pemmican, once 'brewed' up, proved all but inedible. The fatty, sludgy porridge made many of the men gag. They were in desperate need of the nutrition, but even Pritchard and Deane-Drummond – trying to put on a brave face – had problems forcing the abominable stuff down them.

They had 'travelled at a fairly rapid rate over very difficult country', Deane-Drummond would report of that first night's march. Trooper Picchi, their Italian former banqueting manager, 'kept up very well, although he appeared to be suffering from some chest disorder, and coughed continuously. There was, of course, every incentive for him to keep up.' If Picchi were captured, and his real identity discovered, his chances of survival were slim indeed.

Once they'd eaten, Pritchard and Deane-Drummond checked their maps. Incredibly, they realized they'd made no further progress than the village of San Lorenzo, which meant they'd pushed no more than five or six miles west of their target. They'd had several hours of darkness in which to march, and ten times that kind of distance lay ahead of them, if they were to make the rendezvous with the submarine. They figured they'd have to double that distance in the nights to come if they were to make it to the first RV, scheduled for the 16th. They didn't want to risk waiting for the second, for the area was bound to be crawling with hostile forces.

The first sign of the enemy was not long in coming: it was a spotter aircraft. It flew in low over the ravine at just a few hundred feet, quartering its entire length. Gazing up through the branches, those hiding could see the observer, using a pair of binoculars to scan the terrain below. But whether they'd been seen or not, no one could tell . . .

Within gulleys and isolated copses scattered over the

snowbound heights, three other parties of X Troopers – equally frozen, equally exhausted – attempted to lie low and avoid the enemy's gaze. The raiders were starting to be plagued by a distinctly hunted feeling. Yet, in the event, the first of their number to make contact with the enemy would be none of those hiding amidst those inhospitable peaks. It would be the man injured upon landing, Lance Corporal Harry Boulter.

Boulter awoke shortly after dawn on 11 February, his frozen hands gripping the cold metal of his Tommy Gun. Parched with thirst, his first priority was water. He managed to hobble to a nearby stream and refill his bottle. Back in his shack, he kept his eyes on the nearest houses. Finally, there was movement. Nervously, a figure stole forth, dressed in the distinctive uniform of an Italian soldier.

Realizing that the raiders had gone – save the hidden watcher, of course – he grabbed a bicycle and sped off. As he neared Boulter's position, the hidden X Trooper directed a burst of Tommy Gun fire in the cyclist's direction. His pedalling became ever more frantic, as bullets whipped past his head. But it was hard to hit a moving target. Shortly, man and bike were gone, racing off in the direction of Calitri.

Boulter realized that that burst of fire had revealed his position. More soldiers would be coming sometime soon and he had to be ready. Tommy Gun gripped in hand, he began to crawl uphill, dragging his injured foot behind him in great pain. Finally, he found a large boulder behind which to take cover. It was as good a place as any to make a last stand.

Some hours later, two carloads of Carabinieri bumped up the track leading to the Tragino Gorge. They stopped just below

Boulter's position. From there, the shattered form of the aqueduct was perfectly visible, and the roar of the escaping water could be heard. A truck arrived bearing soldiers. Only then did the combined force turn their attention to the shack, from which Boulter had made his getaway.

They stopped short of the hut, yelling challenges and firing rounds into it. When no one responded, they rushed the building, only to find no one inside of course. They fanned out, moving slowly up the hillside towards Boulter's position. Boulter realized if he let them get behind him, he'd be outflanked and vulnerable from the rear. He leaned around the rock, levelled his weapon, and gritting his teeth against the pain he opened fire.

Carabinieri and soldiers alike dropped to the ground, returning fire with their rifles. Rounds pinged off the boulder. Boulter kept trading fire with fire, trying to beat back the phalanx of enemy, but it was always going to be a losing battle. Finally, having unleashed a last burst, he groped in his backpack for spare magazines. There was none. He was all out of bullets.

Realizing the fire from the *paracadutista* had died down, the enemy closed in. First upon Boulter was a Carabinieri sergeant, who wasted no time slapping him in handcuffs, before trying to prod him to his feet. Boulter gestured at his ankle. He was injured. He couldn't move. No one seemed to give a damn. They set about him, using fists, boots and rifle butts to beat him. So fierce was the assault that his uniform was torn open, revealing the corner of one of the secret escape maps.

That may well have saved Boulter's life. Attention shifted from him to the map. Eager fingers grabbed it, ripping it free. It was handed to the officer in charge, who studied it carefully. Finally, Boulter was hauled to his feet, and by gestures and yells it was made clear what was expected of him. Under guard, he was to walk to the nearest town.

Boulter began to hobble. Each time he fell, or limped too slowly for his captor's liking, he was assailed by rifle butts. Finally, they bundled Boulter into a car. Upon arrival at their destination – a large town; maybe a city even – Boulter would get to see a doctor at last, but only after repeating the words 'Red Cross' to every Italian who might listen. Upon inspection, it was found that his ankle had been fractured.

An Italian officer arrived to interrogate him. To every question, Boulter refused to give any information other than his name, rank and serial number. The line of inquiry was clear: the questioner was desperate to know in what direction and with what intentions the *paracadutisti* had disappeared. Boulter was saying nothing, or not until he sensed the chance to have a little fun at his interrogator's expense.

'How many of you *paracadutisti* drop into Tragino?' he asked.

'About fifty-five thousand,' Boulter replied.

The interrogator's face darkened. Boulter was warned not to be 'English comedian'. It was making the interrogator angry, which didn't bode well. He kept the interrogation going for hours, long into the evening. Always the same questions. How many dropped? Where are they headed? Who is in command? How do they intend to escape?

Boulter didn't break and he certainly wasn't telling.

As a bitter dusk descended over the mountain heights, the X Troopers – the hunted fugitives – shook life into stiff, frozen limbs. Pritchard's men shouldered their backpacks, strapped on knives and pistols and began to walk. At first they took a goat track, one spied out by Sergeant Lawley earlier that day. It led to a fast-flowing river, which was forded via a series of stepping stones. There was a gap in the middle. All jumped it bar one, who plunged into the icy torrent. Rescued, he would have to march all night in soaking clothes.

The track led up a horribly steep slope, which was knee deep in mud. When finally they reached the top, Pritchard and his men realized they had arrived at the source of the River Sele itself. Now all they had to do was to follow the river to its outlet, where HMS *Triumph*, with her rum and Navy rations, should be waiting. They pressed on, spirits buoyed a little, dogs howling in villages near and far at their passing. The feeling of being hunted was palpable.

At midnight, Pritchard called a halt to brew tea. It warmed them, but it was only by sheer stubborn willpower that his men were keeping moving at such an unrelenting pace through such punishing terrain. From their position on the high ground he eyed a road. For hours now they'd been moving parallel with its course. For all that time it had remained devoid of traffic. Deserted. It ran in exactly the right direction to speed them on their way.

Finally, Pritchard gave voice to his thoughts. The road was deserted. Not a car, truck, bicycle or pedestrian had they seen on it. It ran straight and true, the way they needed to go. They could move fast along such a highway. The escape plan had always allowed for 'seizing a lorry or bicycles'. Pritchard suggested they make for the road. No one dissented. If they tried to stick to the mountains they would never make the rendezvous, that much was clear now.

Pritchard led his men in a scramble down from the ridge. As

their rubber-soled boots made contact with the firm tarmac of the highway, spirits rose. The men began truly to march now, swinging along in unison for miles, cutting a swathe through the night. Then, out of nowhere, a darkened horse and cart appeared. At the reins hunched the shadowed form of a peasant woman.

Pritchard signalled the interpreter forward. 'As we pass, call out our step in Italian,' he whispered. 'Left, right and so on.' In the thick darkness, it should be impossible for any locals to tell that he and his men weren't Italian soldiers. Sure enough, the phalanx of raiders surged past, keeping time to marching orders cried out in Italian, before pressing on towards the promise of safety.

At the approach of dawn the ruse seemed to be holding good. They turned off the road, and Pritchard and Deane-Drummond began searching for a hideout. The map showed a hilltop apparently thick with forest, but by the time they reached the cloud cover, which lay dense and low around the heights, no woodland was there to be seen. When they did finally discover a small patch of trees, it turned out there was a farmstead right at its very midst.

Deane-Drummond felt his spirits plummet. His limbs had never felt so leaden or so full of aches. Clothes soaked from the sweat of the forced-march were starting to freeze in the chill. They pushed higher, the cloud closing thick and opaque all around them. Finally, they reached a patch of scrub clinging to the hillside, interspersed with a few shallow caves. They collapsed into it, shivering and utterly exhausted, but grateful for the respite and the shelter.

On other hillsides, others of the X Troop had suffered even greater privations during that long night. Captain Daly's force of five had been engulfed by blinding, blizzard-like conditions. 'We ran into a snowstorm and lost our direction, travelling in a circle,' he reported. 'In consequence we were well behind time. We had to be at the rendezvous by 2200 hrs on the 16th Feb.' Under pressure, Daly also made the decision that they had to take to the roads. The race was on.

Other escape parties figured they would do likewise. Captain Lea and Lieutenant Paterson, the Big Canadian, led their party on a punishing night-march, taking to the roads where necessary. Killer Jowett had set a murderous pace over the high ground. Sergeant Clements was with him – the X Trooper who'd got stuck in the Whitley's jump hole – plus Trooper Ross, the baby of the unit, and Trooper Grice, the Australian.

So, too, was the mysterious 'Flight Lieutenant Lucky'. He alone voiced objections, when Jowett suggested they resort to using the road, at least for the few remaining hours of darkness. 'I'm not in the business of getting caught,' Lucky had announced, somewhat confrontationally. As if any of them were, Killer Jowett retorted. In the final vote, Lucky was outnumbered. Their force, too, would march on the darkened highway.

Come first light, Killer Jowett spotted a place of hiding. He'd noticed a thickly wooded island lying in the centre of the River Sele, which by now was broad and sluggish. He and his men waded across the water, crawled into the densest cover and settled down to wait out the daylight hours.

It was dawn on 12 February 1941, and the new day ushered in clearer weather over the mountains. Come mid-morning, an unusual aircraft cut through the thin winter skies to the west of Monte Vulture. Hunched over the controls of the speeding Maryland was Flight Lieutenant Adrian 'Warby' Wharburton. As his aircraft flashed across the Tragino Gorge his cameras were whirling.

From Malta HQ, a message had been sent to London, confirming rescue measures for the raiders: 'Sailing H.M.S. TRIUMPH as previously arranged ... instructed to proceed with utmost care ... to reconnoitre Bay concerned near date of withdrawal to see if there is enemy patrol activity.' Lieutenant Commander Wilfrid Woods was en route, his submarine already due west of Sicily and steaming steadily northwards, bang on schedule.

Upon arrival back at his Malta base, Wharburton's films were rushed off the Maryland, straight through the labs, and the enlargements thrust into the eager hands of Wing Commander Sir Nigel Norman at the makeshift Colossus HQ. The photos showed the target in riveting detail, individual trees being clearly visible. The photos were hand notated: 'Taken <u>after</u> operation. For use with stereoscope.'

The stereoscope resembled an odd-looking set of binoculars mounted in a frame: images examined via the device – two photos, viewed via the two lenses – would 'jump out' at the viewer, appearing as if in 3D. It was a useful means for interpreting reconnaissance photos, a skill perfected at the outbreak of the war. But as the team of photo-interpreters studied Wharburton's images, something seemed to be wrong. The aqueduct stood out clearly, as did the shadow it cast below, but it appeared to be *unharmed*.

The analysts checked and rechecked the photos. No matter how they scrutinized them, they seemed to show the aqueduct wholly intact. How could it be? The raiders had been dropped. There had been little obvious sign of any resistance on the ground. Yet, inexplicably, the photos appeared to show the Tragino aqueduct undamaged. Closer study of the images revealed a group of trucks and cars drawn up at the nearby farmstead, but no vehicles at the aqueduct itself, which would have been expected, had it been sabotaged.

It was a mystery. Finally, at 1810 hours on 12 February, Wing Commander Norman dispatched a coded message to London, outlining the only possible conclusion that he believed he could reach, on the evidence to hand. 'MOST SECRET. Air photographs taken ... Both bridges are intact. Mistake by ground party unlikely since both bridges would be clearly visible during approach from dropping ground. Cannot therefore explain failure of operation.'

In a longer typed report, Wing Commander Norman echoed that mystified, despairing phrase: 'The failure of the operation cannot yet be explained ...' While noting that the Whitleys failed to release some of the arms and explosives, he continued:

The whole of X Troop force was dropped, apparently under good conditions in the vicinity of the objective ... the force could probably give a good account for itself with the arms available ... and in any case no sign of opposition was observed from the air.

'It seems impossible that some vital piece of equipment necessary for the demolition was lost ... The only possibilities that seem to remain are: (i) the details of the operation were known to the enemy and the party was captured immediately ... (ii) that the objective was entirely different in construction from anticipated design, and the equipment available was insufficient for its destruction.

Sadly, no one imagined that the recce photos may have been interpreted incorrectly; that the bridge might appear intact from several thousand feet, but had in fact been blasted apart and severely ruptured. Either way, by the evening of 12 February 1941, Operation Colossus had been branded an inexplicable failure. The news landed like a bombshell in London. But there was worse to come.

The following morning the Chiefs of Staff held a meeting, Operation Colossus being Item One on the agenda. Admiral Sir Dudley Pound, First Sea Lord and Chief of the Naval Staff, was in the chair. Viewed by some as 'Churchill's anchor', Pound was a controversial figure during the war, accused of lacking clarity of judgement, as epitomized by the failed summer 1940 Norwegian campaign.

Regarding Colossus, Pound opened the meeting by stating that 'the enemy would now probably be aware of the rendezvous for the submarine as the message sent out by the aircraft had unfortunately been in simple code . . .' He was referring to S for Sugar's mayday call, after her engines had failed and the Whitley had been forced to make a crash-landing at the Sele estuary. Pound went on to say that he considered it 'wrong to risk the probable loss of a valuable submarine and its crew against the possibility of bringing off a few survivors'.

Sir Charles Portal, the Air Chief Marshal – head of the Royal Air Force – appeared to agree with Pound. 'Latest air reconnaissance reports appeared to show that the objective had suffered no damage,' he was recorded as saying. 'As the Operation had miscarried it was probable that most, if not all, of the personnel had been killed or rounded up.' After a little more discussion, Admiral Pound decided to 'cancel the despatch of the submarine . . .'.

While no one from Combined Operations was present, Item 3

on the agenda that morning was: 'Invasion: Operations by Special Service Troops'. Those present, who still insisted on using the phrase 'S.S. Troops' for the Commandos and the SAS, suggested: 'S.S. Troops would have a very useful role in the reinforcement or recapture of islands, such as the Orkneys and Shetlands and the Isle of Wight . . . It would be . . . difficult to organise and stage counter raids on the enemy embarkation ports during the turmoil of invasion.'

Their mindset was still overwhelmingly defensive – invasion oriented – and lacking in offensive vision. The supposed failure of Colossus – Britain's first ever airborne raid – would have been grist to their mill. As far as they were concerned, it 'proved' that British forces, under the Prime Minister's unrealistic urgings, had overreached themselves. Far better to rein in the raiders – the 'S.S. Troops' – and prepare for the coming of the Wehrmacht to British shores.

At 1541 hours on 12 February, a HUSH MOST SECRET Naval Cypher message was despatched from Admiral Pound to Malta. It read: 'Investigation shows that it is most probable that Syko message made by the aircraft has compromised the withdrawal orders. H.M.S. TRIUMPH is to be recalled forthwith and the withdrawal operation cancelled.'

Unsurprisingly, as soon as Roger Keyes, Chief of Combined Operations, learned of this, he was apoplectic. He had never rated the X Trooper's chances of escape at more than fifty-fifty, but to cancel the submarine left them no chance at all. It was unconscionable. Keyes pushed back with all his might, using every weapon in his arsenal: 'I did everything in my power to get the recall of the submarine cancelled.'

Viewed as a maverick adventurer by many in high command,

Keyes, of course, had Churchill's ear. The two men shared a vision about the promise of raiding and airborne operations. They believed wholeheartedly that British forces needed to go on the offensive; that the boldest measures were the safest. In defence of the Colossus raiders, Keyes penned an appeal addressed directly to his friend, the Prime Minister.

'Prime Minister,' he began, 'The . . . Chiefs of Staff Committee has just informed me that a decision has been taken . . . to cancel the arrangements which had been made to attempt to rescue by submarine the . . . parachutist troops who volunteered for a hazardous enterprise.' Keyes explained how, when and where the rendezvous was planned, and why the decision had been made to abandon the raiders to their fate.

He rounded off: 'I consider our failure to make any effort to carry out the salvage arrangements, promised to the parachutists, amounts to a clear breach of faith.' He signed off begging Churchill to overrule the decision, or at the very least to leave it to the discretion of the Vice Admiral, based in Malta, who Keyes knew would abhor the suggestion they abandon Pritchard and his men.

Churchill demanded answers of his Chiefs of Staff. 'An air reconnaissance has shown the target to be intact . . .' they argued. In other words, the Tragino aqueduct still stood; *Colossus had failed*. They reiterated their standpoint that the 'risk of sending the submarine into the prearranged rendezvous should not be accepted'.

It is a simple adage but true that nothing succeeds like success. It is equally true that nothing fails quite like failure. Colossus had been branded an abject failure, and in the lack of any evidence to the contrary HMS *Triumph* was ordered to make an about turn and return to port that very evening.

'*Triumph* was recalled by the Admiralty; and altered course to return to Malta at 2020 13th February, 1941.' At the point of being ordered back to port, the submarine was 200 miles north of Sicily, so already in position to swing east towards the Sele estuary. Instead, she made an about turn and headed home.

Keyes, overruled, was devastated. Typically, he didn't pull his punches. Of *Triumph*'s recall, he stated:

> It has been a matter of great regret to me that the Naval arrangements to rescue COLOSSUS troops were not carried out . . . every effort would have been made by the submarine to effect rescue and it can only be hoped that no troops arrived at the beach to meet with disappointment.
>
> It is deplorable that the brave spirits and high endeavour of these very gallant soldiers should have been expended upon such an ill-prepared operation . . . [W]hile it is impossible to judge the result of their action until the full history is known, it is certain that . . . their enthusiasm and warlike spirit was admirable . . .

He praised Major Pritchard, 'whose exceptional qualities of courage and leadership have been a constant inspiration . . .'

Similar sentiments were expressed by those in command at Malta. 'It was a cause of much regret to TRIUMPH and to all who had met them that . . . Triumph had to be recalled . . . The position selected for the withdrawal of these men was reasonably good. The water was deep, close to an uninhabited coast, there was a good landmark, no rocks, and a good sea bed for bottoming.'

On 15 February 1941, Churchill penned a personal minute to

General Ismay, his chief military adviser, expressing regret over Colossus. 'I would rather not have opened this chapter, raising as it does all sorts of questions about the status and uniform of these troops. Let me have a report as soon as possible upon the preparation and execution of this plan . . . Make sure that for the future my initial is obtained to all projects of this character.'

General Ismay responded by diplomatically reminding Churchill that 'you approved the Operation on 9th February,' and suggesting one possible reason for the apparently dismal outcome. 'The chances are that the raiding party for some reason failed to reach their objective and the inference is that they have been captured.'

The Tragino aqueduct might hang in tatters, its waters draining uselessly into the river below, yet no one but the raiders – and the Italian forces now hunting them – knew that. Admiral Keyes, Director of Combined Operations, had been absolutely right when he'd counselled caution, stating that 'it is impossible to judge the result of their action until the full history is known.' But based on the scant evidence to hand – the recce photos – the top brass had jumped to the wrong and damning conclusion: the mission had failed.

Failure meant death or capture, and that meant that no submarine should be sent, especially if it risked interception by the enemy. Either way, the Operation Colossus raiders – Keyes, Clarke and Churchill's SAS originals – had been hung out to dry. In that sense they truly had been the expendables.

The supposed 'failure' of Colossus – the first airborne raid ever executed by the Allies – would cast a long shadow over the war-torn months to come.

Chapter 6

Claude Wavell bent over the photograph, studying it more closely. The black-and-white image showed an expanse of sullen, November-grey sea rolling towards towering cliffs of chalky-whiteness some 400 feet high. To the right lay a tide-dark pebble beach, flecked at its lower end with breakers, its upper side leading to a deep cleft running inland, lined with a slew of buildings. But it wasn't those that interested Wavell.

His eyes lingered on the far left of the image, scrutinizing a rectangle of woodland and the paths leading to and from it. The trees sheltered an ancient, fortified French farmstead – part-barn, part-castle, arranged around a courtyard – beyond which lay the reason the pilot had risked his dash through enemy airspace to secure this image. There lay a Freya radar unit – a small, mobile device, looking much like a king-size sprung mattress laid on its side. Of that much they were certain.

Still Wavell kept tracing and retracing the paths snaking to and from the Freya's position. One track branched south, leading to a flamboyant-looking, high-roofed chateau, isolated atop the cliffs, and appearing quite out of place amidst acres of grassland close-cropped by grazing cattle. A smaller path – barely visible at this resolution – led from the chateau towards the very drop to the sea. Why would it do that? Perhaps there was a pillbox or bunker, perched right on the cliff edge – slit windows gazing out balefully across the Channel, in search of Allied warships.

But the more he studied it, the more the path seemed to fade to nothing, stopping just a few dozen feet short of the cliffs. Just where it appeared to end, there was a distinctive black spot - no more than a full-stop when viewed from this kind of altitude. Of course, it could be just about anything. An animal feeding pen. A latrine. An especially fat and dark-coloured cow. A speck of dust caught on the film. The latter, most likely. But something was eating at Wavell. Was there just a chance that this might be the most elusive of all German technology, for which he and colleagues had so long been searching? Might it?

For months much of the talk at RAF Medmenham, the head-quarters of Allied photo reconnaissance work, had been of this mysterious and most deadly German 'paraboloid' radar. The more he stared at the speck, the more it seemed to jump out at Wavell. Was it just his imagination, or did it seem to have that extraordinary bowl-like structure the boffins at scientific intelligence had led him to believe they were looking for? Maybe. Definitely a maybe. He placed the photo carefully to one side. It was something to discuss with Jones, his favourite scientific intelligence expert, just as soon as the man put in an appearance. He was bound to be along to Medmenham sometime soon.

Reginald Victor Jones – known to all as R. V. Jones – was a big, jovial, broad-featured fellow who worked for the British Secret Intelligence Service (SIS) in the field of science, and more specifically that of winkling out the enemy's newest war technologies. Jones's appointment to SIS was an absolutely crucial one for the war. Described as 'a scientist with a special interest in German weapons', many a lesser individual would have failed to make a mark in the secretive and rarefied world of intelligence. Jones proved the exception. Deeply influenced by his parents, who remained hugely suspicious of German intentions following the First World War, he'd also paid special attention to the views of his headmaster at Alleyn's, the Dulwich, London public school, on the theory of repentance and forgiveness.

The Germans had never repented the First World War, he argued. They had only ever expressed regret that they had lost it. 'And mark my words, as soon as they are ready they'll be at it again,' his headmaster had averred. Jones would distinguish himself in the war as being willing to speak difficult and unpalatable truths to those who least wanted to hear them. By his own admission, he might not have survived doing so, 'had the situation not been so serious' – i.e. had Britain not been faced with defeat after defeat in so many theatres of the war.

Jones was fascinated by the craft of photo reconnaissance, and he just couldn't keep away from Medmenham. Indeed, he and his assistant, Charles Frank, had also noticed that strange dot atop the Normandy cliffs. They'd telephoned to say so, and Jones would be dying to find out Wavell's thoughts. Whenever Jones did pay a visit, people tended to pay attention. He wasn't just smart, immensely sure of himself for his comparatively young age and – rightfully – forceful in his views. He was also known to have Churchill's ear.

Why, on occasion even the Prime Minister himself was known to put in an appearance. For a politician, Churchill had a fine grasp of the life scientific, and he was not beyond making the odd leap in thinking or deduction himself, plus he had personal reasons to favour Medmenham. His second daughter, Sarah Churchill, was working as a photo interpreter at Danesfield House, the grand country manor that served as the nerve centre of Allied photoreconnaissance work, situated near the Buckinghamshire village of Medmenham.

You could almost say that Danesfield – more formally known as 'RAF Medmenham', after the adjacent village – had been the making of Sarah Churchill. Famously rebellious as a teenager, she'd been nicknamed 'Mule' by her father, after eloping to marry an Australian almost twice her age. The marriage fell apart and, chastened, she'd decided she wanted to do her part for the war effort. At Danesfield she most certainly had. At one stage, she'd even chastised her father for waxing lyrical about a top-secret operation, one that she had been working on quietly for months without breathing a word even to him. 'I believe there is such a thing as security,' she'd scolded, leaving Churchill most impressed with his once-wayward daughter.

No doubt about it, Danesfield was an extraordinarily creative and vital place and there would be few anywhere to rival it in the war. As early as June 1940, Churchill himself had observed: 'Remember that the photographic machines are of tremendous value in enabling us to find out if any expedition is preparing in the German Harbours and river mouths,' adding that Britain was, 'greatly dependent . . . upon photographs which far exceed what the human eye can discern'.

Danesfield's Central Interpretation Unit (CIU) was unprecedented, utilizing a groundbreaking three-stage process to glean maximum intelligence from images secured over enemy territory. In 'First Phase', specially trained photographic interpreters took films directly from the aircraft, for immediate study at the airfield, so they could check for the most pressing matters. Was a certain ship still in port? Were bombers massing to carry out a raid? Had infantry or armour been deployed?

'Second Phase' took place back at Medmenham, involving a more studied analysis, revealing far more detail. With photo interpreters on hand twenty-four-seven, twice daily they issued their reports, condensing all they had learned during the past twelve hours. 'Third Phase' involved deeper scrutiny by those who were experts in their fields – enemy shipping, armour, aircraft, rocketry, rail-transport, industrial activity and more. It was those Third Phase investigations that provided some of the most spectacular intelligence breakthroughs, allowing Allied commanders incredible insights into almost all aspects of the Nazi war machine.

Claude Wavell had been recruited to fulfil just such a role. Wavell – no relation of Field Marshal Archibald Wavell, who'd done so much to pioneer early Special Service and deception operations – had proved himself a brilliant mathematician, but he was busy pioneering air-survey work in South America when first approached by a friend serving at Medmenham, and was reluctant to return to Britain. After Dunkirk he'd rallied, telegraphing: 'If you still want me, I'll come.' 'Come at once,' was the reply.

Upon arrival, Wavell had proved himself a rare genius at spotting enemy radar. It was Wavell who'd found one of the first Freya sites – identifying two tiny units barely a few feet wide, from photos covering the vast swathe of Nazi-occupied Europe. Incredibly, he deduced from the photos that the twenty-foot-square devices were *rotating*, something then viewed as revolutionary in the field of radar. By contrast, Britain's massive radar towers – called Chain Home – were vast, stationary monoliths. By studying photos taken bare seconds apart, and making the minutest of measurements of their shadows, Wavell was able to determine that the Freyas were indeed turning.

It was an amazing achievement, but Wavell wasn't alone in possessing such talents. RAF Medmenham was populated by the 'Mad Men of Ham', as the locals liked to call them – a cast of brilliant eccentrics and lateral-thinkers, including dons, newspaper editors, writers and ballet dancers. Photo interpretation didn't just require raw intellect: it called for leaps of the imagination and detective-like qualities; minds that could deduce what the enemy might be up to, no matter how he might try to hide it, and from a few sketchy images shot at altitude.

Archaeologists, accustomed to forming impressions from fragmentary evidence – a sliver of a clay bowl, a fire-burned bone, a seam of sediment rich in hand-worked flint – proved especially gifted at such work. Accordingly, the entire Archaeology department of Cambridge University had been relocated to rural Buckinghamshire and put to work. Women proved particularly talented, and uniquely in the war they were often to be found in more senior positions than the men at Medmenham.

In the egalitarian, collegiate atmosphere of Danesfield House, pretty much anything was allowed. The wisteria-draped manor became the centre for photo reconnaissance for the entire British military and the American armed forces, right until the end of the war. Lying just a few miles to the east of RAF Benson, the airfield from where the photo recce squadrons operated, it was especially suited to its task, and as the war progressed it would deal with 25,000 negatives and 60,000 prints per day.

Yet right now, in November 1941, there was one image – one confounding, tantalizing photograph – that was troubling one of Danesfield's brilliant minds. Before Wavell could raise 'the speck' with his confidant, R. V. Jones, he had some unexpected visitors. Two Spitfire pilots from RAF Benson dropped in for a few beers. Prior to heading out for a drink, Wavell showed off his newest gadget, which he'd grandly christened the Altazimeter. He'd designed and made it himself, he announced proudly.

What on earth did it do, the pilots asked? It measured the actual height of an object from an aerial photo, announced Wavell. Height equalled shadow-length times the tangent of the sun's altitude. That, combined with latitude, the scale of the photo, orientation and date gave the exact reading. The principle of 'spherical trig', Wavell explained. Complex for the human mind to grasp. Simple, with the help of the Altazimeter.

The pilots were itching for a beer, but Wavell had one more object of interest he was determined to show them. He pulled out a pair of identical photos showing the mysterious, elusive speck. The prints had an arrow scrawled in black marker diagonally across the sea, spearing the clifftop, and labelled 'SMALL BLACK OBJECT'. He grabbed his stereoscope viewer for a closer, 3D view.

'Come and have a squint at this,' he suggested, gesturing at the scrawled arrows.

Wavell began to wax lyrical about German radar, or 'RDF' – Radio Direction Finding – as the British then called it. It was markedly different from home-grown radar and potentially revolutionary. Its origins, they suspected, were as old as the British form, and the enemy might well be more advanced technologically. Better radar would spell disaster for the Allies, who even now were throwing all into taking the fight to the enemy, sending bombers into hostile airspace.

Wavell slotted some more photos under the viewer. One pair was the high-altitude image of the Freya station, from which Wavell had deduced that the radars were rotating. He inserted a second pair under the stereoscope – incredibly detailed images of the Freya units, secured via a close-up dash executed by one of their fellow pilots. Called a 'low-level oblique', the images had been captured at just a few dozen feet, and with a camera pointing out of the side of the aircraft, hence the name.

Such photo-runs were known as 'dicing missions' by the pilots who executed them. Dicing with death, in other words. Until that particular sortie had been pulled off, Wavell explained, the powers that be had refused to believe the Germans even *had* radar, so blinkered were elements of the British scientific and intelligence community. A picture speaks a thousand words: that dicing sortie had proved the naysayers wrong. But there was a new worry now occupying some of Britain's finest minds: a second German radar type, based upon a compact, mobile 'paraboloid', was feared to be in operation, tracking and nailing Allied warplanes.

He slipped the first two sets of prints back beneath the stereo viewer. Might the mystery speck labelled 'SMALL BLACK OBJECT' be one of those paraboloid discs, he mused? Clearly, there was only one way to find out: someone needed to execute a dicing mission over those clifftops, which lay just to the north of the French village of Bruneval.

'You pilots annoy me,' Wavell needled them, good-naturedly. 'You fly over this place time and time again and never turn on your cameras in time.'

The pilots eyed each other. That was like a red rag to a bull.

One of them, Flight Officer Anthony 'Tony' Hill, had had something of a troubled relationship with 'dicing'. He was immensely fond of the low-level dash, seeming to thrive on the adrenalin rush of running the enemy's guns. Trouble was, he'd very often got the timing off. Dicing took split-second reflexes, and Hill was by his own admission 'a bit slow'. The oblique camera wasn't forward facing; instead, it lay behind and to one side of the cockpit. This took it out of the pilot's range of vision, not to mention his point of view. A pilot executing a dicing mission had to swoop past the target, punching the camera 'shoot' button just as whatever needed photographing slipped past beneath his sleek wing.

It was all about timing, something Hill had found hard to master. That was until R. V. Jones had taken him under his wing. Hearing about this pilot who thrilled to dicing sorties, but had a habit of missing his mark, Jones had paid a visit to RAF Benson and taken Hill for a beer or two in the nearby pub. He'd warmed to the man immediately. Hill was modest, determined, maverick, half-wild – as so many recce pilots tended to be. Invariably, the risks associated with their elite profession drew in such individuals.

Together, pilot and scientist, they deconstructed the dicing craft, until Hill seemed to have the gist of it. He went away and practised relentlessly, until by trial-and-error he had mastered the technique. Nowadays, there were few better, or more-daring, pilots. With his swept-back dark hair, silk scarf and flying jacket, Hill was every schoolboy's ideal hero. Indeed, he had already earned a DFC for a daring recce mission executed in May that year. He rarely ducked a challenge, and evidently wasn't about to now.

'Where exactly is this place?' Hill demanded of Wavell.

About twelve miles north of the French port of Le Havre lay a stretch of high chalk cliffs, Wavell explained, upon which the white tower of the Cap d'Antifer lighthouse was the key landmark. A thousand yards south of the lighthouse was the village of Bruneval, and to the seaward side of that lay the mystery speck.

'I'll get you your answer tomorrow,' Hill promised Wavell combatively.

It was a wintry 4 December morning when Hill took to the skies over RAF Benson, in his sleek, polished, unarmed reconnaissance aircraft. As opposed to Flight Lieutenant Wharburton's Malta operations, which invariably seemed to combine recce sorties with shoot-'em-up missions, the photo recce flights over Nazi-occupied Europe were much more fleeting, covert affairs. Flying comparatively slow Marylands across airspace guarded by the German military's radar sentinels would have been close to suicidal, despite the aircraft's armaments.

Instead, the pilots operating out of RAF Benson relied upon speed, surprise and daring to slip through the enemy's air defences. The Spitfire Hill was flying owed its unique specifications to the father of Allied photo recce craft, F. Sidney Cotton, a man whose sheer brilliance had been such an affront to the hidebound British establishment that in recent months he'd been removed from command of his own squadron – typical of the way Britain so often chose to 'reward' its somewhat unruly and free-spirited heroes in the war.

As a young man Cotton, the son of a cattle-rancher from Queensland, had abandoned the farming life for one of flying and adventure. He'd served with distinction in the First World War, operating with the Royal Naval Air Service, and in the inter-war years had run a commercial flying business in North America, doing remote area mapping, search and rescue missions, and even aerial surveys of seal populations.

Prior to the outbreak of the Second World War, Cotton was commissioned by British intelligence to execute 'commercial' flights over Germany, which were in reality secret photo reconnaissance missions. Cotton did so flying a Lockheed 12 Electra Junior, an all-metal twin-engine commercial passenger aircraft of late 1930s design. He had learned his business the hard way and he truly loved his aircraft. The Lockheed was no exception, and at its controls he mastered the craft of high-altitude, high-speed photo reconnaissance work.

At the outbreak of war Cotton was asked if he might execute some recce missions on behalf of the French Air Force and the RAF. He did so, dashing through the thin and icy blue over German airspace at well over 10,000 feet altitude. By December 1940, the results of his daring sorties spoke for themselves. He'd photographed Cologne, Düsseldorf and much of the Siegfried Line, the massive defences on Germany's western border. The French were astounded at the results. They summed them up in a simple table, which spoke volumes:

i)   The RAF have photographed 2,500 square miles of German territory in three months, for the loss of forty aircraft.

ii) The French Air Force have photographed 6,000 square miles for the loss of sixty aircraft.

iii) Cotton's unit has photographed 5,000 square miles in three flights, without loss. (And these figures do not include 12,000 square miles of Belgian territory ... That also entailed no loss.)

The British military bowed to the seemingly inevitable, and gave Cotton – the upstart Aussie – the rank of RAF Squadron Leader, and command of his own squadron, the No. 1 Photographic Development Unit (PDU). While Cotton had made enemies in high places, he seemed almost to revel in his notoriety. His squadron acquired the nickname 'Cotton's Club,' or more often 'Cotton's Crooks', due to their fondness for flouting regulations. Cotton even had a special squadron badge designed: 'CC-11', short for Cotton Club 11. The '11' signified Cotton's 11th Commandment: 'Thou shalt not be found out.'

On 16 June 1940, even as Britain reeled from crushing defeat in France, the powers that be finally got their way. Under Dunkirk's long shadow, they found suitable cover to sack Cotton. Every effort this fiercely patriotic and gifted individual subsequently made to get back into his own squadron was rebuffed. Despite his enormous contribution to the war effort, he was frozen out, any further role being closed to him.

By his sheer brilliance, he had made those in high places look foolish. They would neither forgive nor make allowances. But of course, Cotton's legacy could not be so easily disavowed. Many of the pilots flying from RAF Benson had been recruited under Cotton's watch: the man who had made their unit what it was would never be forgotten. How could he be? The Spitfire that Hill was piloting to the coast of Normandy had been 'cottonized' – having all unnecessary weight removed. Cotton stripped it of weaponry and radio kit. He removed the lead balancing weights, situated in the rear of the aircraft's fuselage, replacing them with camera kit weighing 64 pounds. He fitted long-range fuel tanks, and polished all external surfaces into an aerodynamic gloss, using a special pale-green paint christened 'Camoutint Green'.

Using such modifications, Spitfires that had been cottonized had a boosted top speed of just under 400 mph, as opposed to the 370 mph of the standard warplane. That, and the photo-recce craft and esprit de corps, were to be Cotton's lasting legacies. But even with their aircraft so adapted, the recce pilots were flying a warplane that was at best able only to equal the speed of the enemy's fighters, the Messerschmitt Bf-109 and the Focke-Wulf FW-190. And on recce sorties such as Hill was attempting, flying down the throat of the enemy's radar, German fighter crews might well have ample warning.

On that December morning Hill hugged the waters of the Channel, as he dashed across the ninety-odd miles that separated Britain from the coast of Nazi-occupied France. Indeed, such was Hill's approach that the first sense the German radar operators had of his presence was when the polished, speeding form of the duck-egg-green aircraft roared above the cliffs. It came in 'very low, and then flew along the coast, prior to twisting and turning immediately above the site', one of them reported of Hill's Spitfire.

Hill darted past the emplacement and on across the woodland behind it, before the startled defenders even had time to react. Of course, such was the intention of a dicing mission. But while his presence hadn't been picked up by the German radar operators, luck wasn't with Hill that morning. Due to a camera malfunction, he returned to RAF Benson empty handed.

Even so, when he spoke to Wavell by telephone he was clearly excited. 'You were right! It must be a paraboloid whatnot . . .' He figured it was about a dozen feet in diameter, adding that 'the Jerries were around it like flies.'

Hill went on to describe to Wavell exactly what he'd seen – a device looking like a giant 'electric bowl fire'. (This was a mobile indoor heater popular in the 1930s, consisting of a filament, set in the centre of a copper dish about the size of an average dinner plate.) His cameras had failed, Hill told Wavell. 'But don't worry. I'll have another go tomorrow.'

No pilot was permitted to execute the same dicing sortie two days running, for obvious reasons. Forewarned is forearmed, and the enemy might be noticeably more alert second time around. But Hill was a Cotton Club veteran. Citing the 11th Commandment - 'Thou shalt not be found out' – he climbed into his sleek aircraft the following morning, only to discover that several other pilots were also preparing to attempt the Bruneval recce mission.

Hill sent a message across to them. The Bruneval job was his, he warned, adding that if he caught any of them within twenty miles of the target, he'd shoot them down. He didn't specify with what, of course, as his Spitfire was unarmed. Either way, Hill duly flew the sortie, kissing the wave-crests and then the edge of the rocks, the howl of the Spitfire's V12 Merlin echoing off the cliffs as he zipped past the chateau at roof-top level for the second time in forty-eight hours, the thrill of the chase coursing through his veins.

He returned from what became known as 'Sortie A/30' in triumph, bearing what would be acknowledged as classic reconnaissance images of the war. Far closer that the original 'speck' photo, the first shot, taken as Hill's spitfire hugged the very cliff-edge, had shorn all of the sea, white rocks and the cleft of Bruneval village from the scene. Instead, dominating the top-centre of the image lay the ugly-looking chateau, presumably the radar-operators' headquarters, a distinct path leading from there to the mysterious paraboloid.

It was far from being a full-stop any more. Hill's photo revealed a grey dish about the size of one of the chateau's bay-windows, pointing directly out over the sea. Indeed, Hill had been flying his Spitfire directly down its guts as he'd popped over the cliff. Photo two was far closer. As he'd dived towards the chateau, banking his aircraft in a screaming low-level turn, he'd fired off an image capturing the device in side-view, plus chateau directly beside it. The image was so detailed that had any sentries been posted at the windows, the surprise and consternation on their faces would have been clear for all to see.

Hill, Wavell and Jones had become good friends over recent months, and they gathered around this extraordinary set of photos, excitedly. Wavell gauged and evaluated the images minutely. Measuring ten feet across, the paraboloid lay in a shallow pit, with a smaller control cabin attached to it. The entire apparatus seemed to be mounted on a turntable, looking capable both of rotation and being tilted upwards.

Radar functions on the principle that when radio waves hit solid objects like ships, buildings or aircraft, they bounce back. By tracking that echo, it is possible to locate the object's position – such as the distance, height and direction of an aircraft. Jones figured the paraboloid could track both altitude and range of whatever was its target – most usually, a flight of incoming warplanes. Increasingly, Allied bombers were being pinned by deadly-accurate searchlights, flak and fighter attacks. Jones presumed the paraboloid played a key function in vectoring the enemy's fearsome defences onto the British, American and Commonwealth bomber crews, not to mention their fighter escorts. Constituting a small, mobile, versatile operating platform, the paraboloid looked uniquely suited to scouring the skies.

But right now, most of this was supposition and informed deduction, as opposed to absolute fact. Via a brilliant combination of scientific rigour exercised by Jones and his team, careful photographic scrutiny exercised by Wavell and his colleagues at Medmenham, plus the daring and skill of Tony Hill, the enemy's

top-secret radar apparatus had been captured on film. But all of
that – and especially the recce images – gave rise to what was the
obvious next question.

It was clear to all who viewed the images that the prized
paraboloid lay a short distance from the cliff edge. More to the
point, some 500 yards to the left lay the open, pebbly expanse
of Bruneval beach, one seemingly devoid of any anti-landing
obstructions. To those studying the photos, it was obvious what
the next step had to be. Capturing the paraboloid on film was an
amazing coup, but stealing it away from under the noses of the
enemy would achieve so much more.

In a sad irony, because Hill's dicing sorties had been 'unofficial'
– they'd come about as a result of an informal chat at Medmenham, as opposed to orders from on high – the photo recce pilots
were henceforth banned from paying visits to Danesfield House.
But that didn't prevent Jones from extending to Hill the highest
praise for what he had achieved over Bruneval.

On 12 December 1941, so barely a week after Hill had
secured his iconic photos, Jones penned a report outlining what
they revealed. 'A new type of German R.D.F. has been photographed . . .' he began. Writing of the photos themselves, Jones
stressed: 'In addition to their striking testimony to the skill of
the pilot . . . they represent the culmination of a long chase . . .
The paraboloid and cabin, which are mounted on a trolley in a
shallow pit, have rotated between the two photographs . . . The
apparatus can determine heights by tilting the paraboloid to
point the beam at the target aircraft, so measuring the range and
target elevation.'

To place in context the revolutionary nature of such technology, Britain's radar defences were centred around Chain

Home – a series of radar stations consisting of 360-foot-high steel transmitter towers, with an adjoining set of fixed wooden receivers 240 feet in height; both anchored, fixed, immovable. The contrast between that and the diminutive German paraboloid spoke volumes. If it was capable of feats to rival or even excel the Chain Home monoliths, the technology involved had to be utterly extraordinary.

Jones discussed all this with his counterparts at Britain's centre for radar research, which went under the cover name of the Telecommunications Research Establishment (TRE), based on the sweeping clifftops just outside the rural Dorset village of Worth Matravers. The experts at TRE – whose top-secret mission was to refine and improve British radar, while countering that of the enemy – could think of nothing better than getting their hands on the newly discovered paraboloid, and they offered Jones their full support in floating a proposal to pilfer it.

Jones's report was circulated to the select few, along with Hill's photos: it was to be the catalyst for the coming raid. 'These photographs, besides adding much to our knowledge of German R.D.F. [radar] technique, and setting a new standard in oblique aerial photography, led directly to the suggestion of a raid,' stated an intelligence report from the time. Regarding the paraboloid, it stressed the priority of securing 'detailed knowledge of its construction and use . . .'

By stealing the mystery dish, the boffins might discover how to defeat it. More to the point, for months now Jones – something of a maverick among the intelligence community – had been arguing that the enemy did have radar. To him, it was increasingly preposterous to suggest otherwise, but still he faced one hell of an uphill struggle. The notion that radar was a wholly British invention – one of the few shining jewels in the so-far largely tarnished crown of Britain's war effort – had proved surprisingly hard to counter.

On many levels, Jones appreciated why. The massive Chain Home radar masts had played a pivotal role in winning the Battle of Britain. That memory was still fresh in people's minds, as was the supposedly exclusive British pedigree of radar – and no matter how the evidence might stack up otherwise. Securing photographs of the Freya – and now the paraboloid – enabled Jones to hammer some nails into the coffin of wilful ignorance. But it was vital to finish the job, for the enemy were in danger of eclipsing the Allies in this war-winning technology.

Stealing something as remarkable as the German radar dish – that would prove it, once and for all.

Chapter 7

Jones and his small team operated out of 54 Broadway, the central London headquarters of the Secret Intelligence Service. The scientists to the spies, they enjoyed far from salubrious surroundings. Despite being a relatively modern office block for the time, 54 Broadway consisted of eight floors of dingy frosted glass and dated wooden partitions, served by brown-painted corridors floored in worn lino, and creaky, clattering elevators. By the winter of 1941/42, it was also grossly overcrowded.

As a foil to its elusive charms, Jones instituted an easy-going work ethic, more akin to RAF Medmenham that to Britain's foreign intelligence headquarters. No one was expected at the office before 10.00 a.m. and Jones's seemingly avuncular presence was reinforced by his habit of pacing about offering advice, while munching on chocolate biscuits. Flocks of pigeons used to alight upon the windowsill. An inveterate practical joker, Jones insisted they were there to enable better communications with the French Resistance. Only occasionally did he fix someone with his characteristically penetrating gaze, revealing the sharp intellect and sharper ambitions within.

Jones's greatest strength – his one undisputed trump card – was his friendship with Frederick Lindemann, his former Oxford University professor and latterly Churchill's chief scientific adviser. Somewhat inexplicably, Lindemann and Churchill were great friends. On the face of it they were polar opposites, and their long and enduring collaboration was something of an enigma. Lindemann was a tall, ascetic, wiry-necked individual, as opposed to Churchill's compact, bulldog-featured, cigar-chomping vitality.

Churchill nicknamed him 'the Prof'. He was in the habit of calling the teetotal, vegetarian and non-smoking Lindemann to lunch with the mischievous cry of 'Beetroot time!' The son of a naturalized German father and an American mother, Lindemann's bluntness and formal reserve made him unpopular with some, but Churchill found him irreplaceable. Lindemann made complex science comprehensible. He could 'decipher scientific developments on the far horizons, and explain to me in lucid, homely terms what the issues were'.

Apart from science, Lindemann and Churchill's bond was their long-standing opposition to appeasing Hitler. To Lindemann fell the lion's share of the credit in ensuring that Churchill gave science the backing it required to help win the war. Lindemann would become Jones's bridge to Churchill, Jones viewing his relationship with Britain's wartime leader as 'a constant invigoration', which went 'far beyond the bounds of science.' It was forged first in the vexing, heated debate over whether the enemy possessed the top-secret, all-seeing, war-winning eye – radar.

Sir Robert Alexander Watson-Watt, a descendant of the famous steam engineer James Watt, was the supposed 'father' of radar. In the lead-up to the war, he'd been asked to investigate the potential of a so-called 'Death Ray' to immobilize aircraft, something the Germans had long been rumoured to be developing. In the process of looking into it he'd stumbled upon the realization that aircraft could be detected by reflected radio pulses – the basic concept of radar. Having discovered radar – in Britain at least – Watson-Watt seemed unwilling or unable to grasp that equally talented individuals might have reached the same conclusions elsewhere.

At war's outset, Watson-Watt's age, superiority and status seemed to trump any dissenters. At forty-seven to Jones's late twenties, Watson-Watt had several firsts under his belt. From tracking the radio signals given off by lightning storms in the 1920s, in an effort to prevent commercial airliners from flying into them, he'd developed Huff-Duff (the name originates from the acronym H/F D/F, which stands for High-Frequency Direction-Finding). Come the war, it was a simple process to adapt Huff-Duff to pinpoint the location of enemy radio transmissions, something that was crucial to finding and sinking Nazi U-boats.

But mostly, his status came about via his mastery of radar. By 1936, Britain's Chain Home masts could detect an aircraft a hundred miles away. It was an incredible achievement in a groundbreaking field of science, and it had led to the sanctioning of the massive financial investment required to build a curtain of such defences ringing the British coastline. The Chain Home system was ready just in time for the outbreak of war.

An invisible wall – a radar barrier – had been thrown around Britain, some 12 miles high and reaching out 120 miles from her shores. No other country had anything remotely like it. The nation's fighter pilots, charged with keeping Britain inviolable, were able to do so in large part due to that barrier. But it wasn't radar alone that enabled the Battle of Britain to be won. It was the meshing of Chain Home into a comprehensive air-defence, early-warning and ground-control system; the means to take the raw data of radar and transform it into squadrons of Spitfires and Hurricanes flying down the throat of the enemy.

That system – Ground Control Interception (GCI) – proved truly war-winning, and it was instituted under the guidance of Sir Hugh 'Stuffy' Dowding, then Chief of RAF Fighter Command. Sincere, visionary, well ahead of his time and famously dedicated to his men – his 'dear fighter boys' – Dowding had played a crucial role in the frustration of Hitler's invasion plans. With radar taking centre stage, and with its giant masts fully in the public's view, the nation was immensely grateful both to Dowding and to the man who had mastered this ground-breaking technology, Watson-Watt. As Churchill surmised, regarding radar, the real achievement lay in how effectively we had 'woven all into our general air defence system. In this we led the world, and it was operational efficiency rather than novelty of equipment that was the British achievement.'

Radar was so secret that only a few categories of intelligence – like the ENIGMA intercepts, the breaking of the Germans' coded communications – had a higher security classification. *In theory.* In practice, it had proven nigh-on impossible to hide such massive structures from public notice. In some instances, the security breaches were laughable. The first Chain Home masts were erected at Bawdsey Manor, which stands at the mouth of the River Deben, in rural Suffolk, some seventy-five miles north-east of London. A favoured holidaying destination, the massive towers were soon featuring on picture postcards with sailing boats in the foreground.

The popular author Arthur Ransome chose to include the towers as navigational aids in his children's book series, *Swallows and Amazons,* which was duly published in Germany in translation. But the real giveaway should have been this: while the contractors employed to build the Chain Home masts were rigorously vetted for foreign shareholdings, no one thought to check from where they might actually purchase the individual components – so much was ordered from Austria, Fascist Italy and even Germany itself.

Little wonder then, when senior Luftwaffe officer Erhard Milch paid a visit to RAF Fighter Command in 1937, he was able to ask: 'Come, gentleman, how are you getting on with your experiments in the radio detection of aircraft approaching your shores? We have known for some time you are developing such a system – so are we, and we think we are a jump ahead of you.'

The truth was that there were many 'discoveries' of radar, in many parts of the world, and the Germans had been at the forefront. In 1904 the German inventor Christian Hulsmeyer had patented a transmitter and receiver that enabled one ship to detect another at distance. It was an early form of radar. In 1931 a pulsed radio system had been fitted to the French liner *Normandie,* to detect icebergs. And in September 1935 the US hobby magazine *Electronics* had carried a feature article on German ship-borne radar.

Yet somehow, by the outbreak of the war all such freely available information seemed to have been overlooked. Then had come two major events, which should have proved decisive. At midday on 18 December 1939, a squadron of twenty-four Wellington medium bombers were on patrol near the German coastal town of Wilhelmshaven, with orders to attack enemy naval units. At this time the Royal Air Force subscribed to the belief that 'the bomber will always get through'. Bristling with gun-turrets, the bombers were 'flying fortresses', and when deployed in self-defending formations they would prove inviolable.

Hence those twenty-four bombers cruising in strict diamond formation in broad daylight off the German coastline. Unfortunately, a Freya radar station had picked them up at seventy-five miles range. Fifty German fighters climbed into the skies, before diving to attack. The Wellingtons were decimated. Only ten made it home, a loss rate of 58 per cent. Even when a dissident German scientist sent a written report to the British Embassy in Oslo, warning that the Wellingtons had been detected by radar, British intelligence concluded that the document was a hoax.

Officially, Germany still did not have radar.

Then came the December 1940 Battle of the River Plate and the scuttling of the German *Panzerschiff* (armoured ship), the 15,000-tonne *Graf Spee*, which should have put German radar centre stage in Britain's war-thinking. With a top speed of 28 knots and armed with six 11-inch guns, the *Graf Spee* was intended to out-gun or outrun any comparable Allied warships. Between September and December 1939 she'd sunk nine vessels in the South Atlantic, totalling over 50,000 tonnes.

But then she was cornered by three British cruisers – *Ajax*, *Achilles* and *Exeter*. In the ensuing sea battle the *Graf Spee*'s guns proved devastatingly accurate and the British vessels suffered heavy damage. But the *Graf Spee* was hit several times, with thirty-six killed and sixty injured from her 600-odd crew. Damaged, she'd put into the neutral port of Montevideo, on Uruguay's southern coast, for repairs. In a cunning deception engineered via false radio reports put out by Naval Intelligence, her commander, Hans Langsdorff, was made to believe that a massively-superior British force lay in wait.

Rather than risk the lives of all his crew, Langsdorff ordered his ship scuttled. On 18 December the *Graf Spee* went down in the estuary of the River Plate, multiple explosions from the charges blowing up the ship's ammunition and sending jets of flame high into the air. A thick cloud of oily smoke obscured the vessel, which burned ferociously for two days. When finally it cleared, the *Graf Spee's* superstructure was still visible, and by then Langsdorff had shot himself in his hotel bedroom, wearing full dress uniform.

The lure of the wreck proved irresistible. Salvage rights were purchased by British intelligence for £14,000, via a Montevidean front company. Under cover of being a scrap-metal dealer, the magnificently named Labouchère Hillyer Bainbridge-Bell flew out to Uruguay. In truth Bainbridge-Bell was a gifted Cambridge maths graduate and a radar expert working for the Navy, not to mention being a veteran of the First World War, where he'd won a Military Cross at the Somme.

Disguised as a 'scrap-man', Bainbridge-Bell managed to clamber about the *Graf Spee's* superstructure, photographing and documenting her radar antennae. His report, authored with characteristic missionary zeal, proved a watershed moment, or at least it should have done, especially as it was lavishly illustrated with photographs. Not only that, but somehow he managed to smuggle back to Britain the burned-out remains of the *Graf Spee's* radar.

Attached to the Aloft Control Platform – a platform set atop a ship's mast or bridge – was an 'Aloft Control "director", recorded Bainbridge-Bell. 'The aloft "director" stood centrally ... and was capable of continuous rotation ... Mounted on the front was a rectangular box-aerial grid.' While this had been 'severely damaged by fire', Bainbridge-Bell was adamant that this was an 'RDF Aerial Array' – a radar unit.

Despite this, Britain's top experts refused to accept that radar could be present on German ships, or at all. In a stupefying reversal of the Emperor's new clothes, the evidence from the *Graf Spee* was ruled 'inconclusive' and shelved, the salvaged radar unit left to gather dust. The official line remained that Germany did not have radar.

Even more astoundingly, the document sent to Oslo warning of how the squadron of Wellingtons had been shot down, had predicted all of this and more. Freya and paraboloid units tracking Allied warplanes; ship-borne gun-laying radar; long-range gliding bombs and rockets (the V1 and V2); the location of Nazi Germany's guided missile and rocketry complex; gliding anti-ship bombs – it was all detailed in what became known as the 'Oslo Report'. Indeed, it was the breadth of the intelligence and the extraordinary advancement of the German weaponry depicted that led British experts to dismiss the report as a plant.

Surely, seasoned intelligence operatives argued, no one individual scientist could know so much about so much. And surely, some of the so-called technologies were just too outlandish to be possible. Jones begged to differ. As the war progressed it became increasingly obvious that the document was genuine. 'I used to look up the Oslo Report to see what was coming along next,' he remarked ruefully. The very genesis of the Oslo Report should have convinced the naysayers. In November 1939 the British Naval Attaché in Oslo, Captain Hector Boyes, received the anonymous package from 'A German scientist who wishes you well'. It consisted of seven pages of closely spaced German type, illustrated with diagrams and sketches.

The very fact that it was unsolicited and went unrewarded, and arose from a revulsion against Nazism felt by the mystery author, should have lent credibility. More to the point, the anonymous scientist had included with it a priceless piece of hardware: an electronic triggering device from a German 'proximity fuse', which detonated anti-aircraft shells when close to their target. Upon getting his hands on the fuse, Jones realized how technologically advanced it was. The device 'proved much better than anything we had', which alone should have been proof enough that the report was genuine.

Jones sensed that the Oslo Report was 'pregnant with warning'. But he was no seasoned SIS veteran. He was a physicist in his late twenties, who happened to have strayed into the world of intelligence. He was a newcomer, comparatively junior and an upstart in such matters. John Buckingham, a senior British intelligence figure, pointed out that Jones was 'innocent in intelligence work', and that 'the whole thing was a "plant"'. The 'German hoaxers had overdone it', Buckingham argued, using the old trick of including something genuine – the fuse – the better to sell a patchwork of lies.

In truth, it was the woeful lack of scientific expertise at SIS that enabled the Oslo Report to be dismissed, by all except Jones and a handful of like-minded visionaries. Jones believed fervently that the aim of his fledgling Scientific Intelligence Service had to be to 'obtain early warning of the adoption of new weapons and methods by potential or actual enemies'. The Oslo Report should have been an absolute clarion call. Instead, 'those in the know' relegated it to the realms of fiction.

Jones demurred. He kept the report at his side, like a bible. And he set out to prove to a sceptical British leadership that much if not all that was predicted therein would come to pass. His first success would be scored in what became known as the 'Battle of the Beams'. Under its offensive mindset, the German military had realized that radio beams could be utilized as pathways, along which a bomber could be guided to its target. The Oslo Report made mention of such extraordinary guidance beams, and due to the accuracy of Luftwaffe missions over Britain Jones figured it might be genuine.

The Oslo Report's author was actually one Hans Ferdinand Meyer, a top German physicist and the director of the Siemens research laboratory in Berlin. An ardent anti-Nazi, Meyer's sole motive in providing the goldmine of intelligence was to halt the seemingly unstoppable march of Hitler's Reich. Meyer's role as its author would not be known throughout the war, but even so, by 1943 he would be arrested for listening to the BBC, and would spend the rest of the war in internment camps.

Jones knew none of this. But by the summer 1940 he felt confident enough to put his head above the parapet. 'In general, where the information can be checked, it has proven surprisingly correct,' he wrote of the Oslo Report, arguing that 'the source was reliable' and 'manifestly competent'. Regarding the beams, the Oslo Report's author had warned in detail of 'a method by which the Germans might navigate their bombers by radio means'.

With Britain's defensive, Chain Home mindset, the nation had nothing remotely like Nazi Germany's guidance beams, which were light years ahead of British capabilities. Even so, Jones set out to prove they existed. He did so utilizing fragmentary intercepts of enemy signals, evidence gleaned from the cockpits of crashed German bombers, interrogations of captured Luftwaffe aircrew and the compelling testimony embodied in the Oslo Report.

On 13 June 1940 he issued a warning direct to a somewhat sceptical Lindemann. Lindemann duly alerted Churchill that there was 'reason to suppose that the Germans have some kind of radio device with which they hope to find their targets'. Lindemann stressed it was 'vital to investigate' so as to 'devise means to mislead them'. Churchill responded by declaring that he wanted the beam issue 'thoroughly examined'.

Barely a week later, Jones arrived at his 54 Broadway office to find a note on his desk, summoning him to a meeting with Churchill. Being a renowned practical joker, he figured it had to be a wind-up. When he realized the meeting was all too real, he raced to Downing Street, but arrived half an hour late. He found Churchill, Lindemann, various RAF high-ups, together with Watson-Watt, gathered around a long table, amidst a decidedly tense atmosphere.

Having listened for several minutes to a heated debate as to whether the German beams even existed, Jones was horror-struck. When Churchill turned to him to ask for clarification on a point of science, he figured he'd best take the plunge. 'Hadn't I better tell you the story from the start, Sir?' Jones ventured. With Churchill's blessing he did just that. The twenty-eight-year-old held those in the room – the nation's top military and political leaders – variously aghast, spellbound and dumbstruck, as he related how German bombers used radio beams to navigate to target and drop their bombs with deadly accuracy.

Churchill would later write of Jones's performance: 'For twenty minutes or more he spoke in quiet tones, unrolling his chain of circumstantial evidence, the like of which for its convincing fascination was never surpassed by the tales of Sherlock Holmes.' If Jones was right, this was 'one of the blackest moments of the war'.

Once the young scientist had finished speaking, Churchill asked what could be done. The RAF needed to fly along the beams and map them, Jones explained, with a view to jamming them, or laying false beams to lure the German bombers off target. The RAF top brass listened with growing incredulity, but Churchill banged the table angrily and silenced their protests. All he got from them was 'files, files, files', he declared angrily. This young man had at least offered a programme of action.

Churchill ordered that Jones's proposals be acted upon. It was a pivotal moment: the Battle of the Beams had begun. On the Dorset coast, one of TRE's foremost radar experts, physicist Dr Robert Cockburn, was propelled into action, playing a pivotal role in the Battle of the Beams. Working closely with the RAF's newly formed 109 Squadron – also known as the 'Wireless Intelligence Development Unit' – Cockburn was to despatch teams of scientists along with brave RAF aircrews, flying Vickers Wellington bombers packed with electronic detection equipment.

In tracing the beams – and later the enemy's radar – the 109 Squadron aircrew were dicing with death, just as the photo recce pilots were, when executing their low-level reconnaissance missions. They were instructed to fly along guidance beams thick with enemy bombers and fighters, or down the throat of the enemy's radar – confronting head-on the very technology used to seek out and destroy Allied aircraft. The risks in doing so were all too obvious, and many 109 Squadron crews – and the scientists flying with them – would lose their lives when engaged upon such death-defying endeavours.

There were further skirmishes for the young Jones. Several times he had to invoke Churchill's authority, to head off his detractors and keep the RAF flights heading into the night skies, to prove the beams' existence. But eventually, the young scientist won through. Towards the end of June 1940, he scored a signal breakthrough: an ENIGMA intercept of enemy communications revealed the existence of 'Knickebein and Wotan installations near Cherbourg and Brest'. Knickebein – crooked-beam – he knew about already and had mentioned during the meeting with Churchill. But Wotan was something entirely new.

From his scanty knowledge of mythology Jones knew that Wotan was a figure of ancient Norse legend. He checked some more. Wotan was actually a one-eyed god of German heroic mythology. Could Wotan be the codename for one of their beam systems? Did one eye equal one beam? It seemed so obvious. Could the enemy really be that direct? In fact, they had a habit of being so. When the Freya radar was duly discovered, Jones realized that Freya was the mythical Norse goddess whose prized necklace was guarded by Heimdall, fearsome watchman of the gods, who could see one hundred miles by day or by night.

Churchill urged Jones to go on the offensive: he was ordered to find the beams and turn them against the enemy. But in a belt-and-braces approach, Churchill also dispatched a cadre of Britain's top radar scientists, with the choicest radar equipment, to North American shores. This act was far from wholly altruistic. In sharing Britain's latest discoveries and inventions, Churchill hoped to draw America further onside. That way, if Britain were invaded by Nazi Germany, at least the leading nations of the free world would be equipped with the best technology to continue the struggle.

Shortly, what Churchill had exhorted regarding the German beams was being done. Under the codename ASPIRIN, a jamming system was developed at the Dorset clifftop establishment of TRE. ASPIRIN counterfeited the German beams, giving the impression they had been bent, which resulted in Luftwaffe aircrews flying off-course and missing their targets. But on the rare occasion when the German beams did hold true, the results proved utterly devastating.

In Operation Moonlight Sonata, the Luftwaffe planned to decimate three major industrial cities in Britain. The first to be targeted was Coventry, on the night of 14 November 1940. Sadly, the beam jamming signals were mistranslated for that night, and as a result the massed fleet of German bombers rained down 500 tonnes of explosives onto the benighted city. Come dawn, Coventry was not quite dead. But the cathedral lay in ruins, some 60,000 buildings had been pulverized, over 500 had been killed and 1,200 injured.

Everywhere, desperate citizens strove to save those entombed within the rubble, and to repair the broken mains and quench fires. Coventry was the first raid that championed the terror bombing of civilians, combined with targeting industrial and military targets. There were to be many more. But thankfully, winning the Battle of the Beams – what Churchill would later refer to as 'the Wizard War' – would ensure that few raids proved as devastating as that over Coventry.

In due course Churchill would hail Jones as being the 'man who bent the bloody beams', helping to win the war. But that victory – one of scientific rigour over wilful ignorance – was just the beginning. The bigger battle lay ahead, and it would concern radar.

*

For Jones, the lessons of the beams were self-evident. If the Germans had the ability to guide their warplanes to within a few hundred yards of any target over Britain, imagine the capabilities of their radar technologies. It stood to reason these would be comprehensive and advanced.

As early as September 1940, Churchill had nailed his colours to the mast, declaring how crucial it was to win the radar war. 'Our supreme efforts must be to gain overwhelming mastery of the air . . . we must regard the whole sphere of RDF . . . as an essential part. The multiplication of high-class scientific personnel . . . should be the very spear point of our thought and effort.'

Considerable effort had been ploughed into teaching British pilots to see better in the dark: developing their natural night vision; squinting sideways at an object, never looking directly at it, to utilize more sensitive cells in the eyes; eating plenty of fruit and veg and keeping off the booze! But radar was set to revolutionize the battle for the skies, and the other spear-point had to be to defeat any potential German mastery of radar. Winning the Battle of the Beams had secured Jones a ready audience with Churchill, thrusting him from 'obscurity to the highest levels of the war'. But in the coming struggle Jones would be frustrated by that old chestnut – experts proclaiming that the Germans simply didn't have radar. The enemy's guidance-beam technology had 'nearly succeeded because of its sheer incredibility', and he was worried that the same might happen with radar.

Of course, the recce photos of the Freya units helped win the argument, especially the close-up, low-level obliques. Jones also got hold of a few frames of precious film footage of a Freya station in action. In June 1941, Danish adventurer Thomas Christian Sneum had made a dramatic flight from Denmark to Britain in an ageing de Havilland Hornet Moth biplane, which had been lying derelict in a farm. He'd taken such inordinate risks because he'd managed to film a Freya station that had been installed by the occupying German forces, and he was desperate to get his evidence into Allied hands.

Unfortunately, upon landing in Britain Sneum was arrested by MI5 – the domestic intelligence service – as a suspected spy. By the time Jones learned of this, the developing of Sneum's film had been botched and only two frames survived. Tantalizingly, they showed a pair of Freyas in operation. Jones had ridden to Sneum's rescue like a 'gentle giant'. Sneum recalled him as a benign figure who treated everyone 'as though they had some good in them, and it was his job to find it'.

Following his daring airborne coup, Sneum would go on to work for SIS as an agent in the field in Denmark. Other 'special agents' would be sent by air from Britain, to try to winkle out the enemy's radar secrets. Occasionally, they had a distinct air of desperation about them. Jones arranged for carrier pigeons to be dropped into Nazi occupied Europe, around where he suspected enemy radar units were operating. Suspended under parachutes in special 'time-release' containers, the pigeons carried the following message: 'Are there any German radio stations in your neighbourhood with aerials which rotate?'

Incredibly, some of those pigeons actually returned to the UK bearing useful intelligence, from which Jones and his team identified three new radar stations. Every fragment of information – the Oslo Report; ENIGMA intercepts; a few surviving frames of film; carrier-pigeon messages – added to the case that Jones was building: the Germans had radar all right, and it was very likely more advanced than our own.

In the early months of 1941, Jones was still being called to high-level meetings with one main purpose: 'To discuss the existence of German radar.' Repeatedly, he let the doubters rattle on, before presenting his evidence. By that winter the situation was becoming critical. The losses suffered by Allied bomber squadrons over Europe were reaching horrific proportions, and Jones didn't doubt that this was mostly due to the enemy's radar.

With the opening of the Eastern Front against Russia, the fortunes of the Allies hung in the balance. In the first six months the Russians had lost more men and war machines than any army in history: over a million men had been taken captive. Any landings to liberate Nazi-occupied Europe were still many months, if not years, away. In the interim, the only means to relieve the murderous pressure on Moscow was via bombing raids, and it was vital that the fleets of Allied warplanes got through.

Writing of Hitler, Churchill declared: 'There is one thing that will . . . bring him down, and that is absolutely devastating, exterminating attack by very heavy bombers from this country upon the Nazi homeland. We must be able to overwhelm them by this means, without which I do not see a way through.'

But during the summer and autumn of 1941 Allied bomber losses kept mounting. In August a report on the accuracy of bombing raids horrified Churchill. It showed that only one in three aircraft got to within 75 square miles of their target. Over the all-important industrial heartland of Germany's Ruhr it fell to *one in ten*. Later statistics on losses made even grimmer reading. By December 1941 some 8,000 aircrew had been killed. More to the point, Britain had lost more highly trained airmen than it had killed Germans, who were mainly civilians.

'The success of German A.A. [anti-aircraft fire] and searchlight systems had been . . . disconcerting – we had lost many bombers,' concluded a report from the time, stamped 'HIGHLY SECRET'. On some raids, losses topped 14 per cent. It was well known that anything above 4 per cent was unsustainable for a long-term bombing campaign. The only way to cut the numbers being lost was to overcome the enemy's defences, and that meant defeating their radar.

Then, in December 1941, Jones had got his hands on those iconic photographs of the mysterious paraboloid dish. He had put a name to it by now: via ENIGMA intercepts he'd learned that it was referred to as a '*Würzburg*'. Perhaps the Germans were getting smarter with their codewords. As far as anyone could tell, Würzburg seemed to have no special significance, other than as the name of a smallish city in northern Bavaria. But that fitted a theme: the Germans had codenamed several of their top-secret radio and radar devices after cities, including Berlin and Ulm.

To all concerned – Jones and his team; Wavell and his Medmenham colleagues; the boffins at TRE – the idea of stealing the Würzburg was so patently obvious and so enticing. It would nail the debate over the enemy's radar once and for all, and in the process save countless Allied lives – those aircrew needlessly being lost over Nazi-occupied Europe. Jones raised the idea of a raid with Lindemann, who took it to Churchill. Britain's wartime leader 'was all for it', but typically, the War Cabinet gave the idea a lukewarm reception.

On 1 January 1942 the proposal got its first airing at Combined Operations headquarters. Sadly, by now Admiral Sir Roger Keyes was no longer in the hot seat. Appalled at the overwhelmingly defensive mindset of the top brass, he had resigned the previous October. In a characteristically uncompromising speech to the

Commons, Keyes spoke of how he had been 'frustrated at every turn in every worthwhile offensive action'. In a devastating critique, he warned that, 'so long as procrastination, the thief of time, is the key-word of the war machine in Whitehall, we shall continue to lose one opportunity after another . . .'

Stinging criticism, and from an impassioned and long-experienced veteran. Casting around for a suitable replacement, Churchill had alighted upon the figure of Lord Louis Mountbatten, the cousin to the King. Though only in his forties, Mountbatten was something of a war hero, due to his captaining of HMS *Kelly*, a destroyer lost off Crete in 1941, while making a dramatic last stand against enemy warplanes. Tall, self-possessed and striking, Mountbatten brought a certain dash and a sense of natural authority to the role.

With his characteristic dauntless spirit, Churchill urged Mountbatten to 'turn the south coast of England from a bastion of defence into a springboard of attack'. In rapid order, Mountbatten expanded Combined Operations headquarters, on London's Richmond Terrace, transforming it into a hothouse of new ideas, where nothing was seen as impossible. Mountbatten described it as 'the only lunatic asylum in the world run by its own inmates'. It proved fertile ground for the newest and most audacious raid yet to be conceived – to steal the enemy's paraboloid radar, on the coast at Bruneval.

In view of the sheer scope and boldness of the proposition, Mountbatten called together his most experienced commanders: General Frederick Arthur Montagu 'Boy' Browning, the new chief of Airborne forces, who'd served alongside Churchill during the First World War, plus Wing Commander Sir Henry Nigel Norman, veteran of the only previous Allied airborne raid – Operation

Colossus. Mountbatten had formed a new Intelligence Section, appointing as its head an old chum, the Cuban-born Marquis de Casa Maury, a former racing driver and the founder of the Curzon Cinema. A one-time playboy, Peter de Casa Maury had joined the RAF when war broke out and was stationed in the West Country. Overnight almost, he found himself spirited to London and promoted to Wing Commander, so he could head up Mountbatten's London intelligence outfit.

Peter de Casa Maury's first responsibility was to be the fledgling Bruneval raid. To him – plus Mountbatten, Browning and Norman – the challenges of launching a smash-and-grab raid were plain to see. 'This part of the coast consists of cliffs broken only by one low defile on which P.R.U. [recce photos] showed there were 8 German machineguns . . .' Cliff-top pillboxes also overlooked the beach: clearly, any assault by seaborne commandos would face withering fire.

The only way to attempt such a mission was via an airborne insertion, parachuting into the open fields beyond the cliff-tops. But that raised a supposedly inconvenient truth: to date there had only ever been one previous parachute-raid by Allied forces, and it had been a disaster. Officially, Operation Colossus had failed and all the men had been taken captive, and that had been in Italy against a largely undefended target.

What chance was there that airborne raiders would succeed now, when facing such defences as menaced the cliffs and beaches of Bruneval?

Chapter 8

Operation Colossus – a mission intended to showcase the prowess of airborne forces – had been characterized as a grim failure. An embarrassment even. It was grist to the mill for those who wished to denigrate and deny the scope for offensive action by any means – Churchill's 'troops of the hunter class', charged with fomenting 'a reign of terror down the enemy coast'. Indeed, the legacy of Colossus had been used to hamper development of airborne forces hugely.

This was doubly unfair, especially as the truth regarding Operation Colossus's fortunes had begun to filter through to Allied headquarters. The first concrete intelligence on the fate of the Colossus raiders had been received as early as March 1941. A reporter with the *Chicago Daily News* – a prominent newspaper in the Midwest USA – had been thrown out of Italy, very possibly because he'd been passing intelligence to London. His report told of a visit to some of the Colossus raiders taken captive by the Italians. 'Their morale was "terrific" and . . . they intended escaping at the first opportunity. They said they had blown up a . . . bridge besides damaging the Aqueduct. Local inhabitants carried the dynamite for them . . .'

It was a first tantalizing clue that the raiders might actually have hit their target. Intercepts of Italian radio reports made further – grimmer – reading. That April, a Rome radio station announced that 'a certain Fortunato Picchi had been taken prisoner, recognized, denounced and shot as a traitor'. It seemed as if Major Pritchard's Italian translator – the former banqueting manager from the Savoy Hotel – had been captured and killed. SOE, whose agent Picchi was, tried to verify the report, with little success. But one thing seemed clear: a significant number of the raiders had been taken prisoner.

Then, on 18 April, a coded message reached London, authored by the mysterious Flight Lieutenant Lucky – the First World War veteran who many had presumed was serving with SOE. Though captured, Lucky announced defiantly: 'Full success. Other prisoners report great scarcity water southern Italy. Will try to make a break for it from next concentration camp.' It was noted of Lucky's missive: 'This somewhat ambitious claim could not be accepted as representing a true picture . . . The air photographs obtained after the event showed the aqueduct apparently intact.'

Six weeks later, Major Pritchard himself was able to get a letter to Britain, which appeared to corroborate Flight Lieutenant Lucky's claims. Pritchard had written it in some kind of DIY schoolboy code, but it was one that his comrades at Ringway felt certain they could master. 'Here at last is something in a letter from Pritchard,' they remarked. Pritchard had written: 'I shall never forget some excellent soup that was distributed among us . . . Made all the difference, as it was cold at the time.' The word 'soup' had to signify guncotton, for that's how all at Ringway referred to the material, in which case Pritchard had to mean that while the explosives proved useful, some was frozen in the Whitleys' bomb-racks.

His next phrase read: 'I knew that the West Wing of the Old Hall was made untenable – no doubt insurance will foot the bill.'

In other words – the raiders had blown up the western end of the Aqueduct, but doubtless not irreparably. Pritchard's letter was deemed to be 'Of great interest, but still no definitive statement of damage achieved.' All that was about to change.

In August 1941 Captain Ryan, of the Royal Australian Army Medical Corps, managed to reach British shores, having escaped from an Italian POW camp. There, he'd spent time in the company of Major Pritchard. Captain Ryan brought with him a report that the Aqueduct had been destroyed, a claim complemented by a hand-drawn diagram, showing the structure ruptured from end-to-end. The sketch was noted: 'Dotted lines show final resting place of masonry.' During what amounted to five months of captivity, Captain Ryan was adamant that no one in the 'SAS Force' had broken or talked. Major Pritchard had asked him to report that Brindisi, Bari and Salerno had been deprived of water for up to ten days, and possibly even longer.

Keyes, who'd never accepted the wanton abandonment of his men, began to agitate for proper recognition. He cited intelligence reports that suggested the mission was 'at least partially successful'. He singled out Pritchard, praising him as a 'born leader. He put his heart and soul into the job, organized the expedition excellently and brought his men to the highest pitch of enthusiasm.'

Keyes proposed honours for the Colossus raiders, including a DSO for Pritchard, for 'considerable success was achieved . . . due to his leadership and inspiration', and despite the fact that he and his men were languishing in POW camps. Keyes also stressed the 'gallant service rendered by the officers and other ranks under Major Pritchard's command'. The War Office felt differently. A rule was in place that POWs could not be given decorations while still in captivity. 'Major Pritchard's case will come up with others for consideration at the end of hostilities,' Keyes was told.

That October, via the US Embassy in Rome, confirmation of Picchi's dark fate came in. The embassy quoted an article from the Italian newspaper *Il Messagero*: 'Amongst the parachute jumpers of the British Armed Forces who were captured . . . the Italian citizen Picchi Fortunato . . . aged 44 was identified.' Picchi was charged with the crime of 'favouring the military operations of the enemy'. Found guilty, he was sentenced to 'death by shooting in the back'. It had been carried out at dawn on 6 April 1941.

By November, the King himself had intervened over the issue of decorations for the Colossus raiders: Pritchard was duly awarded a DSO on the 25th of that month. Other honours would follow. But the final nail in the coffin of the supposed failure of Operation Colossus was this: in early November a Major Middleton-Stewart, who had been captured on operations in North Africa and held as a POW in Italy, managed to escape and reach friendly lines. Like Captain Ryan before him, he had spent time in a camp with Major Pritchard.

Middleton-Stewart's report on Colossus proved even more detailed and convincing than Captain Ryan's. It confirmed that only a fraction of the explosives had arrived on the ground; that all the raiders had been captured, but the Italians believed otherwise; and that one man – Boulter – had been injured during the drop. It also confirmed that the 'Aqueduct was blown . . . and one coln [pier] was destroyed.' Middleton-Stewart provided a sketch of the destruction. It was almost a carbon-copy of that drawn by Captain Ryan.

This was judged to be 'definitive and reliable information as to damage achieved.' The following month a further written report was smuggled out by Pritchard, who was by then being held in Sulmona POW camp, known as PG (*Prigione di Guerra*) 78, in Central Italy. In it he confirmed that 700 pounds of explosives were detonated at the aqueduct, resulting in the complete 'demolishing of one section. Perceptively, he added that this 'might not show up in a vertical air photograph'.

In the coming months Deane-Drummond would be the first of the Colossus raiders to escape (on his second attempt). His eyewitness testimony nailed it absolutely. He brought to Britain a full account of the raid and its aftermath, including confirmation of Picchi's execution. Indeed, all of the Colossus raiders had faced repeated threats from their captors of being shot at dawn. Regardless, none had broken or talked. Deane-Drummond was able to confirm absolutely the destruction wreaked at the Tragino Aqueduct. He was also bullish about the wider successes of the raid: 'We had shown we could breach their homeland and nowhere was it safe to assume that another raid was out of the question . . . Britain, by itself in the war at this time, had shown it was not only capable of aggressive action, but that it could attack targets a long way inland . . . We had done the job and done it successfully.'

By all accounts, reports of the success of Colossus were genuine. Despite being taken captive, the Colossus raiders felt immense pride in what they had achieved. At one stage the 'British parachutists' – 'these terrible men' – had been paraded through the Italian city of Naples in chains, dragging cannon balls. Though captives, they had marched like victors, belting out the songs of the airborne raiders at the tops of their lungs.

The consciences of the Colossus raiders were clear. Theirs had been no failed mission. Their only failure, if it could be viewed as such, was to have been taken captive. More to the point, the Italians didn't know that. As twice as many parachutes had been found on the ground as captives taken, the Italian military presumed that several dozen raiders were still at large. Rumour spread that the Apennines were 'swarming with them'. In reality, those were the 'chutes left over from the container drops.

The Colossus raiders had blown up the aqueduct and cut off the water supplies, just as they had been charged to do, and against all odds. The trouble is, mud tends to stick. Once Colossus had been ruled a failure by those on high, it proved a hard task to turn that impression around. More to the point, thirty parachutists were languishing in captivity. Disregarding the fact that their means of escape, HMS *Triumph,* had been cancelled, any claim to success was unavoidably tempered by their capture.

The War Office had cited the case of Colossus in arguing that 11 SAS should be disbanded. In a herculean battle of wills, Churchill had countered that he wanted many hundreds of such 'small "bands of brothers" who will be capable of lightning action', ready 'to harass the enemy . . . from Northern Norway to the western limit of German-Occupied France'. The War Office parried, stating that it didn't favour such 'irregulars', with their 'unconventional attire and free-and-easy bearing'.

Churchill refused to be beaten. On a bleak Saturday in April 1941 – barely two months after the 'failure' of Colossus – he and his wife gathered at Ringway with a hand-picked group of generals, plus Averill Harriman, US President Roosevelt's envoy to Europe and a man who would play a pivotal role in transatlantic relations during the war. They were there to witness an airborne demonstration. It was a grave and portentous moment. The war was not going well, and the worth of nine months of feverish preparations at Ringway were about to be proven, one way or the other.

Some 5,000 training jumps had been completed, a fanatical zeal being applied to the creation of Britain's airborne army. Even so, the sceptics and critics abounded. They pointed out that with the Blitz still to be defeated, German military and industrial targets to be bombed, and Britain's coast manned against invasion, resources were stretched to the limits, without trying to form an airborne force, the role for which in the larger war was still very far from clear. Today's demonstration was intended to be a powerful riposte to such criticisms.

Wing Commander Norman was in charge of the day's proceedings, and typically, he'd set up a speaker so the distinguished guests could listen in on what was happening. With his wit and charm and off-beat humour, Norman got along with Churchill famously well, but today he was uncharacteristically nervous. This demonstration was absolutely critical. In the nearby control tower a close watch was being kept, in case the enemy chose to launch a surprise raid, threatening the esteemed gathering.

On the runway five Whitleys were warming up, and Norman checked if they were good to go. He asked if Churchill might like to personally give the instruction for the demonstration to start. He'd prepared a card outlining the jargon to be used to get things rolling. But as the two men chatted, Churchill demurred: the Wing Commander should have the honour.

'Hallo, formation leader, this is Wing Commander Norman calling,' he began. 'Are you ready for take-off?'

'No,' came the reply, after a short pause. 'I'm not ready for take-off. Five of the blighters have fainted.'

After an awkward silence, the voice of the lead pilot came back on the air, confirming that those who had fainted had been removed, and they were good to go. As the five aged Whitleys roared down the runway and rose ponderously into the grey skies, Norman gave a sheepish grin to Churchill. They were getting somewhere, at last. Churchill's features broke into a rare smile – there had not been a great deal to laugh about of recent months. The tension was broken, sighs of relief being breathed all around.

Despite such inauspicious beginnings, the drop went ahead in blustery conditions, the men of 11 SAS acquitting themselves well. There was even a fly-past by a General Aircraft Gal.48 Hotspur, a military glider capable of carrying eight troops, plus a landing in formation by five single-seat gliders. While it fell far short of Churchill's grand vision of an airborne armada, Norman and his fellows expounded on the promise of airborne operations to come.

It called for real imagination to believe that such a means of waging war might soon become a reality. Fortunately, that was one thing with which Churchill was blessed in abundance. On observing the means of triggering the 'chutes, he suggested to Norman a modification as to how the static line might be deployed inside the Whitleys. It was acted upon and proved a great improvement.

Having seen the future that morning at Ringway, Churchill sent a note to General Ismay, to raise with the War Cabinet. At the time, it embodied a hugely courageous decision, one full of foresight and vision. With his staunch courage and optimism, he urged: 'Advantage must be taken of the summer to train these forces who can nevertheless play their part meanwhile as shock troops in home defence. Pray, let me have a note from the War Office on the subject.'

By that autumn an Airborne Division was in the offing, consisting of several Parachute Brigades and one Air-Landing, or Glider, Brigade. The commander of this new division was Major General 'Boy' Browning – 'Boy' due to his youthful good looks. Winner of a Distinguished Service Order (DSO) in the First World War, he'd been a member of the British Olympic bobsleigh team during the inter-war years, and married the famous novelist Daphne du Maurier. Unusually for a senior army commander, he'd shown huge interest in airborne operations, and was a fellow believer in their war-winning potential.

Browning was convinced that forging an airborne esprit de corps was vital. He dispensed with the British Army helmet, replacing it with a bespoke paratrooper's version, made of tightly fitted canvas with rubber padding. Close-fitting para-smocks, copied from captured German *Fallschirmjäger* kit, were introduced, as were light-weight jump trousers. Thus attired, Browning's paratroopers stood out as being something different, elite and set apart.

The strange craft of parachuting was also regulated and defined, demystifying it a little.

The length of the static line is twelve feet six inches. The strop has to be long enough to ensure that the parachute will be well below the aircraft before it opens, and short enough so that the 'chute is not caught in the slip-stream ... the strop is attached to a steel cable running along the inside of the aircraft. The strop-attachment is clipped to this cable and moves with the jumpers as they shuffle one by one towards the exit.

The canopy of the parachute is usually made of nylon,

though sometimes of cotton, and has a diameter of twenty-eight feet. In the middle is a circular hole, the vent, twenty-two inches in diameter. The vent prevents undue strain on the canopy when it begins to open . . . The rigging lines attaching the canopy to the harness are twenty-two feet long.

Even so, the craft remained daunting. Typically, Sergeant David Cross Jefferies recalled his first jump with undisguised trepidation.

None of us looked altogether happy. We knew it was 'any moment now', and I felt a dull reluctance creeping into my being, which I tried hard to ignore. Our instructor had told us: 'Everyone feels like that, so don't imagine you're the only one with the wind up.' I thought of those comforting words, and was selfish enough to hope that he was right. It was soon my turn.

The order: 'Prepare for Action', came like a douche of cold water down my back. I stopped singing abruptly. The business of jumping was drawing uncomfortably near.

'Hook up,' ordered the instructor. Feeling like a condemned criminal, tying the slip-knot in the rope, I hooked up. I expected to find my hands trembling, but they were firm and steady. Perhaps I was in that state of fear that goes beyond mere trembling. 'Petrified' is, I believe, the word.

I moved to the door. We were near the dropping zone, and the feeling of reluctance, which the song had almost stifled, returned with increased force. I felt that I could never bring myself to jump. Then I caught the eye of my instructor . . .

The twinkle told me he knew exactly how I felt. He leaned towards me. 'I say,' he said, 'which pocket's your money in?' 'Top left hand,' I answered. And while I was working out just what he meant (my wits were not at their sharpest), he rapped: 'Action stations, GO!' I went.

Sensing that his airborne warriors needed a special emblem, the better to bind them to the brotherhood, Browning delved into Greek mythology, settling upon Pegasus, the mythical flying horse that had born the Greek hero, Bellerophon, into battle, to defeat the fire-breathing Chimera monsters. Pegasus felt somehow just right: from then on it became the distinctive badge of Britain's airborne forces, initially worn as a shoulder flash.

To complete his revamp, Browning decided to rename the most experienced airborne outfit that he had inherited: on 15 September 1941, 11 Special Air Service became the 1st Parachute Battalion. Of course, their original name and their legacy would live on, in North Africa, with David Stirling and his SAS operations in the deep desert. Unwittingly, the Colossus raiders had helped found a legend, but this was truly the parting of the ways.

Right now, priority number one for Browning's embryonic Airborne Division was to lay to rest the ghosts of Operation Colossus. What he needed was a mission of equal daring on which to score a signal success. Thus, on 1 January 1942 he and his fellow airborne commanders gathered to discuss the concept of the smash-and-grab raid on the Würzburg paraboloid at Bruneval. Despite the fearsome machinegun nests and natural defences of sea and cliff, they figured maybe this was the answer. Certainly, they could hardly wish for a higher-profile task: it had come direct from the desk of Churchill.

Together, Browning, Mountbatten and Norman scrutinized what intelligence existed on the target, in a report compiled by their newly installed Intelligence Chief, Peter de Casa Maury. Despite his flamboyant reputation, he seemed to have done an excellent job. In the mission objectives, de Casa Maury concluded: '[T]here was good photographic intelligence of the target ... which was sufficiently near the coast to make the attempt a feasible operation.'

Describing the terrain, he wrote of 'a small beach by Bruneval, a quarter of a mile S of the object. The sea shoals rapidly from 7 to ¼ fathom, the beach is steep and consists of round pebbles and sand.' Any 'landing from seaward appeared suicidal,' leaving parachuting as the only option. But while airborne raiders might drop in on the target, once they were laden down with the heavy radar kit they were only getting out again via the sea. Fortunately, the beach, if it could be taken, looked eminently suitable for such a withdrawal.

The German defences were the make-or-break factor. De Casa Maury listed the following, which immediately menaced any landings: one guard post, two four-inch guns, two cliff-top pillboxes each with two machineguns, plus two more machineguns positioned in the open near the beach. In terms of the identity and numbers of the defenders, he listed two regiments of the German 336th Infantry Division, an artillery regiment, a recce battalion and a tank-hunting battalion, plus a signals detachment and an armoured car unit. The area was also 'heavily defended by numerous Fighter and Bomber Squadrons'. Regardless, de Casa Maury seemed to favour their chances of 'removing and bringing back intact the object and all technical apparatus'.

One of the greatest challenges was that airborne forces still had no dedicated aircraft. Wing Commander Norman came up with the answer: they should call upon the services of 51 Squadron, the veterans of the Colossus raid, 'expressly for this operation'. It made every sense to utilize their experience, just as it made every sense to study Operation Colossus carefully, to ensure that Operation Biting fared well.

The raid to steal the Würzburg would involve a crack unit of airborne troops parachuting in, and attempting to get out again by sea, just as the Colossus raiders had intended. They scrutinized the key lessons-learned document, drafted a month after Colossus. 'As the task was the first of its kind, it will be appreciated that a large number of problems would arise, many of which may be obviated in the planning of future operations of a similar character.' Any lessons needed to be learned and learned quickly.

In the aftermath of Colossus – a raid 1,600 miles from Britain, into the depths of the Italian mountains – they had to presume the enemy believed nowhere was off-limits to such forces. With Bruneval lying just across the Channel, the potential for a raid must have occurred to the Germans. The enemy must have taken appropriate defensive measures: to assume otherwise was inviting a whole world of trouble.

Regarding the aircraft to be used, the Colossus report stressed how it was 'absolutely essential that sufficient time be allowed for modifications and other preparatory work . . .' The 'existing type of containers were of poor design', the release gear being ineffective, unreliable and lacking in accuracy. It required 'new designs of equipment and containers' and for those to be tested. It was also 'absolutely essential that more time and attention should be devoted to the selection and training of pilots for paratroop dropping operations.'

The report continued: 'To enable a reasonable chance of success, full-scale rehearsals must be practised over country, if possible similar to the actual target.' Intelligence on the target had to be detailed, accurate, timely, and ideally to come from numerous sources. After all, the single greatest failing on the Colossus raid was to mistake a reinforced concrete structure for one made of brickwork.

On the positive side, the report noted that 'a long flight does not necessarily have a bad effect on soldiers.' Moreover, 'landing of paratroops in bright moonlight is practically as easy as in daylight, and trained men can be dropped in close country even with moderate winds.' The report pointed out that the 'morale and enthusiasm of paratroops was very high,' and that 'a model of the terrain around the target had proved invaluable . . . Similar models should be made for all future operations of a like nature.'

The lessons-learned document proved a gold mine of information. It was like a cheat-sheet for those planning the coming raid on Bruneval. Much had been learned from the Colossus adventure. On more than one occasion Major Pritchard had wondered if he and his men – his X Troopers - had been the expendables, the guinea pigs. Whatever the truth of the matter, those envisaging a smash-and-grab raid on the enemy's prized radar were going to find themselves hugely in their debt now.

Flesh was put on the bare bones of a plan. A force of ninety paratroopers would parachute into the target, together with some thirty-odd attachments – mostly sappers, charged to dismantle and steal the Würzburg. The raiders would be taken off the beach by a fleet of small boats, most of which would be Assault Landing Craft (ALCs). Designed by the British company Thorneycroft, the all-wooden ALC was being built at small boatyards and even furniture-makers across the nation. Ideal for beach-landings, the shallow-draft, barge-like vessel could be clad in armour plating for better protection.

The absolute overriding priority for the raid had to be to get the purloined loot – the Würzburg – back to British shores. 'Various methods of getting the "apparatus" safely back to this country were examined,' including 'by means of an aircraft landing in the area of the operation for the sole purpose ... Failing that, the "apparatus" should be transferred to a fast boat at the earliest opportunity.' A Motor Gun Boat (MGB), a small, heavily-armed vessel capable of 28 knots, could linger offshore, awaiting delivery of the stolen German radar.

Cunning decoys and deceptions were envisaged, including 'the dropping of dummy parachutes', to mislead the enemy. From somewhere a scientific expert would need to be found who was willing to 'drop with the parachutists and deal with the "apparatus"', and to work out if any 'special form of carrier is required for the "apparatus"'. Bearing in mind the risks inherent in the raid, SOE would need to advise on escape and evasion options for any who might be left behind.

Finally, the right air, sea and land commanders would need to be found, to spearhead the operation. Time was pressing. The raiders would need to hit the moon window, while at the same time striking within the winter months, wherein the long nights would provide enough hours of darkness within which to steal the loot and slip away to safety.

A first priority was to have detailed models made of the target, for the raiders and aircrew to orientate themselves. On 4 January 1942 an urgent request was dispatched, stamped 'MOST SECRET'. It read: 'A model is required by C.C.O. [Chief Combined

Operations], if possible within seven days of today's date . . . The scale required is such as to produce a model approximately 5ft square . . . Full details of houses, woods, paths, fissures in cliffs, woods, etc., are required . . . where possible, the true degree of slope shall be indicated.'

As the pace hotted up, a codename was required for the mission, one as evocative and as inspiring as Colossus – the giant figure of ancient Greece that bestrode the world. Mountbatten set upon OPERATION BITING, for the simple reason that on the coming raid he intended his forces to 'Bite 'em hard.'

That decided, the key priority was to find the right man to lead the raiders into battle. It would need a figure equal in stature to Major Tag Pritchard, one whose men would follow practically anywhere. The X Troopers had dropped deep into enemy territory, knowing in their hearts that their chances of escape were at best slim. They had done so anyway, undaunted. Operation Biting called for similar steely resolve.

While the distance to be covered was far less, the defences were infinitely more daunting. It would require courage, dash and daring to wrest that mystery paraboloid from the enemy's grasp, and at every stage they were sure to encounter fearsome resistance. The German defenders would have just about everything on their side: numbers, firepower, cover, terrain, not to mention early-warning from their very own radar.

And so the search was begun to find a commander whose men would follow him into the jaws of hell.

Chapter 9

Major John Dutton Frost was comparatively new to airborne forces. On his second training jump he'd injured his knee, and had been recuperating ever since. So, while he was officially the CO of C Company, he wasn't capable of any airborne operations just yet. He wasn't unduly concerned. Britain seemed mired in a defensive mindset, things were going abysmally on just about every front, and he didn't expect airborne forces to be making any forays into enemy territory in the foreseeable future.

Today's news that C Company were to move to Salisbury Plain for special training had quickened his pace a little – that was until he'd learned the reason why. It was all for another demo, at which the great and the good would see airborne forces put through their paces. It was all very well proving what they could do in practice, but why not go ahead and hit the enemy for real? It was approaching twelve months since their first ever airborne sortie, and by all accounts Operation Colossus had suffered mixed fortunes.

Frost was far from alone in hungering for action; for a chance to prove their mettle in the red heat of battle. There was something about that explanation – 'special training for a demo' – that didn't quite ring true. As Frost busied himself at Ringway, trying to win his blue 'jump wings', he sensed that something very different might well be in the offing. One or two remarks were let slip that gave him 'considerable food for thought'.

The commanders at Ringway seemed to be paying an inordinate amount of attention to Frost, which a demo just didn't warrant. More to the point, there were several dark references to the 'last time', which Frost quickly realized had to mean Colossus. Why were those in charge referring to the Tragino aqueduct raid, when all C Company were supposedly doing was readying for a demo? Colossus had been no dry-run. It had been the real thing. Not a man had returned. All were either dead or in the bag, apparently.

Frost – stocky, solidly built, moustachioed, dark-haired – climbed into Ringway's 'vile, loathed sausage' of a tethered balloon, sensing there was more to this than he'd been told. If there was even the slightest chance of a mission being in the offing, he was absolutely determined to lead it. C Company was his outfit, and its acting commander, Major Philip Teichman, just wasn't right to take it into battle, as far as he was concerned.

C Company was known as 'Jock Company', for practically all hailed from celebrated Scottish regiments. While both Frost and Teichman were English, Frost was long-steeped in the traditions of Scottish soldiering, having been commissioned into the Cameronians in September 1932, a Highland regiment with a history stretching back to 1881. With Douglas tartan forming part of their dress, the Cameronians marched to the tunes of 'Within a Mile of Edinburgh Toon' and 'The Garb of Old Gaul'.

The Cameronians were 'dour' and 'dogged' and 'as hardy and enduring as any in the world', Frost averred. His Jock Company was cut from similar cloth, constituting 'a rather outstanding body of men'. He was damned if he would let Teichman lead them into their first battle. In which case he needed to complete five jumps in almost as many days, to earn his jump wings and join the Salisbury Plain rehearsals.

But the weather at Ringway was famously fickle, and on that first day the 'vile sausage' was fogged in. Day two proved similar, until, at the approach of dusk, the mist suddenly lifted. Frost managed to cram in two jumps, before darkness descended over the airbase. Only three days remained, with as many jumps still to complete. But in a sense it had been written in the stars that he would join airborne forces, and it would be a cruel twist of fate if he missed this baptism of fire.

Born in India in 1912, Frost was the son of Brigadier F. D. Frost, MC. In his first weeks of life he'd become accustomed to gunfire: his father shot and killed a snake that was crawling up the side of his cot. On further postings to Iraq, the young John Frost learned to ride with the Iraqi Arabs, hunting jackal. At age nine he was sent to boarding school in England, to tame some of his wilder ways. First at Wellington, in Somerset, and then Monkton Coombe, near Bath, he'd followed the 'gentleman's' pursuits of shooting, fishing and riding, and then learned to box at Sandhurst.

At war's outbreak Frost had found himself in the Syrian desert, commanding a unit of the Iraqi Levies, a force manned by locals serving on behalf of Britain. It was a wild, lawless province which evoked fond memories of his childhood, and he would later remark of the Levies that their 'watchword was "Perfection" . . . I shall always remember them.' Even so, he itched to join the 'real war'. Upon learning of defeat in France and Dunkirk, he'd lobbied friends and contacts to secure a posting to the real action.

Having duly wangled a return to Britain, Frost had rejoined the Cameronians in March 1941, but had quickly realized not a great deal was happening. Accordingly, he'd jumped at the opportunity to volunteer for Special Service, professing to have not the faintest idea that airborne operations beckoned. He should have known better. Before leaving Syria, Mr Sethi, his devoted clerk in the Iraqi Levies, had alerted him to a report about the raising of airborne forces. Frost feigned uninterest, claiming he had no desire to get 'mixed up with that kind of thing'. Mr Sethi had fixed Frost with one of his looks: 'You never know all that is to come,' he'd remarked, portentously.

Frost was now twenty-nine years old, and for sure he was mixed up with that kind of thing all right. Mr Sethi's predictions had very much come true. Having made it into airborne forces, Frost had devoured studies of earlier operations, scrutinising the techniques used by the Germans' *Fallschirmjägers*. One thin pamphlet had been issued by the War Office on Britain's previous airborne venture – Colossus. It portrayed the mission as unsuccessful, the raiders being captured en route to the coast, where they 'were to be taken off by submarine'. No mention, of course, that HMS *Triumph's* mission had been summarily cancelled.

Frost's crash course in jump-training went to the wire, his sixth being completed just in the nick of time. He'd most disliked jumping from the balloon, a technique pioneered in the First World War, when those manning observation balloons had found themselves at risk of being shot up by enemy aircraft. Just as soon as the observer spotted a hostile warplane, he would leap over the side of the basket, trusting to his parachute to get him down safely – far preferable to being engulfed by a blazing balloon. The parachutes had become known as 'Guardian Angels' as a result.

Frost, like many, loathed the balloon jumps at Ringway. When leaping from a speeding aircraft, he'd found parachuting offered a similar thrill to horse riding or hunting, albeit utterly alien and new. In many ways – physique; mindset; regard for his men – Frost was similar to Major Tag Pritchard, the lone airborne commander who had trodden this path before, not that Frost was entirely sure what path it was he was following.

At one stage during his recruitment, Frost had worried that he'd blown it. At his October 1941 London interview, he was asked what best defined the airborne mindset. Almost without thinking he had answered that too much discipline tended to cramp initiative, so they should favour self-starters and the independently minded. He worried that the brigadier hadn't appreciated his answer. In fact, it was exactly what he'd wanted to hear. Those were the kind of recruits Frost had sought when forming Jock Company.

His jump-training done, he hurried south to Salisbury Plain, to take over at the helm. Teichman seemed angry, and couldn't hide his frustration at the speed with which Frost had won his wings, especially since an added incentive had been thrown into the ring. If the 'demo' went well – it would take place on the Isle of Wight – C Company were earmarked for a raid on the coast of France sometime soon. Well, what of it? Frost countered. He was here now and it was his company.

From the moment of his arrival Frost faced some probing questions. For many in C Company, much about this 'training demo' didn't add up. Why had they been allotted such inordinate amounts of ammunition, they asked, and why all the new armaments? The men had each been issued with a Sten gun – designed by Shepherd and Turpin and made by Enfield, hence the name – a weapon none had even known existed, it was still so new. It appeared to them like a cross between a carbine and an automatic pistol. Why had they got Stens, if only for a demo?

Frost had his suspicions, but he kept his counsel. The Sten had only just been invented and it was prone to teething problems. As the cold snows and frozen January mud brought Salisbury training to a standstill, Frost and his men seized the chance to iron out the worst of the weapon's faults. Designed to be easy to mass-produce, the rough edges needed filing, to ensure the mechanism didn't jam. They consoled themselves with the fact that at anything under fifty yards it proved vastly superior to the rifle-and-bayonet, previously their standard weapon.

For the 'demo', C Company were supposed to parachute in at night and raid a German HQ, as Churchill and his cohorts looked on and applauded. An area had been selected with steep hillsides, to represent the cliffs upon which the imaginary German headquarters was situated. Frost and his men were to be dropped inland of the HQ and to the rear of its supposed defences, neutralize them and destroy the target, before withdrawing down a steep ravine leading to a 'beach', where they were to be picked up by the Royal Navy.

Frost was told that his company would be divided into four distinct units, each named after a foremost British naval commander – a nod to the role the Royal Navy would play. Divvying up his Jock Company into 'little penny packets', Frost found himself commanding five assault parties codenamed *Nelson*, *Hardy*, *Jellicoe*, *Drake* and *Rodney*. Night after night they practised, fighting their way over punishing terrain and in biting wind, sleet and snow. Frost didn't like the approach or the results one bit.

It was a given that the company commander should be intimately involved in mission planning. But here, Frost had inherited a blueprint from on high. All very well assigning fancy admirals' names to assault parties, but it just didn't cut it with Frost. No plan, however good, survived first contact with the enemy. Frost knew that. It was crucial to keep it simple and flexible, and by anyone's reckoning this plan wasn't that.

More importantly, every one of his men had been trained to function at the platoon level. Everything in the British Army went by threes: three battalions to a brigade; three companies to a battalion; three platoons to a company. That defined the individual soldier's world-view and their understanding of how things worked. Those amorphous assault parties – *Nelson*, *Hardy*, *Jellicoe*, *Drake* and *Rodney* – cut through all of that. It was non-sensical, swirling up his platoons into shapeless, formless units. Frost hated the plan. Loathed it. So, too, did his men.

Remembering his answer at interview – that too much military discipline was a bad thing – Frost redrew the plan from scratch. He rejigged it, so each assault team was formed of an individual platoon, with one central headquarters unit being his to command. That was another thing he disliked about the plan: it allowed for no effective control; no nerve centre; no brain from which to direct the men to fight or to flight. Plan formulated, Frost went and sought out Major Bromley-Martin, the Grenadier Guards staff officer who was running things hereabouts.

Once he'd outlined his alternative plan, a fierce argument ensued. Bromley-Martin was adamant: this had been laid down by headquarters and it wasn't about to change. The two men parted in some acrimony. The following morning Bromley-Martin sought Frost out. Having first sworn him to absolute secrecy, and to sticking to the 'Prime Minister cover story', Bromley-Martin came clean. Frost and his men were training for no demo. Instead, they would be heading into France on a real live raid and 'before February is out'.

The objective was top secret and the enemy were there in strength and in complex positions. All would be revealed to Frost in good time. But if he wanted the job, he had to stick to the plan, even if it disquieted him. Those were the terms. Frost was left with the distinct impression that Bromley-Martin was planning *his* raid, something he didn't particularly appreciate. Even so, he felt he had no option but to accept – for no matter what the plan of attack, no one else was leading his men into battle.

'Right, it's up to you to see that everything works properly,' Bromley-Martin announced, once Frost had agreed his terms. 'Ensure that your Jocks are so fit they'll be jumping out of their skins, or you won't have a hope of bringing them out alive.' Well, at least now he knew.

After endless days slogging through icy storms and clinging mud, Frost was well aware what impression his Jock Company tended to make. The newspapers had hailed Britain's parachutists as being men who 'drank blood and crunched glass'. One look at Frost's men seemed to prove it. They were by his own admission 'a wild crew'. For months they had focused on fitness, toughness and weapons training, plus learning the paratrooper's craft. 'We had little time for drill,' Frost noted, and even less 'for making ourselves look glamorous or even clean'. The truth was his Jocks 'looked horrible.' Piratical almost.

They lined up for inspection by General 'Boy' Browning, a man known to be something of a stickler for proper turnout. He moved slowly down Frost's thin, ragged line – supposedly the British Army's finest. When he was done, Browning took Frost aside for a quiet word. He told him to see Bromley-Martin right away and get every man issued with new uniform.

'And see here, Frost,' he added, 'that is without question the filthiest company I have ever seen in my life!'

Frost didn't doubt it, but he didn't particularly care about appearances. Now that he knew they were training for a raid for real, he cared more about bringing his men out alive. And for that, the more ferocious their demeanour the better, as far as he was concerned.

Thankfully, it wasn't solely up to him to bring his Jocks out unscathed. Frost was blessed with a raft of officers who couldn't be bettered. At the heart of it all lay his Company Sergeant Major (CSM), Gerry Alexander Strachan, a man of huge experience and salt-of-the-earth good sense. Hailing from Dundee, Strachan – bull-necked and tough, with broad, plain-spoken features – had served with the Black Watch, more informally known as the 'Ladies from Hell' (due to their habit of charging into battle wearing tartan kilts, of course).

Strachan had long been suspicious of the huge quantities of weaponry arriving for a so-called 'demo'. Frost had had to argue, somewhat unconvincingly, that nothing was going to be spared for Churchill. He didn't particularly enjoy lying to Strachan, whom he viewed as 'the very best sort of senior NCO in the world'.

Captain John G. Ross, Frost's second-in-command, was another of the famed Ladies from Hell. Level-headed, unflappable, indefatigable, Ross was in charge of supplies for the Company, which were coming in thick and fast at any time of day or night. He was blessed with a fine intellect, and Frost sensed he would be leaning on Ross to get them through the coming raid. He was the kind of officer to hold a vital road or a beach, calm and resolute under fire, until every last man had been evacuated.

After Ross came Lieutenant John Timothy, like Frost a recent volunteer for Airborne forces. A native of Tunbridge Wells, Kent, Timothy had been a keen rugby player and cricketer at school, taking a job with Marks & Spencer as a sales manager just before the war. On the day hostilities were declared, Timothy had joined a long queue of eager recruits, only to be turned away due to numbers. He'd kept badgering the local recruiting sergeant, until eventually he was allowed to join up.

After a spell in the Grenadier Guards and the Queen's Own Royal West Kent Regiment, Timothy had volunteered for Special Service, as not a great deal seemed to be happening. When asked at interview why he had done so, he replied: 'Well, as the war wasn't coming to me, I thought I'd better go and meet it.' It was just the kind of offensive spirit airborne forces favoured. It was also the kind of direct, honest answer that typified the man. Dark-haired, dark-eyed and with an intense look about him, there was little doubt that Lieutenant Timothy meant business.

Then there was Lieutenant Peter Naumoff, a man who had a very special reason to want to fight the Nazis. Although he kept it very much to himself, Naumoff was Jewish and keenly aware of the hatred being spread by Hitler and his cronies against his people. Although news of the concentration camps wouldn't break for two years or more, the dark rumours had spread within the Jewish community. Naumoff was actually a 'supernumerary officer' in the British Airborne Division then being formed, so akin to a reserve officer. But Frost had warmed to his unbridled enthusiasm, coupled with his steadfastness and sheer nerve. He'd not had the heart to refuse Naumoff a place on the coming mission. He'd been placed in command of the *Drake* assault party, which was to help spearhead the assault against enemy forces defending the 'German HQ'. Payback time.

Last but not least came Lieutenant Euan B. Charteris, at just twenty years of age Frost's youngest officer, but by no means the least capable. Indeed, Charteris – known to all as 'Junior', for obvious reasons – struck Frost as being ideally suited to leading the charge. Having served with the King's Own Scottish Borderers, headquartered in Berwick-Upon-Tweed, whose men first saw action in 1689, he had that regiment's long and glorious tradition to uphold.

Charteris was in command of *Hardy* section, and his objective was to seize and secure the beach. His men were mostly Seaforth Highlanders, whose cap badge displays a highland stag, above the motto, in Gaelic, *Cuidich 'n Righ* – Aid the King. They were seen as having tremendous offensive spirit. Not only that, but they were devoted to their young and charismatic commander. If any party could clear and hold Bruneval beach, it was Charteris and his men.

It was a fine crop of officers to lead Jock Company into action. But equally, Frost favoured his men – his Jocks – to bring themselves out of enemy clutches unscathed. The self-starting, boisterous, independent mindset ran deep within the C Company ranks. Sometimes, a little too deep. Frost had already experienced one or two incidents wherein such spirits had got just a little out of hand.

One night, some of the wilder elements of the company returned from letting off steam in a nearby hostelry. They'd marched behind an improvised band, one formed of their fellow paratroopers and bearing trumpets, drums and trombones 'borrowed' from the

Just days after Dunkirk, Churchill asked for
volunteers for Special Service, those willing
to take the fight to the Nazi enemy by
all possible means, to step forward.
Thousands flocked to the call.

Churchill's Special Service volunteers
undergoing highly realistic training. Recruits
learned survival, orienteering, close quarter
combat, silent killing, amphibious and
cliff assault, weapons use (including captured
enemy arms) and demolitions.

In the summer of 1940, Churchill called for 5,000 men to train as airborne forces, pioneering a form of warfare the likes of which the world had never seen. The word 'Air' was inserted into the Special Service volunteer's name, and the fledgling Special Air Service (SAS) was formed.

Christened No. 11 SAS Battalion, the 450-strong unit had few aircraft with which to train. They had to make do with a handful of obsolete Armstrong Whitworth Whitley bombers – nicknamed the 'Flying Barn Door' – plummeting vertically through a hole cut in the floor (a C47 is pictured in the background).

Despite having to invent airborne operations largely from scratch, the relentless training paid off. Here, in a sketch from the time, 11 Special Air Service operators seize the limousine of the Crown Prince of Norway, during an exercise on Salisbury Plain, prompting one observer to remark: 'Our parachute men are . . . of considerable resource, initiative and daring.'

Special Operations Executive (SOE) training. In June 1940, Oxford classics professor and SOE recruit Colin Hardie, came up with a mission of untold audacity – to blow up an aqueduct in Italy to paralyse the country's key ports. Codenamed Operation Colossus, it would be the first airborne raid by Allied forces – the fledgling SAS.

Operation Colossus was commanded by Major Trevor 'Tag' Pritchard. Fiercely loyal, his men would follow 'Old Tag' anywhere.

Pritchard's second-in-command, Lieutenant Anthony Deane-Drummond, had been urged by his schoolmaster: 'Put your heart and soul – as well as brains – into anything you do.'

The Op Colossus team included the unshakeable Sergeant Percy Clements, a former Leicestershire miner (*below, left*), Sapper James Parker (*below, centre*), a demolitions expert, and Lance Corporal Robert B. Watson (*below, right*) who volunteered for the SAS in 1940.

On 10 February 1941, the 36 Colossus raiders took to the skies. After braving 1,600 miles of enemy airspace thick with flak and German fighters, the pilots dropped them with near pin-point accuracy in the shadow of Mount Vulture, where they proceeded to wreak havoc on their target, as illustrated in the commemorative postcard below.

Major General A. J. Deane-Drummond
CB DSO MC

Philatelic Officer
RHQ
The Parachute Regiment
Browning Barracks
Aldershot, Hants

Due to faulty intelligence, High Command ordered the recall of HMS *Triumph*, the submarine tasked to whisk the SAS men off enemy shores . . . And so they were abandoned.

All the Op Colossus raiders were captured or killed. Pictured here in Italian POW camp Campo di Lavoro 102, from left, top row: Lance-Corporals Henderson, Pexton, Maher and Tomlin. Next row: Lance-Corporal Watson, Troopers Phillips, Samuels, Humphreys and Pryor, plus Sergeant Durie. Seated row: Trooper Parker, Sergeant Walker, Corporal Grice. Bottom row: Corporal O'Brien, Trooper Nastri and Sapper Davidson.

In November 1941, King George VI – here shown inspecting airborne troops - intervened over the issue of decorations for the Colossus raiders. Major Pritchard was awarded a DSO and other honours followed, but still Colossus was branded a 'failure', casting a pall over airborne operations.

On 17 December 1939, following the Battle of the River Plate, the German warship the *Graf Spee* was scuttled. Her gunnery had proven devastatingly accurate, and a British scientist-spy was smuggled aboard the wreck to salvage her radar, the wire lattice that can be seen atop the forepart of her superstructure. But top experts argued that only Britain had invented radar: they discounted the Graf Spee evidence, and much more besides.

Physicist Reginald Victor Jones – known to all as R.V. Jones – worked for the British Secret Intelligence Service (SIS) winkling out the enemy's newest war technologies. Described as 'a scientist with a special interest in German weapons,' Jones – still in his twenties at war's outbreak – would argue vehemently that the Germans had radar, and that we needed to do all in our power to defeat it.

On 5 December 1941, Flight Officer Tony Hill returned from 'Sortie A/30', a daring low-level dash by reconnaissance Spitfire – known as a 'dicing' run, as in dicing with death. Hill's photo captured the elusive Würzburg, a mobile radar capable of vectoring lethal flak and fighters onto Allied aircraft. Stealing it from the French cliffs was seen as being crucial to winning the war.

Hill's photos were studied intensely. The Würzburg turned out to be a mobile radar capable of vectoring lethal flak and German fighters onto British aircraft.

SOE agents were dropped by Lysander light aircraft in France to spy out the top-secret radar. Pictured third from left is Percy Charles 'Pick' Pickard, tasked to lead the airborne side of the coming mission.

Bruneval beach lay just a few hundred yards from the German radar site. Pre-war postcards were studied, to see if assault boats could land. But the beachside villa (shown) and cliffs had been turned into a fortress by the enemy, making seaborne landings suicidal.

5957. SAINT-JOUIN-PRUNEVAL (Seine Inf.) – Plage et Falaises d'aval

Far from prying eyes, at Loch Fyne, on the rugged west coast of Scotland, 120 men of
C Company, of the 2nd Parachute Battalion, began training for the mission,
now codenamed Operation Biting.

But full-scale exercises
for Op Biting along the
Dorset coast proved
disastrous. By zero hour
– the mid-February '42
'moon window' – not
one dress rehearsal had
proven successful.

On the night of 27–28 February 1942, the raiders flew towards the French coast. Subsequently commemorated in the *Victor Book For Boys*, the mission proved fraught from the very start as parties were dropped in the wrong place and German defenders fought ferociously.

On the evacuation boats parties armed with Bren light machineguns and Boys anti-tank rifles – nicknamed 'the elephant gun' due to its heavy bore - raked the enemy clifftop positions with fire.

The raiders' heroic return (*above*), showing Major John Frost, far-left on the bridge. German captives seized (*left*) included young *Infanterist* – infantryman – Tewes (*left of photo, facing camera*), and *Flieger* – aircraftman and radar-operator – Heller (*right, facing camera*). They would yield priceless intelligence.

Two radar experts went on the raid. The first was Flight Sergeant Charles William 'Bill' Cox, (*above, second left of photo*), a radar technician, here shown talking to Group Captain Sir Nigel Norman, the Air Commander of Op Biting, immediately after the raid. The second, Donald Preist, was one of the 'boffin boys' serving at the Telecommunications Research Establishment (TRE), Britain's top-secret radar research facility (*below, wearing glasses*).

The morning after the raid, Wing Commander Pickard examines a captured German helmet. On the eve of departure, he'd confided in Frost: 'I feel like a bloody murderer dropping you poor devils over there . . .'.

Major Frost, facing camera, had been sent a message by Lord Louis Mountbatten, Chief of Combined Operations, on the eve of departure: 'Best of luck. Bite them hard.' Frost, shown here immediately after the raid, talking to Lt. Col. J. A. Goschen, a future 1st Airborne Division luminary, had made Mountbatten's urging a hard reality.

Eight of the Op Biting raiders would not make it back. This photo shows Lance-Corporal McCallum and Privates Thomas and Willoughby, who were cornered by German troops in a cave along the French coastline and captured.

For the majority of the raiders Op Biting spelled a welcome 'V-for-Victory', at a time when all was not going well for the Allies. The British and American press lapped up the story.

By rebuilding and studying the stolen radar, Britain's scientists worked out how to blind it. The top-secret technology – codenamed WINDOW – involved scattering bales of tin-foil strips, which replicated radar echoes as if thousands of Allied warplanes filled the skies. By using WINDOW – today called 'chaff' – British and American bombers were able to pound targets deep inside Germany.

On D-Day, WINDOW technologies were used in the greatest fakery ever, creating a procession of landing craft, destroyers and battleships where none in truth existed, while the real D-Day fleet steamed unnoticed towards the Normandy beaches.

local Royal British Legion. On another evening, Sergeant Jimmy 'Shorty' Sharp – 'short in stature, but very great as a soldier' – arrived back at camp, with a gaggle of other sergeants, laden with an enormous pilfered cheese.

To their ale-befuddled senses it seemed to make more sense to shoot it up, as opposed to eating it. An explosion rang out, followed by cries of 'Shorty! Shorty!' All presumed Shorty had been shot. No such thing. Amidst peals of laughter, the men – now brandishing Stens – began to hotly debate how best to dispatch the cheese. One suggested shooting it out of the rafters of a hut. Another suggested he hold it, while one of his fellows shot it out of his hands. 'Don't be bloody daft!' the putative shooter replied. 'I might hit your hand!'

All were young and high-spirited, and their antics had in them the 'excuse of youth and the heat of blood', as Frost observed. But he had to keep a close eye. Security was everything for the raid. 'If the enemy has an inkling of the project we shall be doomed,' Frost reflected. The only aspects favouring the raiders were speed, aggression and surprise. Take those away, by forewarning the enemy, and they were all as good as dead.

When General Browning learned of the high jinks, he was less than impressed. These men 'did not appear to realize that their carelessness or desire to "show off" might result in a disaster and loss of life . . . no hints of inside knowledge; no showing off and no bravado to fond relations, can be allowed.' There was even a suggestion that 'security personnel' might be planted 'amongst all ranks of all the Services taking part, their identity not being known even to the Commander of the forces'. That, it was argued, might kill such behaviour dead.

Frost, with Strachan's steely backing, had a simpler solution.

He resorted to the single most powerful sanction for any who might step out of line – that of a swift and ignoble return to their unit. That threat alone proved enough to curb the worst excesses, and to silence the wagging of tongues. Frost understood his men absolutely. You couldn't make an omelette without breaking a few eggs. Likewise, you couldn't raid a heavily-defended target on the French coast without a bunch of wild toughs with which to do so. It went with the territory.

Frost also had absolute confidence in those who were tasked to fly his 'Jocks' into action, if not exactly their airframes. British Airborne forces were still jumping from the Whitley, via its reviled hole. There was nothing any of them could do about that. But in 51 Squadron RAF, they were blessed with pilots who had achieved the seemingly impossible on Colossus, navigating the X Troop hundreds of miles across enemy airspace, to drop them with pinpoint accuracy deep into the Italian mountains.

Having won a DSO on Colossus, Wing Commander Tait had moved on to 35 Squadron, the first to be equipped with the Handley Page Halifax, a four-engine heavy bomber. In June 1941 he'd led a daring daylight raid over Kiel, in northern Germany, for which he'd won a bar to his DSO. In his absence, Wing Commander Norman provided the continuity. He'd commanded the air side of Operation Colossus: likewise, he was in control of the air aspects of Operation Biting. And if anything, Tait's replacement at 51 Squadron was an even more impressive and striking figure.

Wing Commander Percy Charles Pickard's reputation went before him. Born in Sheffield and educated at Framlingham boarding school, in Suffolk – motto: 'Wisdom grows with study' – Pickard had spent time farming in Kenya before the war. In the mid-1930s, he'd driven from there to England with three friends, almost dying from malaria en route. Commissioned into the RAF, he'd fought over Norway and France, during the evacuation of Dunkirk, winning both a DFC and a DSO.

But his real claim to fame was his appearance in the Academy Award-winning film (1942, 'Best Documentary'), *Target For Tonight*, directed by Harry Watt, which showcased a fictional mission by RAF bomber crews over Nazi Germany. Pickard had played the role of 'Squadron Leader Dickson', piloting Wellington 'F for Freddie'. The film opened with an RAF photo reconnaissance aircraft dropping film by parachute, to be examined by the kind of team that Wavell led at Danesfield House. Indeed, the film actually featured real live photo interpreters from Medmenham, who discovered a complex of oil tanks and terminals where there had previously only been fields.

On identifying the installations, one of those featured declared: 'It certainly is a peach of a target, isn't it, Sir!' Pickard – posing as Dickson – led the resulting bombing raid, which was a run-away success. The film was a huge hit with the public, giving the impression that RAF bombers were wreaking havoc on the enemy and Pickard became something of a celebrity. Even Frost was impressed. Pickard commanded a 'crack bomber squadron,' he remarked, 'and we felt if anybody was going to put us down in the right place, they were the people to do it.'

There was a certain dash about Pickard, with his fair hair worn longish and somewhat ruffled, as if he'd just been running his fingers through it. He would need it, for what was coming. It hadn't escaped the notice of anyone that not only would the Whitleys be braving the enemy's guns, they would be flying down the very throat of their all-seeing eye – their radar. On this mission especially, the chances of remaining undetected were slim indeed.

For Operation Biting, Norman demanded 51 Squadron better their record on Colossus. Preparations were to be exhaustive. Nothing was to be left to chance. As soon as possible the aircrews began to 'practise [the] dropping of dummies from 400 feet', the kind of altitude at which Frost and his men would jump. Only once they'd mastered that were they permitted to get live bodies into their warplanes. They had to study the area intimately, 'until they could all draw the coastline and landmarks free-hand, without reference to the map'.

Norman demanded that he and Pickard fly a reconnaissance mission over the target, within the first two weeks of February, to avoid any confusion on the night of the attack. He ordered a 'surf reconnaissance flight along the French coast', the very night of the assault, to check the sea conditions. Plus he wanted a flight over the target just hours before the raid, to take an 'altimeter reading at . . . 350' above ground level', and to gauge 'parachuting conditions . . . including drift and landing, and visibility on the ground'.

New containers were designed and tested. They were ingenious, being 'specially marked and fitted with coloured lights turned on by impact, for easy identification'. Those lights were bright enough to be seen from 100 yards, the colour of the illumination signifying the contents. A red lamp meant weapons. Green was for signals kit. Purple denoted explosives and wrecking gear. And yellow meant trolleys. As the sole purpose of Biting was to steal away the prized paraboloid, three foldable wheeled carts, made of canvas stretched over metal frames, were to be parachuted in.

But there was little point in making such exhaustive preparations on the air side, if the withdrawal from the beach wasn't equally carefully resourced, rehearsed and husbanded. In that, Frost and his men were blessed with having something of a secret weapon at their disposal: a shore establishment called HMS Tormentor.

Based at the venerable Household Brigade Yacht Cub, at Warsash, on the mouth of the River Hamble, near Southampton, Tormentor was a top-secret training facility for covert raiding operations, one led by a most remarkable individual. Royal Australian Navy (RAN) Commander Frederick Norton Cook had already survived two ships being sunk beneath him, when, in July 1940, he'd been asked to found Tormentor.

The first, HMS *Royal Oak*, a Revenge-class battleship, had been torpedoed in the supposedly impregnable naval base of Scapa Flow, in Orkney, by a German U-boat shortly after the outbreak of the war. Of *Royal Oak*'s 1,234 crew, 833 were killed, perishing in horrific circumstances in the freezing Scottish waters. The surprise strike by *U-47* made her captain, Gunther Prier, a celebrity in Germany, where he was the first submarine commander to be awarded the Knight's Cross of the Iron Cross, the highest award instituted by Hitler's Reich.

Six months later, on 26 May 1940, Cook was aboard the light cruiser HMS *Curlew*, when she was attacked by a squadron of Junkers JU88s, a twin-engine aircraft more commonly known as the *Schnellbomber* – fast-bomber. *Curlew* was sent to the bottom, and after two such horrifying brushes with death, Cook, certainly, had no reason to love the enemy. Having joined the navy at the age of thirteen, the sea was in his blood. Thirsting to hit back, Tormentor presented the chance to do so.

It was a month after HMS *Curlew*'s sinking when Cook was

summoned by Admiral Keyes. Keyes wanted cross-Channel raiding operations expanded by any means. Cook was to form a strike centre, at which regular soldiers could be trained to launch irregular hit-and-run attacks. Asked to think up a suitable name for his new command, Cook suggested 'Impossible' and 'Incredible', before one of his freshly-recruited officers came up with HMS 'Nobby'. Why Nobby? Cook had asked. It stood for 'Night Operations by Bloody Yachts', the officer explained. Cook figured that was about the gist of it. But they settled upon Tormentor, for they intended to prove a torment to the enemy along the coast of occupied France.

One of Tormentor's earliest recruits was Lieutenant Bill Wescott, an infantry officer selected for a 'very hush-hush mission'. Posted to the former Brigade Yacht Cub, he was told they were to transform 'ordinary infantry soldiers' into those able to execute 'night raids on France'. Issued with 'special weapons, ammunition, explosives and rope-soled [silent] boots', Wescott was introduced to their raiding craft – American-made all-wood Eurekas, or R-craft (raiding craft), capable of carrying thirty troops at pushing 10 knots.

The R-craft were developed as Louisiana swamp boats, by the Eureka Tug Boat Company of New Orleans. But due to the vessels' shallow draft, they also proved perfect for beach landings. They'd first come to the attention of Lieutenant-Colonel Dudley Clarke, founder of the Commandos, who'd ordered 136 of the vessels in the summer of 1940. The first fifty had been delivered by October that year, and they proved well suited to hit-and-run attacks.

Cook instructed Wescott and fellows to create 'an assault course, a training programme ... recce sites for landing and exercises for night operations, physical training and unarmed combat'. In November 1941 they received their first intake, a Company from 7th Battalion the Wiltshire Regiment. The first raid was already being planned. Fittingly codenamed Operation Curlew – after *Curlew*, the cruiser sunk under Cook – it involved probing the coastal defences around the village of St-Laurent-sur-Mer, 'Omaha Beach' in the D-Day landings.

Tormentor's second and even more hush-hush role was to scope out possible landing grounds, for when the Allies might be ready to liberate occupied Europe. Operation Curlew went ahead on the night of 11/12 January 1942, a hundred raiders sneaking towards the beaches under cover of darkness. The Eureka boats possessed no landing ramp, so those riding in them had to vault over the bows, laden down with all their assault gear. Omaha Beach was duly recce'd, Curlew proving a 'great morale booster to both Tormentor and [the] Raiding School'. Two years later the beach would be stormed by US troops from the 1st and 29th Infantry Divisions, plus US Army Rangers.

Immediately after Operation Curlew, Mountbatten came to observe Commander Cook's flotilla and his men in action on the Solent. Clearly, he must have been impressed. Days later, Cook found himself summoned to Combined Operations headquarters in London. Mystified, he found only three people in the meeting room: himself, Commander David Luce, a Planning Officer, and Captain John Hughes-Hallett, Mountbatten's Chief of Staff.

Hughes-Hallett began to wax lyrical about a raid scheduled for that February, on the cliffs above a French village called Bruneval. Troops were to go in by parachute, but to come out via the sea. Cook wondered what on earth it had to do with him. After a while, Luce intervened. 'Shouldn't we tell Cook that he is to be the Naval commander of the operation, Sir?' he queried. Reining in his enthusiasm for a moment, Hughes-Hallett agreed that they should.

Cook was told that his outfit – the men and vessels of Tormentor – had been chosen to bring the paratroopers off the coast. Upon hearing this news Cook 'pulled out the thumb and really took notice of what was said'. He was warned that secrecy was absolutely paramount. A few careless words or a throwaway remark in a pub could be reported back to France within minutes, after which enemy forces would be quadrupled along that stretch of coastline.

The more he heard of the coming mission, the more Cook's main concern wasn't of loose talk costing lives. First of all, he wondered how on earth they were going to 'find the tiny, 400-yard rocky beach under the high cliffs, after travelling 100 miles across the Channel'. His last navigational fix would be the Isle of Wight, after which they'd be reliant upon charts and the ship's compass. Needless to say, that stretch of French coastline was dotted with innumerable pebbly beaches sandwiched between towering cliffs of chalk.

Second, he reckoned the latest time he could abort the raid due to 'bad weather, gales, swell, fog, breakdowns or whatever was 2200', which was around the time the Whitleys would have to take off. Timing would be everything. Third, inter-boat communications were abysmal, relying upon temperamental walkie-talkies. Fourth, he needed the Tormentor flotilla to 'go in on a rising tide', crucial to ensuring they got off again with their cargo of 'tired or excited paratroopers'. He also pointed out that any wind above Force 2 or 3 would make conditions treacherous when embarking from the beach.

Fortunately, two conspicuous landmarks bracketed the shore at Bruneval. One was the Cap d'Antifer lighthouse to the north, with the large square belfry of St John's Church to the southern side. But still, finding either of those after a long sea-crossing at night had the makings of a nightmare. Of course, none of that meant that Cook didn't want this command. After his experiences with HMS *Royal Oak* and HMS *Curlew*, he was desperate to hit back. Having landed the naval side of Biting, he had the perfect opportunity to do so.

Air, sea and land forces sorted, there remained one hurdle facing Operation Biting: winning the official seal of approval from on high. At the start of the fourth week of January 1942, the War Cabinet gathered. News from elsewhere was universally calamitous. Defeat, after defeat, after defeat. Surely, something like Biting could be no more than a pointless pinprick, in light of such disasters? Fortunately, Mountbatten was there to present the case personally.

The Chief of Combined Operations faced a disbelieving Admiral Pound – he who had so summarily recalled HMS *Triumph*, the submarine tasked with collecting the Colossus raiders from the Italian coastline. Sir Charles Portal, the Air Chief Marshal, was also there. He seemed to favour the raid, for the RAF were getting mauled and in large part due to German radar. General Ismay, who basically represented the interests of Churchill, was also present.

No matter how Mountbatten argued his case, the mood seemed overwhelmingly defensive; defeatist almost. Britain faced a lightning advance by the Japanese down the spine of Malaysia; Rommel counter-attacking in North Africa; Burma under siege, which threatened India thereafter; and approaching a hundred

Allied merchant ships being sent to the bottom by German U-boats every month. The Chiefs of Staff even had before them a proposal from the Commander-in-Chief in Singapore that Allied forces pursue a 'scorched earth' policy, fearing that Britain's fortress in the Far East would fall.

This was something they agreed was 'the best line to take in the circumstances'. In truth, Singapore was but days away from a mass surrender, something Churchill would lament as 'the worst disaster and largest capitulation in British history'. Privately, even he was losing heart. The fall of fortress Singapore would stun him. He'd find it stupefying. Facing defeat on all fronts, it seemed futile and pointless to hit back. But that was exactly why a mission like Biting should get the go-ahead, Mountbatten argued. The War Cabinet put the decision back to Churchill, but with little sense of urgency: 'the Prime Minister should be informed at the next convenient opportunity.'

Of course, Churchill needed this raid. The *nation* needed this raid. The Allied war effort needed such a boost as never before. Two days later the War Cabinet met again. In light of the propaganda value of such a mission, those gathered granted 'general approval for the proposed Operation'. Now it just required Frost and his Jock Company to make of Biting a bloody reality . . . plus there was also the small issue of finding a radar expert willing to drop into battle alongside the Ladies from Hell.

Somewhere among TRE's clifftop laboratories, surely there had to be a scientist who was also something of a fearless adventurer.

Chapter 10

Due to its vital importance to the war effort, TRE was subjected to maximum security restrictions. It was almost as difficult to enter its fenced Dorset 'campus' overlooking the Channel, as it was to get into Churchill's War Rooms in Whitehall. Only high-ranking military officers, top politicians, radar boffins and technicians were permitted access.

Arthur Percival Rowe – short, bespectacled, pipe-smoking, modest, self-effacing – ran TRE. Known formally as 'A. P. Rowe', but as 'Jimmy' to his fellow scientists, he'd been one of the first to warn that unless Britain mastered radar, it faced defeat at the hands of Nazi Germany. Each of TRE's laboratories had its team of dedicated specialists. One dealt with perfecting cutting-edge systems to improve bomber navigation. Another, with developing radar to hunt for U-boats. Another, with technology to aid night fighters to find and kill enemy aircraft.

A quiet maverick at heart, Rowe had imbued TRE with a special ethos typified by his 'Sunday Soviets' – informal gatherings at which all were welcome, no matter how lowly or exalted, for brainstorming sessions on how technology might help win the war. Frederick Lindemann – Churchill's 'beetroot time' scientific adviser – was a regular, and in a delicious irony a portrait of Hermann Goering was said to hang on the wall of the meeting room. The chief of the Luftwaffe, Goering was in many ways TRE's nemesis, or at the very least their foremost target. Invariably, the Sunday Soviets would spill over into the nearby pub at Worth Matravers, the Square and Compasses, which the boffins had nicknamed the 'Sine and Cosine'.

As with all such establishments, recruiting for TRE proved something of a challenge. It was hardly possible to advertise for positions within a top-secret research base that supposedly didn't exist. One early recruit was Laurie Hinton, and his story typifies the methods by which TRE got its people. In his teens when war broke out, Hinton had had several friends shot down in the Battle of Britain, and had made up his mind that he 'wanted to go into the RAF'. But that didn't happen. Others in positions of power had other ideas.

Having completed a degree-level course in engineering at Imperial College London, the scientific acumen that Hinton had demonstrated drew considerable attention. At interviews with several 'prominent people', he was quizzed on his views of the war and how he might help. Shortly, instead of a summons to join the RAF, he received a buff envelope containing mysterious instructions: he was to take the train to a certain destination at a particular time and date. 'There was nothing about what I might be doing. I could have been digging potatoes for all I knew.'

So it was that Hinton was unwittingly selected to join the boffins at TRE. No reason was given as to why he'd been denied a shot at the RAF. 'You wouldn't dare argue about it or ask why,' he remarked. 'At first I was disappointed that I wasn't going to fly and fight. But when I started at TRE I realised how important it all was.' In time, Hinton would work on centimetric radar, which was inspired in part by the German technology that lay behind the Würzburg. It was 'very, very new', he recalled. 'At first, I knew nothing about what I was doing, but I learned fast . . . '

Hinton kept a leather-bound ledger, in which he recorded his ground-breaking work, key breakthroughs and inspiration. Inscribed simply 'RADAR & E.W.' on the spine (EW stood for electronic warfare), the contents were broken down thus: '1. Propagation. 2. Aerials and Transmission Lines. 3. Transmission and Reception. 4. Circuits and Circuit Elements. 5. Valves and Thermionics . . .' The opening page read: 'ATMOSPHERIC ATTENUATION OF MICROWAVES 0.1CM TO 2.0 CM. a) Permanent effects (Van Vleck). At wavelengths in this band water vapour and oxygen absorb energy from electromagnetic waves, the former because of its electric dipole moment and the latter because of its magnetic dipole moment . . .'

Crammed full of complex diagrams, graphs and formulae, from there on it became more and more mind-boggling, at least to the layman. Needless to say, Hinton had to guard that file with his life. From the very first he realised how stringent was security. 'You were not allowed to go wandering around and peering into other labs and asking what they did. That was not allowed. I knew nothing about what went on in the next room . . . It was an absolute culture of secrecy and there was no talk to your family even about what you did there.'

Innovative, pioneering, groundbreaking – research at TRE was still something of a Heath Robinson affair, John Hooper, a lab technician, recalled. Typically, Hooper had been recruited into TRE by the nod-and-wink method. His headmaster had earmarked the seventeen-year-old school leaver for a job at Lloyds Bank. 'No fear,' the plain-speaking Hooper had told him. 'I'm not going into a bank.' While serving as a machine-gunner in the First World War, Hooper's father had been shot in the head and confined to a wheelchair. Working in a bank wasn't exactly Hooper's idea of how to help the war effort.

A school friend offered an alternative. 'John, you're interested in radio, aren't you. Apply for a job where I am.' 'Where's that?' Hooper asked. 'What do they do?' 'Oh, you know, wireless sets, radios, that kind of thing,' his friend responded, vaguely. When Hooper went for an interview, the main issue seemed to be how he'd found out about TRE at all.

'How do you know what we're doing here?' the interviewer demanded.

'Well, I don't,' Hooper countered. 'A school pal of mine said he worked here, and you made wireless sets and that kind of thing.'

'Is that all he told you?' the interviewer pressed.

When Hooper convinced him that it was, the interviewer finally relented. Hooper was in. He started working in one of the laboratories. 'Whenever the "boffin boys" designed some new circuitry, they didn't really make it themselves,' he explained. 'We'd set about making it up and they'd test it out and they'd say, "Oh, that's all right," or "No, that's no good at all." But *their* lash-ups on the benches were terrible: they were "bread-board lash-ups", with wires going everywhere and valves glowing red hot, that sort of thing!'

Hooper recalled one morning when his boss announced that the Air Commodore was paying a visit. 'Who's he?' Hooper asked. It all meant very little to him. Getting on with his tasks, he made up a power unit two feet square and got it running on his bench. Typically, his boss had his hands tucked into his waistcoat pockets as he showed the Air Commodore around, and somehow he managed to back himself into Hooper's power unit. 'All of a sudden a shriek of 500 decibels went up: "*Ye gods!*"' Hooper recalled. 'His hair was standing up vertically two inches on his head.'

Later Hooper's boss asked of him: 'Why have you got all these things on your bench running with all these voltages, with no warning signs. Anyone can come in and touch them.'

'Well, they shouldn't, should they,' Hooper countered. There was zero health and safety, and they got a great deal more done as a result, he reckoned.

Despite the informality of the Sunday Soviets and the free-wheeling nature of TRE's research, the work rate was relentless. Hooper recalled many a Monday when he'd clock in at 8.45 a.m., only to find a 'chap in the lab all bleary-eyed and unshaven. I'd say: "Oh, you're here early." He'd respond: "What d'you mean, early? I've been here all weekend!"' The TRE scientists were beavering away seven days a week, night and day, for they understood the urgent need to stay one step ahead of their counterparts, those boffins on the opposing side slaving away to secure victory for Nazi Germany.

From somewhere among those driven, workaholic scientists a volunteer needed to be found to join the Operation Biting raiders. Donald Preist was seemingly as unassuming and studious a man as you could ever hope to meet. Balding, shy-looking behind his thick, horn-rimmed glasses, and with a buck-toothed grin, Preist had been at TRE for several years, pioneering the technology behind Chain Home. In the dying days of January 1942 he was at his desk, when he took an unexpected call. He was asked to head over to a military base not far from Salisbury, to meet some people from the First Airborne Division.

As he drove north in his fine Alvis coupé, Preist had no idea what lay behind the mystery summons, but he wasn't overly concerned. His scholarly air concealed a man with a surprisingly flamboyant taste in motor cars . . . and a certain impetuosity. This was as good an excuse as any for a bracing winter's drive, and Preist sensed adventure was in the air. He followed the twisting road that snakes across the wintry expanse of Salisbury Plain – the rolling chalk downland upon which British military exercises and manoeuvres have taken place since time immemorial – wondering what might lie behind the mystery summons.

'All this history, undisturbed by invaders since 1066,' he remarked of the moment. 'We had just escaped another invasion, thanks to the RAF and radar. But Hitler was still at large and undefeated. What was to happen next?'

For Preist, the answer wasn't long in coming. Upon arrival, he was met by Major Peter Bromley-Martin, the staff officer with whom Frost had had his run-in over the planning for Operation Biting, before being whisked off to lunch with General 'Boy' Browning himself. Still without the faintest clue as to why he was there, Preist was regaled by Browning with stories of how Churchill had telephoned that very morning, asking him to accept his son, Randolph Churchill, into airborne forces.

'The Old Man wants me to take his son,' Browning confided. 'I told him under no circumstances would I take his bloody son into my Regiment!'

Browning left the reasons why unsaid, but it was easy enough to hazard a guess. What commander would relish the prospect of sending the Prime Minister's son into action behind enemy lines? After lunch, and still without the faintest clue as to why he was there, Preist was shown to a table scattered with aerial photos. They had been taken over coastal France, he was told. Then he was asked what he thought of the small, paraboloid-like object visible on the images.

Preist studied it for a few seconds. 'It could be a radar,' he ventured, 'working at a rather high frequency.'

'I'll tell you why we're so interested,' Bromley-Martin enthused. 'The Germans have been shooting down our bombers over the Ruhr . . . Their accuracy is amazing.' The paraboloid – known as a Würzburg – was believed to be a ground-breaking piece of enemy radar, he explained. 'We intend to make a raid and bring it back here. Would you like to come along?'

Though the offer had come utterly from out of the blue, Preist barely hesitated before replying. 'I certainly would. When do we start?'

'Come back here in a couple of days. We'll train you in parachute jumping.'

On the drive back to TRE, Preist's 'feet were already a long way off the ground'. In fact, his elation would prove a little premature. Behind the scenes, there was much manoeuvring. R. V. Jones, chief scientist to the spies, had volunteered for Operation Biting. He had been ruled out. He knew too much, and it would be a calamity if he were captured by the enemy. Preist was about to be blocked, for similar reasons. The day after his whirlwind visit, he took a call from Bromley-Martin, expecting to get his marching orders for parachute training. There was to be no such luck.

'Sorry to disappoint,' Bromley-Martin began. There was too much of a risk sending Preist, especially with his Chain Home expertise. 'If you fell into the hands of the enemy it could be a bit awkward, possibly very unpleasant for you.' They had a back-up plan, Bromley-Martin explained. Instead of parachuting, Preist would wait offshore with the Tormentor flotilla. That way, at least he could ensure 'the radar gear is brought back safely'.

'Disappointing, but I see your point,' Preist replied, trying to hide his dismay. 'What do I do next?'

Preist was summoned to London. At Combined Operations headquarters he was briefed by Peter de Casa Maury. He was to take a specialized radio receiver in one of the Tormentor boats, with the aim of spying on the Würzburg. Tuned to what they suspected was its frequency, this was a chance to gather crucial intelligence. If the raiders failed, Preist could still secure an up-close trace on the mystery paraboloid. In addition, if it suddenly stopped transmitting, that might signify that Frost and his men had succeeded in stealing it away.

Preist was to join the Tormentor flotilla, to rehearse the seaborne side of things. But first, he was to learn how to steal such 'a piece of delicate equipment, without wrecking its contents'. They would have precious little time at the target: raid planners were budgeting for thirty minutes maximum in which to dismantle the paraboloid and spirit it away. From his SIS offices, in a scene reminiscent of Bond's 'Q', R. V. Jones had issued a detailed list of instructions on exactly what he wanted stolen. It read:

Objects required to be collected:
1) The box behind the paraboloid.
2) All panels, switchboards etc.
3) All spare parts – or samples of them, particularly valves.
4) The safe, or its contents, if there is one.
5) The SCREEN on which grid squares or a map may be traced. Cathode ray tubes. Take care to preserve fluorescent powder; water spoils it.

6) Any scales in miles or Kms on the switches.
7) All diagrams – circuit diagrams especially, and Manuals.
8) Aerial complete (this is probably in the centre of the paraboloid).
9) The aerial probably connects to 'something'. Bring me the 'something'.

This was Jones's ideal wish-list and it was a tall order indeed. If nothing else, it revealed the immense care that was supposed to be taken by the looters, and presumably while they were under fire from the enemy on all sides.

Preist was dispatched to meet Lieutenant-Colonel Basil Schonland, a man whom the young scientist, still only in his twenties, would learn to 'respect very much . . . He was genial in a fatherly way, and full of humour.' Schonland's kindly demeanour hid a core of inner steel. South African of origin and a fellow physicist, he had been wounded in the First World War during the spring 1917 battle of Arras, which had cost approaching 300,000 lives. Schonland had just the right combination of sol- diering skills and specialist scientific knowledge for what had been asked of him. He was busy building a mock-up of how the paraboloid might appear, complete with a dish approximating to the size revealed in the air photos.

Schonland was clear about his priorities. While the sheer effrontery of the raid might satisfy Churchill's demands that the enemy be harried at every turn, its key purpose was to steal vital scientific intelligence. Schonland proceeded to instruct Preist on how to blow the paraboloid apart, but in a wholly controlled fashion. 'He showed me how, by wrapping a small piece of plastic explosives, rather like putty, around a long piece of steel bar, and then detonating it, the steel would be cut exactly where the plastic was placed.'

After his instruction, Preist reflected of the raiders who were to learn such skills: 'I wondered how many of them would make a dishonest living cracking safes, once the war was over.' There was little time to dwell on that now. The plan for Operation Biting was fast evolving, including Preist's own role. He was told that if he could hazard a dash ashore without any risk of being captured, he was to help dismantle the paraboloid and spirit it away.

With the possibility of making a landing on enemy shores, Preist needed a suitable cover. He certainly couldn't risk alighting on the beach in his normal civvy attire. Any man captured out of uniform was sure to be shot as a spy. Accordingly, Preist was given a temporary commission in the RAF at the rank of Flight Lieutenant and issued with uniform to suit.

Unbeknown to Preist, Frost and his raiders had been given very explicit instructions concerning their venturesome scientist. Their Operational Orders read: 'IT IS OF THE UTMOST IMPORTANCE THAT FL.-LT. PRIEST [sic] SHOULD NOT FALL INTO THE ENEMY'S HANDS.' The exact interpretation of that was left open, but their orders regarding the enemy were chillingly clear: 'No prisoners will be taken other than Offrs [officers] and technical personnel.' Only those who could render real value were to have their lives spared; the converse was very likely true of Donald Preist.

The sensitivity of those orders was reflected in the level of secrecy applied to them. They were stamped: 'To be destroyed by fire on completion or cancellation of the operation . . . NOT TO BE ALLOWED TO FALL INTO THE HANDS OF THE ENEMY . . . NOT TO BE TAKEN TO SEA IN COASTAL OR

LANDING CRAFT.' It was hardly surprising. The order not to take prisoners (bar officers) was controversial, to put it mildly. It wasn't exactly in keeping with the Geneva Conventions. But desperate times called for desperate measures . . .

There were layers upon layers of secrecy surrounding Operation Biting, most of which few were privy to. Unpacking those was like peeling an onion. At the very heart of it lay the most secret and risk-laden undertaking of all, one masterminded by SOE. Only so much could be surmised from aerial photos of the defences at Bruneval. To better assess the enemy's strengths, and to maximize the raiders' chances, it required boots on the ground. To send in the spies was incredibly dangerous; the greatest single security threat of all. But still it was felt a risk worth taking.

So, on the evening of 24 January 1942, Gilbert Renault settled down in his rented Paris apartment to decode a message from SOE. It was unusual for an agent of his standing – one who ran the entire Confrérie Notre-Dame; the Brotherhood of Notre Dame network – to do so personally, but he adored codes. As usual, the message was split into two halves, as a security precaution: neither should signify a great deal without the other.

The first read: 'No. 49: Need information indicated . . . inform us within forty-eight hours delay necessary obtain this information observing following conditions firstly do not act yourself nor gravely risk members your organisation secondly do not compromise success operation julie stop to deceive boches in event your agent taken be ready to reply same question not only for place chosen but for three of four other similar places on coast . . .'

Gilbert Renault – more commonly known by his codename, 'Remy' – was being asked to activate his resistance network to secure certain urgent information, but not to do so in such a way as would endanger himself or his fellows, nor Operation Juliet, which was Remy's own forthcoming extraction by Lysander, to London. If any of his agents were captured, they were to offer cover stories to their interrogators, to disguise their real focus of interest.

The continuation message read: 'No. 50 . . . firstly position and number of machine-guns defending cliff road at theuville on coast between cap antifer and saint jouin . . . secondly what other defences thirdly number and state preparedness defenders stop . . . first class troops or old men stop fourthly where are they quartered fifthly existence and positions barbed wire . . .' And so it continued.

Of course, Remy was being asked to sound out the calibre of the defences around Bruneval. It was an area that had already drawn the attention of his Confrérie Notre-Dame. Indeed, it was one of his men who'd been the first to spot the Freya station, alerting London to its existence.

'There was a great insistence on a certain track that went down to the beach,' Remy remarked of the messages. 'Was this path guarded, did it have barbed wire protection and was the beach mined?' It didn't take the brains of a rocket scientist to surmise what might lie behind such queries. London was considering some kind of a raid on Bruneval; that much was clear. To entrust such a sensitive assignment to such a man reflected the status Remy had earned in Allied eyes.

The son of a philosophy professor, Remy had had a strict Catholic upbringing, and he believed the struggle against Nazism was nothing less than one of good versus evil; his resistance network to be likewise blessed by God. But as with many in the French resistance, his had been a long and convoluted journey to join the Allied cause. When war was declared Remy had been refused service in the French military, because he was a thirty-six-year-old father of four – Catherine, Jean-Claude, Cécile and little Manuel, just a few months old. Frustrated, he had witnessed the lightning advance of the enemy with horror and dread. With Paris about to fall, he had confided in his wife, just a few weeks pregnant with their fifth child, that he wanted to try to reach British shores.

There was no option but to continue the struggle, he had declared. If not, it was clear what would happen. 'Our children will be torn from us, and their German masters will bring them up in the teachings of National Socialism. Wouldn't it be better to die?'

Stifling her sobs, his wife had insisted he go. 'Go,' she'd said, simply. Then: 'But I am so tired.'

For a moment Remy had softened, taking her in his arms. 'If you say "stay", dearest one, I won't go.'

'No, go!'

Together with his brother, Remy had headed for the chaos of the ports, catching a ride in *La Barbue*, a trawler making a bid for freedom. The boat's skipper had won a Croix de Guerre, a high-valour French medal, in the First World War, by ramming a U-boat and sinking it. In recent days he'd been at Dunkirk, commanding a destroyer that had been sunk under him. Even so, he was damned if he was going to buckle or break, or allow himself to be taken under the Nazi yoke. The spirit of resistance was blossoming, even in this, France's darkest hour.

During the cold of that night voyage Remy had thrust his hands deep into his raincoat, seeking warmth. He'd found something even better. In the recesses of one of his pockets he'd discovered a carefully folded note. By the light of a match he'd managed to read it. It was from his wife. 'I believe in you. I'll wait as long as it takes.' Upon reaching England, Remy had learned the very worst news. Marshal Pétain, the so-called 'Lion of Verdun', had signed an armistice with Nazi Germany. Remy could not believe it. Pétain – who'd declared: 'They shall not pass.' Pétain, who should have been incapable of treachery. 'If you were too old or too tired, Pétain, why did you not retire?' Remy railed.

At the Falmouth reception centre where he and his shipmates had made landfall, a little old lady wearing an enormous flowery hat was serving tea. She was very English. She'd fixed him with a kindly look. 'Don't worry, my boy . . . everything will be all right.' Then she'd cleared her throat, and told him – ordered him: 'Have a cup of tea.'

His resolve thus stiffened by an ally that his country's leaders had betrayed, Remy had headed to London where the French Resistance was rallying under General Charles de Gaulle. In the following weeks he'd got to meet the General several times, but the first gesture of resistance that he was asked to undertake was somewhat unusual. Having a background in the movie business, Remy was asked to broadcast a message into France via the BBC, to act as a rallying cry for like-minded people everywhere; for all patriots of France. For Remy, it would also be one directed to the hearts of his wife and children.

It was an evening broadcast, and with his voice breaking with emotion Remy announced: 'Our children are probably asleep. Before you go to bed, without waking them, kiss them for me gently, and last, more tenderly still, the littlest one . . . Know that my thoughts never leave you for an instant, and that the living remembrance of you is here by my side. When the day comes, it will lead me into battle.'

That was the power of Remy's message. On the one hand, he could not live without his wife and children. On the other, he was bound by heart and soul to the cause; the struggle. Indeed, so were his family. In time, many of them would suffer terribly for it. But for now, it was a rallying cry to those who would risk all to fight, and with little more than the armour of their convictions.

For that very reason, because of that very spirit, they would be victorious, Remy argued. 'What was an SS man without his whip? Mussolini without his balcony, Goering without his medals, Himmler without his torture chambers? Nothing. What was Gilbert [Remy] without arms, without his family, without even his own name? He was a whole man in the freedom of his sacrifice.' And he would overcome.

True to his word, Remy was dropped back into France, to raise an underground network. Under instructions from his British handler – a man 'whose fine intelligent black eyes looked out at me from a thin face'; a man whom he was only ever to refer to as 'Q', but who became a close friend – Remy's mission was to establish an intelligence network covering the vital ports of northern France. Before leaving London, he had indulged in the purchase of a fine tweed overcoat, and enjoyed a personal send-off from De Gaulle, now commanding the Free French army in exile.

'Au revoir . . .' he was told by the tall, gaunt Frenchman, as they shook hands. 'I rely upon you.'

In due course Remy had established his Confrérie Notre-Dame, which would become one of the largest underground intelligence networks in France. In England, he had been taught basic code, but London preferred to send him an expert radio operator. In time that man, Bernard Anquetil, was captured by the Gestapo and tortured. It was one of the earliest blows to the Confrérie Notre-Dame, and they had to presume that the imprisoned man had talked. In fact, he remained silent, no matter what the Gestapo did to him.

Remy would remark of Anquetil's unfathomable courage, and the countless others who were to follow: 'Words fail me when I think of the girls and boys who went out on missions for us. The final test of a person is what he does under torture . . . and not one of the agents who were captured gave a comrade away prior to execution. Not one.'

By the untold bravery of others, the Confrérie Notre-Dame endured. But, Remy lamented, 'So may faces, scarcely glimpsed, have disappeared into the night.' In the summer of 1941, SOE sent a replacement radio operator. By now it was too dangerous to use any real identities. In time, the Confrérie Notre-Dame would assign only code numbers to agents, in an effort to safeguard them and their families. The newly arrived radio man would be known only as 'Bob'. His was one of the most dangerous roles of all. The enemy operated mobile radio-direction-finding units, based in vans and trucks, to track down the secret W/T operators.

Six months later, it was Bob who received the 24 January message about the mission to recce the defences around Bruneval. Having decoded it, Remy called in one of his most trusted agents, Roger Dumont. Remy had chosen the codename 'Pol' for Dumont, after the famous brand of Champagne, Pol Roger. A former officer in the French Air Force, it was Pol who had first alerted Remy to the closely guarded Freya station on the cliffs above Bruneval.

In Remy's Paris apartment they studied the radio messages, together with their maps of the area. Pol suggested he team up with another of the 'brothers', Charles Chaveau, codename Charlemagne. Not only was Charlemagne local to the area, he was one of the few Frenchmen permitted to drive through the Coastal Zone, access to which was heavily restricted. Charlemagne happened to own a garage in the area. In the business of repairing and servicing vehicles he needed to travel, hence his precious permit.

Charlemagne was summoned to Paris. He drove there in his smart Simca 5 car, the then Franco-Italian rival to the VW Beetle. Fortunately, when the target of their mission was explained, Charlemagne announced that he knew 'those corners like my own pocket'. Bruneval and its surroundings were old stalking grounds. Setting out early, he and Pol drove north-west, Charlemagne stopping at one point to fit snow-chains to the Simca's wheels. The steep hills around Bruneval were said to be a foot thick with drifts.

As they neared the coast, Charlemagne stuck to the minor roads. It made good sense for the two Frenchmen to keep off the main highways, which in this area were particularly heavily patrolled. Neither relished the thought of being stopped and questioned. They made it into the eastern outskirts of a snow-bound Bruneval village, stopping at one of the first buildings on the left – the Hotel Beauminet.

'Very good people,' Charlemagne remarked, as he parked in the pristine snow to the hotel's rear.

The hotel's proprietors, Paul and Madame Vernier, were a Franco-Swiss couple. More importantly, they were staunch supporters of the Resistance. As they ran the village's only hotel, the

Verniers were bound to know all there was to know about their target. Having sought them out, Charlemagne and Pol settled down with the Verniers to talk. Sure enough, they proved a mine of information on the radar installations and their German defenders.

The entire clifftop site was a closed military area, but the Verniers had been up there as far as one could go delivering food, including to the Gothic-style chateau that sat atop the cliffs. It had been built by a renowned surgeon, Professor Antonin Gosset, in the 1930s – hence its name, the Château Gosset. Nowadays it was occupied by the Germans. To the north lay the fortified farmstead, known as Le Presbytère, with the Freya station immediately beyond it. The Verniers knew the exact number of enemy troops stationed there, for they'd had to supply them with food.

Down on the beach was another strange-looking building – a mock-fort some three storeys tall, complete with towers and battlements. It was called the Stella Maris villa. There was a guard force of a dozen permanently on duty, the villa being surrounded by trenches that could be manned 'within minutes'. In Bruneval itself the Verniers knew the German troops well, for they quartered themselves at their hotel. The force consisted of thirty men, under command of an energetic and efficient sergeant. They were kept permanently on their toes, for the coastal area was infested with German units some of which were armoured, and they were forever involved in one kind of exercise or another.

Of course, the Verniers risked everything if they were caught divulging such information. They had spoken so openly only because they knew Charlemagne so well. If they were found out, they faced transportation to the dreaded concentration camps, or worse. They were careful not to ask any questions of Pol and Charlemagne. The less they knew, the less they could tell. It was better not to know. Once they were done talking, Pol figured that he and Charlemagne should head for the beach. The hotel proprietors warned them not to go. It was a forbidden area and anyway the beach was mined.

Pol was typically resolute. 'Let's go take a look anyway,' he declared.

Wrapping their coats tighter to guard against the icy wind, the two figures wandered down the snowbound gorge that led to the sea. To either side the slopes rose steeply, honeycombed here and there with rabbit warrens. As they neared the beach, a path climbed up to their right, towards the cliff-top radar stations. To their left, the weather-beaten expanse of the Stella Maris villa sat right on the rear side of the beach, its painted windows peeling, its façade reminiscent of better days.

This had once been a popular tourist destination. Now, the route ahead was blocked with a barbed-wired barricade. As the two Frenchmen approached, a tall figure dressed in German army uniform appeared. He had an air about him as woebegone as the villa in which he was stationed. He eyed the two of them suspiciously. Charlemagne, being the local man with the permit to travel hereabouts, took the initiative. It helped that he spoke good German.

'Good morning,' he announced, all smiles. Gesturing at Pol, he explained that he was taking a pleasant stroll with his cousin, who came from Paris and was locked in a dark office all day long. He was dying for some fresh air and to get a glimpse of the sea. 'Lucky you're here,' he continued. 'We wouldn't have dared go any further. We've heard there are mines . . .'

There were, the sentry confirmed, gesturing at the signs to either side: *Achtung – Minen*. '*Tellerminen*,' he added – anti-tank mines.

Redoubling his charm offensive, Charlemagne asked if the guard might do them a huge favour and escort them to the beach, just so his cousin could get a glimpse of the sea. The sentry seemed to be softening. Charlemagne stressed how it would be only for a few seconds, and how much 'innocent pleasure' it would render to his poor, city cousin. Finally, the sentry relented, pulling aside the movable section of the barrier so the two men could pass through. He closed it after, warning them to stick closely to the path. Shortly, they were standing on a stretch of pebbles that shelved steeply to the sea. Charlemagne knew the beach well. Even in the calmest of conditions there was a considerable swell. The undertow was said to be fierce. Those who holidayed here were best restricted to paddling.

Charlemagne offered their guard a cigarette, as Pol stood gazing out over a sullen grey sea, apparently captivated. The tide was low and he couldn't see any underwater obstacles. He turned about seemingly to speak to his fellows, his eyes sweeping the heights above. Two machinegun posts were visible, set to either side of the gorge. He could see the black snout of the nearest, menacing the full sweep of the beach. Nasty. He spied a figure dressed in forage cap and great coat, trying to ward off the chill. If they were up there even in these conditions, he could only think that the guns were permanently manned.

As they retraced their steps across the beach, Pol noted there was no sign of any barbed wire, apart from at the road block. He also suspected the 'minefield' was a bluff. The sentry forgot to stick to the path, walking right across where the field of *Tellerminen* was supposedly sown. The enemy clearly felt the beach was impregnable, even without mines or wire. Pol was inclined to agree. Storming this place: it would be suicidal.

Having thanked the obliging sentry, they hurried back to the hotel, where Charlemagne had arranged to meet some of his regular customers. Everything was in short supply, as the Germans requisitioned vehicle spares for the war effort. Tyres, in particular, were like gold dust. His orders taken - perfect cover for their visit – Charlemagne headed for the Hôtel des Vieux Plats, a renowned black-market restaurant a few miles inland. It was the kind of place where you could still enjoy a fine meal, even in the midst of rationing.

Charlemagne frequented the place whenever he was able. So too did the German officers posted to this region – those that could afford its prices. Having eaten and drunk well, he and Pol lingered over coffee and calvados. He called for the visitor's book, so his 'friend' could leave a message of appreciation. In a private moment, they managed to copy down all the names of the recent German diners. Those individuals could be tracked and traced to their respective units, once the information was transmitted to London.

While Charlemagne and Pol were so engaged, their boss had also been busy. From a remote snow-swept field Remy had been embroiled in Operation Juliet – his pick-up by Lysander. He had with him two suitcases stuffed full of intelligence of explosive value: the latest German military maps, delineating their positions, plus reams of documents spirited away from German naval bases. Bob kept him company, an aerial slung around the attic in which they were hiding, the wind howled and the snow swirled. No flights were possible, and Operation Juliet had to be postponed.

On 9 February Remy met Pol in Paris, to compose their vital message. They tried to condense the details gleaned from the Bruneval recce into the shortest wording possible, the better to avoid the *Funkabwehr* – German Radio Defence Corps – vans that cruised the city streets. Once they were done, they checked the wording one last time. Pol eyed Remy worriedly. 'Even so, it's going to make one hell of a vacation,' he warned – 'vacation' being their codeword for a radio-transmission.

Satisfied, Remy handed the paper to Bob. Wireless operators in the Confrérie Notre-Dame had taken to bicycling about the streets, their radio sets dismantled and cunningly concealed, so they never transmitted from the same place twice, in an effort to evade those who hunted for them. But the present message was inordinately long. It had to convey a great deal of information. After all, that was what London had asked for. Plus there were real gems of intelligence that could not be wasted.

'Be careful,' Remy warned his radio operator.

'Don't worry,' Bob replied, affecting his carefree air. 'The Boches are very stupid.'

Remy hoped that Bob was right. He was amazed at the level of detail Pol and Charlemagne had secured. That same evening, he took a telephone call from Bob, who confirmed that both halves of the Bruneval message had been safely transmitted to London.

The message from the Confrérie Notre-Dame gave chapter and verse on the Bruneval defences. It described the paraboloid itself being sited in a pit 'fifty metres from the cliff', and 'surrounded by barbed wire and a number of dugouts'; a 'platoon of about thirty soldiers', based in the Hôtel Beauminet; the beachside Stella Maris villa being manned by a dozen soldiers, armed with 'two machine guns . . . surrounded by wire ten metres thick'; and it warned that a 'reconnaissance battalion with armoured cars was twenty-five kilometres to the east,' and could 'arrive within one hour.'

The message included details of the individual units and the names of their German commanders. The force manning Le Presbytère, adjacent to the Freya station, were from the 2nd Company of the 23rd Luftwaffe Air Reconnaissance Regiment, and their commander was *Oberleutnant* (lieutenant) Hans Melches. The troops billeted in the Hotel Beauminet hailed from the 1st Battalion of the 685th Infantry Regiment, whose overall commander was a long-experienced professional officer, Colonel von Eisenhart-Rothe. Those stationed at Stella Maris villa, on the beach itself, were also from the 1st Battalion, and the commander in charge there was *Oberfeldwebel* (Sergeant) Huhn.

As the details made their way into the hands of the Biting commanders, Major Frost marvelled that in some cases 'the strength, the billet, the weapons and even the names of some of the Germans were known.' Learning the identity of the individual enemy commanders made their presence more concrete somehow, bringing the threat they and their troops posed to life.

A posting to the French coast was seen as a comparatively cushy number for German troops. This area, Haute Normandie, was relatively prosperous, with farms producing rich local produce. No one was going hungry, that was for sure. Few units sought the alternative – to be sent to the Eastern Front, to face the freezing ice and snow and the Red Army. The Bruneval radar installations were top-secret facilities, and they were to be fiercely guarded. But to date, the main enemies for the German garrisons had been boredom and routine.

To combat this, commanders organized regular patrols and

exercises, which could take place at any time of day or night. Passwords were changed daily, and anyone who got them wrong could be shot on sight. The challenge to be cried out was: '*Halt! Wer da? Halt! Halt! Kennwort!*' – (Halt! Who goes there? Halt! Password!) Halt! entries were to fire on sight, unless the password was given. Recognition signals – flares – were also to be fired at any boats passing close inshore, as a defence against incursions from the sea.

The radar sites were totally off-limits to the German Army. They were Luftwaffe installations, and most of the Wehrmacht guard forces would have little idea what they were protecting. But none would want to mess up and face a punishment posting, especially as the Eastern Front was said to be akin to a death sentence. Learning all of this made the coming mission very much more real, the intensity of the training all the more relentless.

By now, Jock Company had moved on from Salisbury Plain. They'd headed to Loch Fyne, situated on the rugged west coast of Scotland, to rehearse the seaborne side of the operation. For the journey north they'd removed all Airborne Division insignia, so as not to attract any unwanted attention. No one wanted word getting out that a British parachute company was on the move. Likewise, aboard the ship that awaited them all mail had been cancelled, as had all leave. The vessel was in total lockdown.

Upon arrival at Loch Fyne, three big surprises would await. First, the men of C Company were to learn for certain what many had long suspected: their training was in deadly earnest. They were heading into hostile territory, to hit a target of the utmost sensitivity and secrecy. Secondly, they were to realize just how much time was set against them: the mission was to take place in just three weeks' time. Thirdly, they were to meet the German who had unexpectedly joined their ranks.

Having a 'Hun on the strength', as Frost would describe it, proved hugely unsettling, especially when embarked upon an operation of such stringent secrecy. At that moment in the war, the German military seemed universally victorious – in Russia, North Africa, in Poland, France and Norway. German troops had attained something of an omnipotent reputation, backed as they were by the apparent power and reach of German intelligence.

Even a man of Frost's standing and temperament was daunted. 'The Germans then seemed invincible. Their armies knew no halting . . . So many things could go wrong with our little party and we had been taught to fear the enemy's intelligence.' Having been told he was to take a German on the mission, he couldn't help but wonder if this was somehow a spy who had inveigled his way into British forces. He worried that the 'enemy probably knew all about us and what we were training for'.

If they did, Frost and all his men were very likely done for.

Chapter 11

Along the remote, sparsely populated expanse of Loch Fyne, Frost and his raiders could train without risk of being watched or spied upon. RAN Commander Cook was there, together with his Tormentor flotilla. Two dozen men from the Royal Army Medical Corps (RAMC) were there, for they had been chosen to travel in the assault boats. Casualties were expected, and there was only so much medical care the paratroopers could perform for themselves.

Combined Operations had decreed that each assault boat should double as a medical station, 'equipped with one or two stretchers, a medical satchel, thermos flasks of hot tea or soup and at least one medical orderly'. Of Frost's men, four in each platoon were given basic medical training and issued with bandages and morphine, in case any life-saving care was required on the field of battle, and before the wounded could be got to the boats.

A force of men from the South Wales Borderers and the Royal Fusiliers – tough infantry regiments, each with two-and-a-half centuries of tradition to their names – were there, selected to act as fire teams on the assault boats. Each would carry four men armed with Bren light machineguns or Boys anti-tank rifles, a .55-calibre long-range weapon capable of penetrating light armour, which came complete with a bipod, but had the kick of a mule. As the assault boats approached the shore, the gunners were to rake the German positions with murderous fire, so as to doubly secure the beach. The boats were fitted with 'armoured shields' as added protection for those riding in them.

A group of about a dozen sappers were also at Loch Fyne. Hailing from the Royal Engineers (RE), they were a recent addition to Frost's party. With their mottos *Ubique* (Everywhere) and *Quo Fas et Gloria Ducunt* (Where right and glory lead), the Royal Engineers had a two-hundred-year history of providing their specialist skills to whatever unit might need them. They had long been at the cutting edge of technological developments in the military, pioneering the use of mapping, telegraphy, observation balloons, tanks and aircraft in warfare.

The party of RE sappers was commanded by twenty-four-year-old Lieutenant Dennis Vernon, who'd been educated at the Leys, a Cambridge boarding school, and after that Emmanuel College, Cambridge. Smart, bright, quick-thinking, Vernon had a lively interest in technology. He'd picked up the essentials of the groundbreaking field of radar pretty swiftly. While some of Vernon's sappers were to act as an anti-tank party, laying mines on the road leading to the beach, most were to concentrate on dismantling the radar.

Like Preist, the scientist now slated to ride in an assault boat brandishing his radio receiver, Vernon and his men had been schooled by Schonland, using his replica paraboloid. Under his expert tuition they'd been treated to 'a practical trial of "robbing" a mock up R.D.F. set'. They'd been warned about the dangers of electric shocks; how those working 'in the proximity of H.T. wires should have rubber gloves and insulated-handle implements'. They'd been provided with the tools of their new trade:

'for opening doors and windows ... for opening [the] set and removing parts ...' and for 'wrecking set after work is done'.

Specialist burglary bags were furnished by SOE. The contents included: '2 jemmies, 2 axes insulating handles, 1 claw hammer, 1 Cold Chisel, 1 Hacksaw and spare blade, 1 Pr side-cutting pliers, 2 Prs rubber gloves, 1 Head torch, 2 Hand torches, 1 shifting spanner 6" handle ...' Vernon and his sappers had also trained with the foldable, two-wheeled trolleys, which were for 'carrying away objects of interest' – in other words, the purloined parts of the radar.

Once the paraboloid had been properly looted, the remains were to be blown sky high, so as to hide all evidence that its constituent parts had been spirited away. The aim was to make it look as if the raiders had simply sabotaged the Würzburg, in the hope that this would win the boffins extra time to work out how to defeat it. To that end, the explosives provided in each SOE wrecking bag included: '3 made-up charges, 8 short lengths of safety fuse, 2 Tin boxes of Tysules [incendiaries], 1 Box of fuses.'

The forces gathered at Loch Fyne practised rendezvousing with Tormentor's assault boats and disembarking 'under fire'. It proved surprisingly difficult, and particularly at night. Rarely did things go to plan. Sometimes, the boat crew failed to locate the right stretch of rocks. It was challenging finding dark figures on a dark Scottish shoreline. At other times, men were left behind. Radio communications from shore to ship proved patchy, and signalling with torches or Very lights – flare rounds – frustratingly hit and miss.

'We found evacuation of the beaches ... extremely difficult,' Frost remarked, 'and if the weather was bad, sometimes dangerous . . . For several nights there was not a single successful evacuation.'

It didn't bode well, and especially as the rehearsals had been in relatively sheltered, friendly waters. Frost certainly didn't relish the thought of 'getting abandoned on the coast of France', and all because the assault boats couldn't find the right beach, or making radio contact had proved impossible.

Their 'mother ship' was anchored on a hidden expanse of the Loch, among a flotilla of assorted Combined Operations vessels. HMS *Prinz Albert* was a former Belgian passenger ferry that had plied the Ostend to Dover route from 1937 until the outbreak of hostilities. When the Germans had overrun Belgium, *Prinz Albert* had been requisitioned by the War Office. She was re-engineered to carry eight Assault Landing Craft (ALCs) – very similar to Eureka swamp boats in design, only being equipped with a ramp at the bows, for ease of landings.

Known as 'Lucky Albert' to those who crewed her, *Prinz Albert* was armed with guns and cannons and had yet to suffer a hit during the war, despite her deployment on several commando-style raids. She was relatively fast, with a top speed of 22 knots. *Prinz Albert's* role was to piggy-back the Tormentor flotilla across the Channel, dropping the assault boats near the French coast under cover of darkness. After that, it was up to Commander Cook to steer them to the beach, to pick up the raiders and skedaddle with the loot.

With room to carry 340 troops, there was more than enough space for Frost and his men. Indeed, after the freezing mud and huts of Salisbury Plain, the vessel seemed like a veritable floating hotel. She was spotless, and there was ample food and drink. There were even real eggs in real shells, something the raiders hadn't seen for months. This was a time when the milk ration in schools had been reduced to a third of a pint per pupil per day, and the adult butter ration was two ounces per week. Breakfasting on fresh eggs went some way to making up for the botched rehearsals and the frequent tumbles into the icy waters of the loch.

Frost had one other issue troubling him at Loch Fyne. Just prior to their departure for Scotland, the mysterious Peter Nagel had joined their number. Frost had studied the man carefully. Nagel was small, dapper and handsome, with brown hair and blue eyes. He'd been sent to Frost dressed in the uniform of the Pioneer Corps, the 'King's Own Loyal Enemy Aliens'. Dispatched from Combined Operations headquarters, Frost's instructions were to enter Nagel on his Company strength as a 'Private Newman'.

Though he spoke fluent English, Frost knew very well that Nagel was German. In the paperwork, General Browning described him as 'a German fighting against Hitler', stressing how his 'knowledge of the German language and of the psychology of Germans' should prove invaluable. Nagel was a man of the world and Frost noted his obvious toughness, intelligence and humour. Apparently, his father had fled the predations of the Nazis, after which he had travelled widely, including to London, Paris, Vienna, Budapest and New York.

Frost figured he could slip Nagel – *Newman* – into C Company, with none but him, CSM Strachan and his second-in-command, Lieutenant Ross, being any the wiser. But still he felt uneasy. That unease had stayed with him in Scotland. 'There was a distinctly eerie feel' to having a German join his party, Frost remarked, no matter what arguments were made to justify his presence.

In truth, Nagel had more reason that most to want to fight.

Born in 1916 to well-to-do parents in Berlin, he was half-Jewish. At first the young Nagel had excelled at his fine Protestant school, the Hansa Vorschule, situated in north-west Berlin. But with Hitler's rise to power had come the rise of anti-Semitism. Peter and his elder brother, Lothar, had often found themselves in fights. Even the school's principal had told him, 'People like you are not wanted in Germany.'

Eventually, Peter's father, Morny Nagel, had found a way to fool the Nazis. The family had split up, making their separate ways to England. But by the time they got back together, Nagel's mother had been detained in France and would spend the entire war there. His father, meanwhile, re-established the family fabric business in Leicester. Nagel, then in his late teens, joined him, working first on the factory floor to learn the trade from the bottom up. Then had come the war.

Nagel had signed up on 8 March 1940, as a private in the Pioneer Corps, but with his fluency in several languages he'd quickly come to the notice of SOE. At the SOE's top-secret Special Training Stations dotted around Britain, he was taught to use every weapon imaginable and to communicate in Morse code, excelling in fieldcraft, hand-to-hand combat, but most of all explosives. He scored 92 per cent in one SOE demolitions test. He was judged as being 'very keen all round, extremely reliable and very courageous . . . will always find a way out.' It was also noted that Nagel was an 'inveterate and successful womaniser' and 'kicks hard against injustice'.

When Combined Operations had searched around for a German-speaking candidate with elite-forces training, Nagel had been the obvious choice. He was a perfect fit for Operation Biting, possessing not only the language skills but also the boldness and front to confuse the enemy by yelling orders in German, as the raid went ahead in near darkness. That was one of Nagel's foremost roles. He was also to be Frost's interpreter, interrogating any prisoners should they need to be questioned on the finer points of the paraboloid radar.

Frost was privy to little of Nagel's background or training, not to mention the source of his motivation. Fortunately, he was about to have his mind put at rest about the German recruit, and in the most emphatic way. Several days into their Loch Fyne rehearsals, Frost was asked to get his men – his 'horrible crew' – off the ship. It was 12 February 1942, and the top brass were due for an inspection, the captain of the *Prinz Albert* asking Frost if 'he wouldn't awfully mind taking his men up into the hills for a few hours.'

It turned out that the visitor – a senior commander, with royal blood no less – was none other than Mountbatten, and his primary reason for visiting was to make an address to everyone, Frost and his raiders included. Frantic hooting from the *Prinz Albert's* sirens alerted Frost that they were very much needed on the ship. They hurried down from the hills and slipped back aboard.

A gifted orator, Mountbatten made a short, stirring speech in which he pretty much gave the game away. Prior to this moment, none of the *Prinz Albert's* crew had been any the wiser that they had paratroopers aboard. Now they certainly knew. Not a man among C Company, and the various attachments, was left in any doubt that they were training for a real mission. Mountbatten's speech left little doubt that the Winston Churchill demo story had been just that: a fiction, to cover up the real nature of what they were here for.

Once Mountbatten was done, he and Frost had a private word. Both men were relatively young, Mountbatten especially so for the burden of responsibility and command that he carried. He asked Frost if he had any concerns. Two, Frost explained, in his typically direct fashion. First, the rehearsals at Loch Fyne had clarified the risks of C Company being left on the beach at Bruneval, for the pick-up had proven tricky. Second, he remained unhappy about the German on their strength – Private Newman; Peter Nagel.

Nagel was sent for. Mountbatten was fluent in German and he subjected him to volley after volley of questions. What did he do before the war? Where were his family now? What were they up to? Why did he want action? What compelled him to fight his fellow countrymen? To each, Nagel answered in a calm, matter-of-fact way. At the end, he and Mountbatten shook hands and Nagel was dismissed.

Mountbatten turned to Frost. 'Take him along. You won't regret it . . . I judge him to be brave and intelligent. After all, he risks far more than you do . . .'

Nagel had also been thoroughly security vetted, Mountbatten pointed out. With that, the matter was closed. Nagel would vow: 'If you had asked us, we would have gone on another hundred raids.' In the days and weeks to come, he was to more than prove true to his word.

During their time on Loch Fyne, Frost encouraged every man, no matter his unit or rank – *or nationality* – to speak his mind. All were free to make suggestions and to propose modifications to the plan. Nothing was off limits, and for sure they had need of every bit of inspired thinking. Timing was critical. Frost commanded 119 raiders: 120, himself included. He was to thrust those few score men into the heart of one of the enemy's most heavily defended and prized installations.

That enemy, meanwhile, would have every road and track at his command, with the capacity to bring overwhelming strength to bear in short order. Mortars; armoured cars; panzers; fighter aircraft – the German commanders had it all at their beck and call. Frost and his men were to remain on the ground only for as long as it took to spirit the paraboloid away. If they were delayed, the tide and the sea would turn against them. The assault craft could not be left stranded on the rocks, as had so often happened during training. If they were, the consequences would be hugely costly for all concerned.

Having got his sappers, plus his mysterious German recruit, Frost's party was all but complete. All bar one, in fact. At the eleventh hour, a radar expert of sufficient expendability had been press-ganged into joining the Ladies from Hell. While Frost and his men were being put through their paces at Loch Fyne, that lone radar specialist had been learning to do something that he'd never once imagined, not even in his wildest dreams – to drop through a hole in a Whitley's floor and to parachute to earth . . .

From the start, the summons had been an odd one. Sergeant Charles William 'Bill' Cox was serving as a radar mechanic at one of the Chain Home stations situated on the North Devon coast. On Sunday 1 February 1942 he'd been ordered to catch the train to London, post-haste. He'd left that very afternoon from Bideford railway station, without the faintest clue what might lie in store.

He'd reported to the Air Ministry at Whitehall, still none the wiser. There he was teamed up with a Corporal Smith, like himself a radar mechanic but serving on an Isle of Wight Chain Home station. The two men were led before Air Commodore Tate, a Canadian First World War veteran who was serving in the RAF's Technical Branch. Marched into his office, they stood to attention before the man's desk.

Tate eyed Cox. 'You are Sergeant Cox, radar mechanic?'

'Yes, Sir.'

Having asked similar of Corporal Smith, Tate announced: 'You two NCOs have volunteered for a dangerous job.'

'Yes, Sir,' Smith confirmed.

'No, Sir,' Cox countered, most firmly.

Tate glanced at him in astonishment. 'You have not volunteered?'

'No, Sir.'

Tate seemed confused. 'There must be some mistake. I particularly asked for volunteers from amongst the comparatively few with exactly your qualifications . . . But now you are here, Sergeant, will you volunteer?'

'Well, Sir, what exactly would I be letting myself in for?'

'That I cannot tell you. There is a war on and people get hurt in wars, but I promise you, you have a pretty fair chance of surviving.'

'Very well, Sir,' Cox conceded, 'I volunteer.'

Having been promoted on the spot to Flight Sergeant Cox and Sergeant Smith, the two men were dispatched to Ringway Aerodrome, still none the wiser as to what they'd let themselves in for. They arrived, to see the letters 'No. 4 PTS' emblazoned on the hangars. It still didn't mean a thing to them.

While they were being processed through the guardroom, Cox posed the obvious question: 'What is this place?'

'This,' the figure on duty explained, 'is No. 4 PTS.'

Cox sighed. 'I know. I can see "No. 4 PTS" in big lettering on that hangar over there. But what is No. 4 PTS?'

'No. 4 Parachute Training Squadron.'

Cox felt his heart 'drop, then start pounding like a trip hammer'. What on earth had he got himself into? They carried a sealed letter from Air Commodore Tate. It read: 'These two NCOs are as yet unacquainted with the duties on which it is proposed they should be employed, or the training that will be required to prepare them for carrying out such duties.'

Cox and Smith were led before Group Captain 'Stiffey' Harvey, who commanded Ringway. He glanced over the letter, before casting the two recruits an almost pitying look. 'You don't know why you're here?'

They shook their heads.

Having given all the usual warnings about the utmost secrecy of what he was about to tell them, the Group Captain explained their mission in a nutshell – that they were to form the radar-dismantling party of Operation Biting, and all that would entail. 'We cannot force you to jump,' he added. 'You did not originally know what you volunteered for, so if you refuse there is nothing we can do.' They were advised to have a look around and a think about it.

Cox and Smith did just that.

Before the war, Cox, who hailed from Wisbech, the Fenland market town in Cambridgeshire, had never been to sea or ridden in an aeroplane. In fact, he'd never strayed more than a hundred miles from home. Not long married to Violet, and with an infant son and a five-month-old baby daughter, he'd been a cinema projectionist prior to signing up. Small and slight in stature, he

214

wasn't everyone's idea of a hero, and with his young family he had every excuse to turn tail and run. Regardless, having had a nose around, both he and Smith decided they'd best get on with it.

They made two jumps from the 'vile, loathed sausage' – the tethered balloon, which Cox found 'rather nerve-racking'. On the second, Sergeant Smith sprained his ankle. There was no way he could complete his six jumps in the time remaining, so from then on Cox was on his own. He made two jumps from a Whitley at 800 feet, followed by one as part of a stick. His final qualifying jump was to be at night, from the hated balloon. It was an 'eerie experience, for everything was dark and quiet', the hole in the floor looking like 'the bottomless pit'. Cox managed it with no sprains or bruises. He'd earned his wings.

It was 15 February, and he would be leaving the next day to link up with the raiders. The earliest date the mission might go ahead was the 22nd, so just six days hence. Cox had an awful lot to cram into the remaining time. He made for Tilshead, a tiny village slap bang in the centre of Salisbury Plain. Just outside of it lay RAF Tilshead, an airbase in use by Combined Operations. Amidst the Lysanders and the Hotspur gliders scattered around the airstrip, Cox sought out Frost and his men. Once he'd got over the fact that he could barely understand a word of their thick, Scottish accents, his impressions were of a 'grand bunch of fellows'.

Frost made the new arrival welcome as best he could, but everything seemed fraught and hurried. From Loch Fyne, Frost and his men had taken the train south, while the *Prinz Albert* steamed along the west coast of Scotland making for Southampton harbour. That was where the seaborne armada for Operation Biting would set sail from, as long as the mission got the final go-ahead. That all depended on the weather during the five days of the 'moon window' – 22–26 February – and the English Channel in February was hardly renowned for its calm or its clemency.

At Tilshead, Cox was introduced to Lieutenant Vernon and his sappers. Together, they would effectively form the radar-dismantling party. But their role was far more complex than simply being a gang of thieves. They were to take a Leica 35mm camera and notebooks with them, so they could sketch, annotate and photograph the paraboloid, before attempting to tear it apart. It was a belt-and-braces approach. If they damaged it beyond repair, or ran out of time, at least the boffins would have something to look at, to try to gauge how the thing worked.

Frost, meantime, put Cox on a crash course of 'hardening-up' training. By day he had fierce PT, route marches, navigation, unarmed combat instruction, weapons practice, plus learning the drill for crossing barbed wire. The first man had to lie over the wire, while the others proceeded to run over his prostrate form. Come nightfall, he was busy studying recce photos of the terrain, using a 'special optical device that gave details in three dimensions' – the stereoscope viewer.

Two models had been constructed in papier mâché at RAF Medmenham, and shipped from there to Tilshead. One showed the paraboloid with the distinctive Château Gosset behind it, and all the immediate defences. The other, built to a smaller scale, showed the wider terrain and approaches. Somehow, Medmenham's Model Making Section – sited in Danesfield House's rambling basement – had brought the targets miraculously to life.

In Danesfield's cellars they'd interpreted the recce photos, translating them into a different language entirely – that of three dimensions; of slopes, hedges, hills, trees and bunkers. A team of former sculptors and artists had set to work with fretsaw, spatula and paint-brush, with tiny hammers and nails, slicing out the contours from hardboard, and nailing them into an approximation of the relief. Smoothed over with a special covering, a massively enlarged photograph of the terrain was wetted, made flexible and eased into place.

In that way, the towering cliffs of Cap d'Antifer had been given precipitous form, the steep valley of Bruneval given its plunging drop to the sea. Next, the dun-hued tones of a winter landscape were added in paint, plus tiny models of buildings, fences and the paraboloid itself were lowered into place, using tweezers. Everything over three feet across was included, so that an observer could crouch down and glance across the 'landscape', as if he or she were actually there.

Lit via an approximation to 'moonlight', the models were photographed as if from a Whitley pilot's eye-view, the cliffs, sea and surrounding landscape appearing as they might on the night of the assault. Wing Commander Pickard and his fellow pilots studied those images closely, committing to memory the contours and landmarks they would need to watch out for, and the means via which they would find the drop zone, a flat patch of open ground lying to the rear of the chateau. After hours of such study, it felt almost as if they had flown the mission already, the raid itself being but a repeat performance.

Having studied the models and spent a few days with Jock Company, Cox – the reluctant parachutist – found he rather liked the men's 'come-what-may, I'm okay' attitude. This late in the day, Frost and his men had been issued with no special orders regarding the danger of Cox being captured. Perhaps none were necessary, after the warning regarding Preist: 'SHOULD NOT FALL INTO THE ENEMY'S HANDS.' Perhaps it was a simple matter of, for 'Preist' read 'Cox'.

In any case, any sensitivities over Operation Biting had been largely swept away, after the events of recent days. From Paris, Remy and his Confrérie Notre-Dame had radioed through a warning. One of the network's key tasks had been to keep a close watch over the German battle-cruisers *Scharnhorst* and *Gneisenau*, plus the heavy cruiser *Prinz Eugen*. During the battle for Norway, the *Scharnhorst* and *Gneisenau* had sunk the British aircraft carrier HMS *Glorious*, and damaged the cruiser HMS *Renown*. For months they had been bottled up in the French port of Brest, where they could do little further harm.

But the worry was they might slip out and cause havoc among the Atlantic convoys. Remy had sent through just such a warning: evidence from the shipyard workers suggested all three vessels were preparing to make a break for it. Unbelievably, they had done just that, and more to the point they had got away. On 12 February, in broad daylight, they had steamed at top speed east through the English Channel, and it wasn't until they were past Dover that what became known as the 'Channel Dash' was finally rumbled.

How had it been possible? Under Hitler's direct orders, they had slipped away in broad daylight, which no one on the Allied side had been expecting. The Führer's gambit had worked, and he boasted that it proved how his habit of acting differently from what his enemies expected paid off. But more than that, the escape of the warships was due to the German military's ability to evade Britain's watchers. Somehow, all those giant Chain Home towers lining the southern coast had been blinded, to such an extent that they had missed the massive warships.

Hitler had demanded total radio silence for what had been codenamed Operation Cerberus, after the multi-headed dog from Greek mythology that guards the gates of the underworld. Fittingly, Cerberus had been a many-headed operation. Not expecting a daylight breakout, and hearing no radio chatter to suggest otherwise, the watchers had been lulled into a false sense of security. Just as soon as the warships began to move, the Germans had launched a complex electronic warfare (EW) plan, beginning with a Luftwaffe mission disguised as a bombing raid, but which actually deployed airborne decoys to confuse British radar.

Two Heinkel 111s, a fast medium-bomber, flew towards Plymouth, each carrying five *Garmisch-Partenkirchen* jammers, which together simulated a flight of fifty warplanes. To Britain's radar operators, it appeared as if a major bombing raid was targeting the south coast port, drawing their attention that way. As the warships raced eastwards, so the EW measures shadowed their progress, jamming the Chain Home stations and shielding the vessels from view. It wasn't until 1131 hours that a Dover radar station picked up the ships, by which time they were steaming through the Strait of Dover and almost in the clear.

British warplanes dashed after them, but all were repulsed or shot down. As the warships slunk into the thickening gloom of bad weather, there was no need for any further EW measures. A straight run to Norway, and friendly waters, beckoned. The Channel Dash proved a major propaganda victory for the Germans. Britain had been hoodwinked most comprehensively, and in her own back yard. After all, this was no Singapore or North Africa. This was the English Channel.

The shock value was enormous. It provoked uproar. *The Times* described the escape as 'the most mortifying episode in our naval history, since the Dutch got inside the Thames in the seventeenth century'. Across the Channel, in Paris, Remy was fuming. Why did he and his fellows in the network keep risking their lives, if their warnings were simply to be ignored? In London, Churchill seethed. 'The Brest question' had 'settled itself by the escape of the enemy', he observed in disgust.

More to the point, the Channel Dash had proved just how sophisticated were the enemy's technologies, demonstrating most powerfully their capacity to jam British radar. If that was the offensive capability of German radar, just imagine what technologies might underpin the electronic defences ringing occupied Europe, not to mention those of the Fatherland. The Channel Dash provided a huge impetus to Operation Biting. If nothing else, the British public were desperate for a morale boost. For a shot in the arm.

With the first day of the February moon window approaching, minds turned to the war of words that would result from the raid. De Casa Maury penned a memo entitled 'Biting Publicity', stressing the need to strike first and to strike hard. 'These days are particularly dangerous as the enemy has a series of Axis successes to exploit . . . However successful Biting may be, the enemy could very quickly put out a story to the world that an airborne invasion of France had been attempted and repulsed . . .'

The answer was issuing a press communiqué 'as early as possible after the operation, without waiting to know the actual results'. It needed to be ready for the noon broadcast of the BBC, and for publication in the evening papers, 'so as to forestall any efforts made by the enemy'. It would have to be prepared well in advance, Biting requiring an aggressive PR offensive to scupper any enemy propaganda.

A press announcement was drawn up, outlining the bare bones of the operation and its success. Of course, this was a high-risk strategy. To strike first required a story going out before the full details were known. For Biting, timely information – not just timing per se – was going to prove vital. To that end, three press men were sworn to strictest secrecy, before being brought into the know. Lieutenant L. Puttnam was an official War Office reporter: he would fly in Wing Commander Pickard's aircraft. Mr A Humphreys was a journalist with Reuters, and he was allocated to the Tormentor flotilla. Mr A. Edmonds, a cameraman with Gaumont-British, would shoot newsreel footage of the final rehearsals.

Edmonds was dispatched with his film cameras to join Frost and his men. At Lulworth, on the east Dorset coast, three stretches of remote beach had been cleared of anti-invasion barriers and mines: Redcliff Point, Bowleaze Cove and Arish Mell. It was no coincidence that the small pebbly coves and towering chalk cliffs were very reminiscent of the terrain around Bruneval. After their exhaustive preparations on Loch Fyne, the raiders hungered to strike back, but they were to be terribly frustrated in the dog days of February 1942.

Like Salisbury Plain, the Lulworth area was a long-standing military exercise ground, so the raiders could make their final dry runs without too much risk of being observed. Between 17 and 20 February there were daily rehearsals, as the assault craft tried to link up with the raiders in those steeply-shelving coves. Not one went to plan. At one stage, the assault craft made it into shore, but got trapped on a falling tide. The raiders leapt out and heaved and shoved in the freezing water, but the boats were stuck fast. 'We got a bit browned off during those practices,' Frost remarked drily.

On another day the raiders were scheduled to leap from the Whitleys, but the wind proved too fierce. Instead, the aircraft roared along the Dorset cliffs dropping only the containers, after which Frost and his men armed themselves, assaulted the imaginary radar station, before heading for the beach, laden down with a trolley loaded with boulders. But there the plan went awry. The assault craft landed in the wrong place and the raiders lost their way in a minefield, which had been laid to deter German invaders.

This time, Frost and his men were lucky to escape with their lives. That rehearsal 'could not have been a more dismal failure', Frost recalled. It was a sobering moment. They were just days away from zero hour, yet not a single practice had been successful. If anything, the dry runs both here and at Loch Fyne had gone to show how impossible it all might prove.

Frost wasn't the only one who was worried. Wing Commander Norman declared the Lulworth rehearsals 'fruitless'. There was one possible consolation. It was 'a poor show, but it taught us a lot. 51 Squadron are trying hard and will, I'm sure, make a good try.' Despite such attempts at reassurances, the men of C Company were beginning to lose heart. Those they relied upon most – the aircrew and the boat crews – just didn't seem able to pull it off.

Meanwhile Cox – Biting's eleventh-hour volunteer – had been granted leave in which to visit his young family. He travelled home to Wisbech, remaining blissfully unaware of the dramas and frustrations playing out on the Dorset coastline. His wife,

Violet, asked no questions, although she knew he was attached to a parachute squadron and that something of the utmost secrecy was in the offing.

The day Cox reached his home town, 19 February 1942, the Allies suffered another cruel blow. In the largest ever attack against Australia, over 180 Japanese carrier-based warplanes struck the harbour at Darwin, sinking 11 ships and destroying 32 aircraft, while suffering negligible losses themselves. Defeat seemingly plagued the Allies on every front. But Cox had more parochial matters on his mind. He bade a lingering farewell to his family, knowing in his heart that 'perhaps I should never see them again.'

Cox caught the train to London, heading for the Air Ministry – the place at which he had first been persuaded to 'volunteer'. There he found Lieutenant Vernon, the commander of the sapper party, who had also just enjoyed a few days' leave. Awaiting them were Donald Preist, the radar expert who longed to risk a dash ashore from the assault boats, and R. V. Jones, the scientist to the spies. There was much to discuss, apart from the technological aspects of the coming raid. A mysterious Frenchman joined them, dressed in full uniform. Cox and Vernon were briefed on how they should comport themselves if captured, and how they were to guard their secret radar knowledge.

They were allowed only to give name, rank and serial number. 'Don't be worried too much about physical torture,' Jones reassured them, 'because I don't think they're using it.' But they were to be wary of trickery and deception. 'We were told that the enemy occasionally put an apparently English person in the room,' remarked Cox. 'This man proceeded to get into conversation and very cleverly drew out the things they wished to know. A concealed microphone relayed the conversation.'

They were also warned of the 'kindness treatment'. After days of solitary confinement in a dark damp cell, a new officer would appear as the prisoner's apparent saviour, offering to get him moved to a far nicer room. 'He will give you cigarettes, a decent meal, a warm fire and something to drink,' Jones warned. 'After a while you will feel such a glow and be so grateful to this very decent officer, that when he starts asking you questions you will hardly be able to resist telling him everything . . . So for God's sake . . . be on your guard against any German officer who is kind to you.'

Cox joked that he could 'stand a lot of that sort of thing'.

Cox and Vernon were also briefed on how to evade the enemy. Raid planners had decided that 'even though the party was large, it might easily split up into twos or threes and attempt to escape that way.' It might be possible to signal in a boat for a clandestine coastal rescue. The French Resistance networks were primed to help, and any farmer or local villager might come to their aid. They were to memorize various addresses, which acted as safe-houses, and passwords were provided. Lastly, they were given maps of France printed on silk, tiny compasses and saw-blades, plus wads of French cash – escape aids, courtesy of SOE.

The chief worry for Jones was that Cox would be the only one of the raiders wearing an Air Force uniform – blue, in a sea of khaki. If he were captured, it was bound to provoke some difficult questions. Cox suggested a solution: he would claim to have been one of the Whitley's dispatchers and to have got carried away in the rush, falling out of the aircraft pretty much by accident. Jones wondered whether that would wash with the enemy.

Jones had tried to get Cox re-assigned as an Army serviceman, with uniform and papers to suit, but the War Office had baulked.

They argued that they couldn't break the rules by willy-nilly shifting a man from one service to another. Jones felt a real sense of responsibility towards Cox – the young radar mechanic risking his life, arguably in the place of Jones himself. But either way, it was too late to do anything about it now. From London, Vernon and Cox caught the train to Tilshead.

Operation Biting was scheduled to be launched the following evening – 22 February 1942.

Chapter 12

February the 22nd dawned storm-grey and sullen, a bitter wind whipping the sea into angry troughs. The raid was delayed. It was Commander Cook, of the Tormentor flotilla, who argued they should make a virtue out of necessity. There was still the driving need to have at least one fully successful dress-rehearsal. Taking advantage of the bad weather they should give it give it one last try, holding a dry run along some sheltered stretch of coast.

The Solent – the narrow neck of sea separating the Isle of Wight from the British mainland – was the obvious choice. It was a Sunday evening as the raiders – Cox and Vernon now with them – were trucked from Tilshead the forty-odd miles to that stretch of water. It was a rerun of the Dorset rehearsals, only now they were shielded from the open sea by the bulk of the Isle of Wight. Even so, the exercise proved a fiasco.

At 2015 the assault craft hove to, some fifty yards offshore, figures calling for the raiders to wade out to them. 'It was freezing cold,' Cox remarked of the night, 'and I kept going until the water reached my unmentionables, then I had to rush for the boat or I knew I should not make it. When we were aboard, the Navy could not draw them off the beach . . .' Figures jumped back in and tried to wrestle the assault craft free, battling the creeping cold and cramps, but they were stuck fast on a falling tide.

Cox and his fellows were forced to wade back to shore, hugely dispirited. After that a journey back to Tilshead beckoned in icy, draughty trucks and soaking wet clothes. Fortunately, Frost had ordered the men to leave their weaponry, plus a trolley laden with rocks, on the shore. At least all of that had escaped a ruinous dunking.

Trying to bolster the spirts of his men – in truth, even their commander was losing heart – Frost delivered what he hoped was a final, uplifting briefing. Despite his best efforts, the original plan with its *Nelson, Hardy, Jellicoe, Drake* and *Rodney* parties still stood. Frost did his utmost to try to break it down and make it comprehendible to his men.

All 120 were landing on the one Drop Zone (DZ) – the field lying some 500 yards to the rear of the chateau – so that was simplicity itself. From there, they were to break out, Frost leading one party towards the paraboloid, with Ross in support. Once all were in position, Frost would blow a sharp blast on his whistle, to signal the start of the assault, his force hitting the chateau and the radar pit. Of course, thanks to Remy's intelligence, they even knew the name of the German sergeant in charge there.

Junior Charteris, meanwhile, would make a dash for the beach, his Seaforth Highlanders' guns blazing, seizing it in short order. Lieutenant Naumoff would take his section, and face off against the German troops stationed at Le Presbytère, the fortified farmstead and Freya station lying to the far side of the paraboloid. That left only Lieutenant Timothy's party, which would block the road leading through the gorge, so preventing the troops quartered at Bruneval from causing any trouble.

Explained like that, it really wasn't so complicated. All agreed the DZ was a good one: clear, obvious and seemingly unmenaced by the enemy. It would be a cheery feeling seeing Donald

Preist, the radar scientist riding in the boats, come hurrying up from the sea below. That would signify both the beach and the radar station were under some kind of firm control. One soldier, studying the recce photos of the area, asked Frost how they'd maintained the element of surprise, with so many assorted RAF reconnaissance planes zipping about the area.

'Oh, telephoto lens, you know,' Frost answered. 'Taken from miles away.'

In truth, he shared the man's worries, but he wasn't about to let on. He added that there was a small *estaminet* – a bar-café – in Bruneval, and they just had to hope that the German garrisons would be drinking the night away as Frost and his raiders put in an appearance. After all, wasn't that what bored soldiers tended to do?

Another man had a question. What would Frost do when he got to the door of the chateau? 'You blow your whistle, what do you do if the door's locked?'

Frost pondered this for a moment, before someone piped up: 'Ring the bell?'

Maybe he'd do just that, Frost figured – but that was only if they got the chance to deploy . . . The weather closed in, becoming truly dirty and dark. Monday 23 February delivered a horrible anticlimax. With the forecast such as it was, no raid was possible for the next forty-eight-hours. Time was running out and all were beginning to lose heart.

Churchill himself was being kept acquainted of the fortunes of Operation Biting. He took an extraordinary personal interest in what was but a tiny undertaking in the greater scheme of things. General Ismay had sent him a copy of the full Operational Plan, on which Churchill had noted in red pen: 'Borrowed by me.

WSC. 23/2.' Churchill had taken the document to peruse at his leisure, but with all the delays he was demanding answers . . . and action.

'Unfortunately, the weather has delayed the final training of the parachute troops,' Ismay wrote, by way of explanation, and a 'postponement has been unavoidable'. Ismay stressed how all commanders agreed that 'so hazardous an enterprise must not be undertaken without the most complete and thorough rehearsal.' Mountbatten added his own briefing as to why the delays were necessary, but still Churchill was chafing at the bit.

For the nights of 24 and 25 February the weather remained storm-lashed and wild. It left one chance for the raiders to go into action: 26 February, a Thursday. Frost fretted that they didn't just face a seemingly invincible Nazi war machine: even the weather seemed set against them. Only one figure appeared resolute. It was CSM Gerry Strachan, who once again proved Frost right in thinking him 'the very best sort of senior NCO'. Despite all the frustrations, Strachan proved a tower of strength, convinced that no matter what, they were going in.

At anchor in Portsmouth Harbour, the crews of HMS *Prinz Albert* and the Tormentor flotilla were likewise unsettled. Donald Preist – who by now had been given the operational codename 'Noah', doubtless an ironic reference to the biblical ark – complained that 'there was a lot of waiting. Somebody once wrote: "A soldier's life is mainly waiting." What we were waiting for was a combination of moonlight, a calm sea and favourable tides . . . In England, in February, this combination is somewhat rare.'

At Tilshead, the men of Jock Company were irritable; brooding. All this time for thinking, locked in the February mud and darkness, wasn't healthy. Frost and Nagel, the lone

German on the mission, seemed to have settled their differences by now. Both were itching for action. For Cox, the wait proved interminable, giving him time to dwell upon his young family back in Wisbech that he might never see again. 'We waited for the day . . . Monday too rough. Tuesday foggy. Wednesday . . . again too much wind.'

On Thursday morning the raiders packed the containers to be loaded aboard the Whitleys and checked over their weapons, seemingly for the umpteenth time. Most were convinced that with the raid being watched from the very highest level, no one would countenance another delay. Not tonight. This was the last opportunity, so if not now, then when? Surely, even if the winds blustered and howled over the French cliffs, they would get to leap into battle. But not a bit of it.

That afternoon, news reached the raiders that they were yet again to stand down. What did that signify? Was it all over? If they had to postpone to the March moon window, would it even furnish enough hours of darkness in which to prosecute the attack? No one seemed sure. As dusk descended over the camp, the mood was fittingly dark. No enemy had defeated them: they had been vanquished by the weather. It was a bitter blow. They tried their best to sleep. Tomorrow, after all, was another day.

Oddly, Friday 27 February dawned calm and crystal clear. It was bitterly cold, but the sun shone from a cloudless sky. It was as if southern England were another country. Frost felt in limbo. What was he to do? In theory, they were past the moon window, but today's conditions seemed perfect. Around lunchtime, a messenger arrived from Airborne headquarters: they were to give it one last try. Frost gave the orders. No one could quite believe it. CSM Strachan was the one exception. He bounded about with endless enthusiasm, urging all to get to it, for tonight was the night.

Unbeknown to them, a drama had played out in Portsmouth that morning, determining the change of plan. Cook, the Australian navy veteran and commander of the Tormentor flotilla, had presented a powerful argument as to why the raid should go ahead, regardless of the moon window having closed. From somewhere he'd unearthed a picture postcard, which showed Bruneval in pre-war days, the calm sea lapping at a picturesque beach.

That morning, he'd presented it to Admiral James, who was in overall command of the seaborne side of operations. Having been bombed out of his office, the admiral was working out of Lord Nelson's old cabin on HMS *Victory*, the venerable warship of Battle of Trafalgar fame. *Victory* had been placed into dry dock in 1922 as a living museum, but come the outbreak of war and Portsmouth suffering heavy air raids, she was back in military service.

Cook's postcard showed two fishing boats drawn up on the pebbles, and a beach hut to the rear. No machinegun nests or bunkers were visible on the cliff-tops, for none had existed at the time. But it was the throng of bathers that were of chief interest. Cook pointed out that even those figures standing just a few yards from the beach were up to their waists in water. In other words, *they showed how steeply the beach shelved.* The gradient was fierce enough to get his boats off, Cook argued, even on a falling tide. He reckoned this was his 'trump card'.

Admiral James studied it for a long moment, but there was little time to vacillate. Nelson-like, the admiral decided to turn a blind eye to the orthodox view – that they had missed their chance. He telephoned Norman and Browning to talk it over.

The postcard was the clincher: all were in agreement. Just before lunchtime, James scribbled out a secret cypher message by hand, one full of portent: 'Proceed with Operation Biting Tonight, 27th Feb.' Mountbatten, on hearing the news, was more forthright. He despatched a message to the force commanders, to be delivered by hand. It read: 'Best of luck. Bite them hard.'

There was now a flurry of activity. Top-secret codewords were issued, to be used by 51 Squadron. WALNUT was the Whitleys' call-sign, followed by the aircraft number. SCRUB signified a cancellation of the mission, and that all aircraft should return to base. OAK would mean that all Whitleys had dropped their parachutists successfully; THORN – that the aircraft had failed to drop the raiders on their objective at all.

In case of any aircraft getting into trouble, 'special care was to be taken not to compromise the coastal R.V.' – in other words the beach from which the raiders were scheduled to withdraw. The lessons of Colossus, the Sele River pick-up and of HMS *Triumph*'s abortive mission seemed to have been well learned.

Aboard HMS *Prinz Albert*, Humphreys, the Reuters reporter, recorded how 'glumness and depression were very rapidly trans-formed into jubilation, when word came around . . . "the job's on tonight".' The mother ship had to get under way with her flotilla in double-quick time. On deck, the sun was shining brightly. It seemed bizarre, after the dark days just gone.

Donald Preist – Noah – found himself aping what the rest of the Tormentor crews were doing. 'We put on our battle dress and warm clothing, because at sea the nights were bitterly cold,' he noted, 'blackening our faces with a burned cork, because white faces would be too visible in the moonlight.' They had their final briefing about the naval plan of action. Having been dropped by the mother-ship, the assault craft would motor in to around three miles of the coast, there to loiter with an escort of Motor Gun Boats (MGBs).

When called in, the assault boats would pluck both raiders and radar loot off the beach, and if time and circumstances allowed, Preist would risk a quick dash ashore. That done they would withdraw, rendezvous with the MGBs, pass the loot across to one, at which point it would make a fast dash to England. Preist thought it a fine plan. But he then chose to paraphrase Robert Burns: 'The best laid plans of mice and men are usually about equal . . . as so often happens, things did not go quite according to plan.'

Prinz Albert set sail and at 2147 reached a point some twenty miles short of the French shoreline. She'd navigated to this spot using a taut-wire measuring apparatus, consisting of a lead weight attached to a reel of piano wire. With that dropped at the last known point of reference, and with the wire paying out over the stern, the distance travelled could be recorded with pinpoint accuracy. It gave no indication of direction, of course, which was all down to charts, compass and dead-reckoning.

Prinz Albert began to lower the assault craft. Weather conditions were 'as near as perfect as could be expected: no wind, sea or swell, and a bright moon with a little cloud and a very slight haze'. Within five minutes all the boats had been dropped and the Tormentor flotilla was ready for the off. Commander Cook gave the signal and the craft set out, heading into the night. Each was loaded with duffel coats, bully beef, biscuits, condensed milk and a jar of rum, for the parachutists when they were brought aboard.

'We were well within "enemy waters" when the light landing craft left the mother ship,' wrote Humphreys. 'Small dark shapes in double line they looked, seen against the moonlit sea, like a team of huskies on the trail . . . Small and defenceless . . .' Just before the boats were out of earshot, Humphreys could hear echoing across the water 'the stirring melody "Land of My Fathers", sung by the Welshmen who formed a large part of the . . . crews'.

He stood in *Prinz Albert*'s bows, watching as the boats 'merged in to the silver greyness of the far distance'. Beside Humphreys was a member of the ship's gun crew, likewise glued to the distant silhouettes. He gazed 'with envious eye at the departing flotilla. His attitude was typical of those who had to stay behind. One man's quiet utterances summed up how all were feeling: "I'd give quids to be going with you . . ."'

When the little boats were all but gone, *Prinz Albert* flashed a final message of good speed, before turning towards British shores. En route, she would act as if laying mines, in case her presence had been detected by the enemy.

With the assault craft puttering towards the French coast, Preist broke out his specialist radio receiver, 'tuned to 550 MHz, the frequency of the Radar', or so they strongly suspected. Almost immediately, he picked up the signal from the German device. 'It got louder and softer, rhythmically, because . . . it was sweeping automatically through an arc of about 180 degrees.' The all-seeing eye of the enemy was beaming out to sea, searching, searching – scouring for targets.

As Preist crouched in that freezing assault boat, spying out the enemy's radar, so Frost and his men were enjoying tea, cake and bully beef sandwiches, at the departure aerodrome. A last supper? It felt nothing like as fateful as the departure of the Colossus raiders had done, launching the Allies' first ever airborne raid. That was just over a year ago, and how things had changed. Spirits were sky-high. They might well be a lonely little armada striking back, but they were resolved to do as Mountbatten had urged, and to bite the enemy hard. Frost, certainly, was determined to bring his men back alive. For their part, they were ready to fight to the last bullet and battle their way to the Spanish border, if need be.

Nagel joined Frost and Strachan as they did their final rounds, chatting and joking with the men. Fragments of song echoed through that glorious night. An aircraft engine coughed in the winter stillness. A vehicle motored steadily around the base perimeter. All seemed beguilingly peaceful. Frost paused here and there, urging the figures to uphold the finest traditions of their – mostly Scottish – regiments. In the nearby huts were neat lines of parachutes, each line corresponding to one of the twelve Whitleys that would fly on tonight's mission. The raiders wanted only one thing now: to jump over France and get on with it.

Frost took a last-minute call from Group Captain Norman, a man whom he viewed as the brilliant grandmaster of the air side of the operation. 'Just wanted to say good luck, Frost. Latest information is that there's snow on the other side and I'm afraid the flak seems rather lively.'

Frost felt a twinge of annoyance. The RAF had flown recce flights over beach and cliffs, checking surf and air pressure, but also disturbing what he imagined to be 'a sleeping hive'. Their aircraft had come under fire, and the batteries of gunners appeared armed and ready. He would have preferred it if they had been left unmolested, on this of all nights. The news of the snow also discomfited him. There was none on the ground in southern

England. They had white camouflage smocks back at base, but he'd had no idea they might be needed. Too late to do much about it now.

A piper began to play. As the skirl of the bagpipes skittered across the aerodrome, it brought the raiders to their feet, almost unconsciously. The call of the pipes: it ran deep within the ranks of the Highland regiments. As each stick marched towards its respective aircraft, Piper Ewing shifted the tune to better suit the regiment most in their number hailed from. Cheers rang out through the darkness. It was immensely stirring, just as Frost had intended.

Riding with Pickard in the lead aircraft was Puttnam, the official War Office reporter and the eyewitness to the coming parachute drop. He described the raiders as 'stepping out to the bagpipes', bearing 'an astounding assortment of lethal weapons – grenades, knives, tommy-guns and so on'. Perhaps in the excitement of the moment he had mistaken their Stens for Thompson sub-machineguns.

Still, his prose captured the spirt of the departure magnificently. 'Most seemed to be Jocks and merry as "grigs" at the thought of a fight,' Puttnam wrote. 'Grigs' is an archaic term for a very lively, cheerful person of dwarf-like stature and of mythical origin. 'The largest accused the Captain of our aircraft of dropping him on his head at the last rehearsal . . . The Captain strongly denied this.'

It was only now that the raiders realized where they were heading. 'It was not until this moment that we learned that the objective was near the village of Bruneval, itself near Le Havre,' Cox noted. 'Major Frost also told us there was snow on the ground and that the password was "Biting" . . . To the sound of the pipes . . . we saw twelve huge black Whitleys outlined in the moonlight . . . I remember wondering if my luck would hold.'

It was 2200 hours, and there was a short pause in proceedings, as the aircrew made their final checks. It gave the men the chance for a last vital act. To save weight, the Elsans – portable loos – had been removed from the Whitleys. In the semi-darkness, turned away from the warplanes and the runway lights, ranks of men took a final opportunity to have a good long pee.

Wing Commander Pickard – the star of *Target For Tonight* – wandered over to have a word with Frost. Pickard's aircraft would lead the pack, carrying Lieutenant Charteris and his stick into battle, as one of a first flight of four Whitleys. Behind them would come two further flights, each dropping their forty men at staggered intervals, with Frost riding in aircraft number six. This was the last chance for the two to have words.

Pickard struck Frost as seeming unusually subdued. He'd grown used to the swagger and insouciance of the 51 Squadron aircrew, which always served to bolster one's spirits. Pickard – pipe permanently jammed between his teeth – had always seemed so solid and unshakeable. Frost gave voice to his main misgiving, about the snow on the ground: 'Damn, we could have worn our whites!' But he wondered what might be eating at Pickard.

The tall, distinctive Squadron Leader bent closer to Frost, so they wouldn't be overheard. 'I feel like a bloody murderer!' he hissed. 'Dropping you poor devils over there in a foreign country, when we are all nice and peaceful . . .'

This wasn't what Frost needed right now, and he felt distinctly unnerved. At this stage in the war the 'Germans were to us terrible . . . formidable in the extreme.' His was 'no grand armada. We were so very much by ourselves.' So much could go wrong, but mostly he feared the enemy's intelligence, and that the mission was already blown. Even as he waited to board the aircraft, 'one could almost imagine an agent reporting from the edge of an airfield.'

Frost had been hoping Pickard would crack a joke or something. The last thing any of them needed was the Wing Commander becoming 'windy'. His words were also an eerie echo of Admiral Keyes's sentiments, almost a year to the day earlier, when he had dispatched the Colossus raiders. *A pity*, he had remarked. *A damn pity*. And not a man among that party had returned.

Frost shook off his unease. Forcing that unsettling remark – *I feel like a bloody murderer* – to the back of his mind, he climbed aboard his own aircraft, 'Y for York', settling down into the 'draughty, uncomfortable, cold and seemingly most vulnerable' hold.

CSM Strachan was acting as the dispatcher, being No. 10 in the stick – last man out – which made it his role to liaise with the aircrew. A rock as always, Strachan began calmly running through the pre-take-off routine, checking if the intercom was working properly, if the jump lights were functioning and if there were enough kapok 'silk' sleeping bags for the men in the stick. Did all have their silk gloves – crucial, if they were to hit the DZ with hands which were warm enough to function and to fight.

As Y for York's engines revved higher, the fuselage vibrating horribly, Strachan ordered all to move as far forward as possible, assuming take-off positions. Once they were airborne the pilot would signal 'Rest Positions' and the men could spread themselves out fore and aft of the jump hole. But for now, they had to remain bunched up against the bulkhead. Small things, seemingly, but vital.

As their orders had stressed, 'pilot will be unable to control the aircraft unless "TAKE-OFF POSITION" is correctly taken up. The alternative is a crash.' The Whitleys were loaded to the max, each laden down with paratroopers, weaponry, ammo, radios, looting kit, explosives, plus 715 gallons of fuel. The make-up of each stick of parachutists had been carefully calculated to balance the aircraft's load, the containers positioned to maintain the correct centre of gravity.

Frost sensed their Whitley start to move, as it began to bump its way along the perimeter track. He felt his stomach contract with nerves. At that moment, as tension ebbed and flowed through the dark, coffin-like hold, he 'almost longed for some last-minute cancellation or for some last reason to delay our going'.

He had been killing time by studying one of the close-up recce photos of the target. It had only served to convince him that the enemy must know he and his men were coming. It was a horrible sensation, and it was only in getting airborne – almost the point of no return – that Frost would shake off such haunting feelings. Oddly, it would be Cox – the reluctant parachutist; no obvious hero, certainly – who served to lift his spirits.

'Somewhere ahead we could hear an aircraft revving its engines, and then it was away', Cox noted. 'The others followed at one-minute intervals. I counted them, and when No. 5 was away, I knew we were next. One minute then, with engine throbbing, our plane moved forward slowly but gathering speed, and . . . we were airborne.'

Cox described the Whitley dragging itself off the ground, as if it had 'great big heavy sloppy feet'. In spite of the silk gloves and sleeping bags, it was bitterly cold. 'No one slept in that dim-lit metal cigar . . . Ten men in an enclosed space, hardly lighted, going to they knew not what . . . but were we downhearted? I don't think so. A group of three in the nose were playing cards. I rendered a song or two, "The Rose of Tralee" and "Because" . . .'

Somehow, the thrum of the engines seemed to make it easier for Cox to sing, beating out a rhythmical accompaniment to his words. For Frost, those songs provided the magic, lifting the despondency: 'Above all the din, the voice of Flight Sergeant Cox of the RAF filled that gloomy fuselage with ringing, cheery tones.' Getting into the spirit, Frost passed around a flask of rum, and each man took a gulp. Courage, for what was coming.

The lead Whitley, with Pickard at the controls, clawed into the winter skies at 2215. All twelve were airborne by 2230. At that moment, the codeword was given over the radio: 'Walnut Twelve' – signalling that all planes were airborne, en route to France. They made for the muster point, Selsey Bill, a distinctive headland jutting into the sea on the southern English coastline. Pickard's aircraft circled above that spot, until all were present.

With no stragglers, at 2315 he turned his warplane south and set a bearing for Fécamp, a fishing port directly across the Channel and situated a few miles to the north of the target. The Whitleys dropped to just a few hundred feet above sea-level, thundering onwards through the darkness in tight formation.

There was cloud cover, and they needed to get below it. 'We came down very low,' Pickard noted, 'the lowest flying at 50 feet and the highest at 600.' At that kind of altitude they also hoped to slip beneath the enemy's all-seeing eye – their radar; or at the least, to remain hidden for as long as possible.

As the warplanes flitted across the moonlit waters, so the holds of several likewise rang with song. What was becoming the airborne 'theme tune' proved the most popular – 'Come Sit By My Side If You Love Me', the last two verses (of the printable version, at least) being:

When we land in one certain country,
There's a job we'll do very well,
We'll fire Goering and old Adolf Hitler,
And all those bastards as well.

So come stand by the bar with your glasses,
Drink a toast to the men of the sky,
Drink a toast to the men dead already,
Three cheers for the next man to die!

Those not singing played cards, rummy and pontoon. In Lieutenant Timothy's aircraft, the former Marks & Spencer sales manager handed around what appeared to be a bog-standard water bottle. Those who took a sip quickly realized it was practically neat rum! In one aircraft, the men chatted about the morphine one or two of them – those given basic medical training – were carrying. If anyone took a hit, at least they had that powerful painkiller to hand. The very thought served to bolster spirits.

On Junior Charteris's aircraft – the lead Whitley – three men were playing a fiercely competitive card game. The big winner, as so often tended to be the case, was Corporal Stewart. On stuffing his winnings into his wallet, he remarked that if he copped it on the raid, whatever man was next to him should take whatever he'd won and put it to good use. They certainly would, his fellow raiders told him with a grin.

Charteris, meanwhile, had made something of a startling discovery: he and one of his men were just a day apart in age. 'We had spent our time in the aircraft mostly in talk,' he remarked. 'I discovered the man sitting next to me was one day older than myself and that we should both be 21 in a few days' time; we swore that we would celebrate our birthdays together.'

By the time the air armada was approaching the French coast, Frost could tell that 'spirits were very high'. Even the lone German among them – Nagel – seemed in fine fettle, despite the fact that he was flying in to attack his own countrymen. Frost had to give it to Mountbatten: so far, his upbeat assessment of Nagel and his qualities seemed to be entirely justified.

With headphones on, CSM Strachan provided a running commentary, relating what he was hearing from the cockpit. A squadron of RAF fighters were flying escort, matching the Whitley's steady, 125 mph cruise speed. Knowing that was comforting, and it boosted spirits still further. But zero hour – jump-time – was fast approaching.

At 2340 hours Strachan gave the warning: 'Prepare for action stations.' Thirty minutes to target. Figures lingered for a few moments in their 'flea-bags'. It was blissfully warm nestled among those silky folds. Once the cover was removed from the Whitley's hole, it was going to be cold as hell. One by one they crawled out, passing the sleeping bags forward, so they could be stowed by the bulkhead. Nervous hands checked static lines, giving a tug on the nylon. Frost passed his flask of rum back and forth. All took a swig.

As the light gleamed off moonlit cliffs, thin and white in the distance, the aircraft lost height, dropping to no more than 300 feet above sea level. Like this, they intended to hug the very clifftops, the pilot turning right – onto a southerly bearing – to flit along their heights, using their contours, twists and turns as cover, and their landmarks as a countdown to the drop.

Strachan gave the order for 'Action Stations'. The plywood

doors were wrenched free of the Whitley's hole. Instantly, an icy blast roared through the hold. The noise of the aircraft's engines could be heard more clearly now, bouncing back from the sea just below. Strachan relayed their progress. 0010: just a few minutes to target. Frost peered through the hole, searching for the cliffs. No sign of anything. He turned to Strachan, asking him to enquire of the pilot if they were in sight of land.

Strachan did so, and relayed the pilot's response: in moments they would be over the French cliffs. Barely had he finished speaking, when the night was torn apart by the powerful thud of gunfire. A *Vorpostenboot* – a German flak ship – sitting off the coast had opened up on the fleet of British warplanes, all guns blazing. Four such *Vorpostenboote* were anchored just to the west of Fécamp, the point at which the fleet of Whitleys were approaching landfall.

All four let rip, unleashing volleys of fire from their 20- and 40mm cannons and from scores of machineguns. The pilots of the Whitleys threw their aircraft into violent action, as they tried to frustrate the gunners' aim, but this close to cliffs and sea there was precious little room for manoeuvre. Via the open hole in the Whitley's floor, Frost could see the incoming tracer, chasing after them like a 'pleasant firework show'. But there was nothing remotely pleasant about the hits the aircraft were taking.

From the cockpit of the lead Whitley, reporter Puttnam had a bird's-eye view of the unfolding action. 'We were sailing down the French coast, with moonlit cliffs and a snow-covered background ... The light flak came straight for our tail, very close indeed. We must have been a sitting target, at the height at which we were flying.' Indeed, his aircraft, B for Bravo, was taking a pounding.

Locked in B for Bravo's hold, it sounded to Junior Charteris as if a giant figure was 'hammering a piece of tin below us'. Those poised at the hole could see what was causing the fearsome racket, the dark silhouettes of the *Vorpostenboote* wreathed in smoke and flame, their guns spitting fire, the surface of the sea alight with burning muzzle-flashes. But even those who were blind to the action caught the expressions on the faces of those gazing downwards: many had turned deathly pale.

'By the time they opened fire we'd gone down to 350 feet and throttled back to 100 mph,' Frost reported of the moment. 'The flak was damned accurate and hit three of the aircraft . . . The pilots had to take evasive action, and they dived to under 100 feet.'

Skimming along the wavetops, the Whitleys were chased by fire. One took a direct hit from a cannon shell in the main spar – the beam-like structure running through the wings, which carries most of the aircraft's load. Miraculously, it was still flying. Another had taken a burst to its rear gunner's turret. That aircraft, too, was still airborne. Ugly the Whitley might be; uncomfortable she most certainly was; but she was also able to take a huge amount of punishment, and remain airborne.

Shore guns joined in the turkey shoot now. In Frost's aircraft, Y for York, there was a new and deafening noise: the rear gunner opened up with his four Browning machineguns. The hammering thud of the percussions filled the hold with a thunderous roar, as he traded fire with fire. A long burst found its mark, a nest of enemy gunners falling silent. But whether he'd hit them, or they'd bolted for their bunkers, he wasn't entirely certain.

*

Unbeknown to the British raiding force, the German troops standing the night shift at the radar stations had been on high alert for some time. Having come on duty at 1900 hours, it wasn't long before the first alarm had been raised: a fleet of Allied warplanes had been detected, making for the nearby port of Le Havre. The Würzburg's beam had groped across the night sky, picking up the aircraft twenty-five miles out to sea and closing fast.

Every two minutes the operators called through an update to headquarters, giving height and direction. Not long after that first flight, another had been tracked across the sea. These were diversionary raids, mounted by the RAF in an effort to distract the defender's attentions. But all were on alert now. At Bruneval beach, in the Stella Maris villa, Corporal Georg Schmidt was manning the telephone in case of urgent calls from headquarters. It looked like being another long, cold and sleepless night.

At shortly before midnight a new alert was raised. The Würzburg team rushed into action. The Freya operators had picked up a flight of twelve aircraft, some forty miles out. The paraboloid swung onto the bearing, moving left and right, up and down, searching for the strongest trace. At five minutes to midnight, the operators sent through their first reading: the twelve aircraft were twenty miles out, and making for Fécamp, it seemed.

Every mile or so, the Würzburg operators sent a new height and bearing reading, tracking the air armada's every move. They saw it turn south at Fécamp and race along the clifftops, the speed and formation being that of a flight of bombers soaring in to attack – at which point the unavoidable conclusion was that, tonight, *they* were the target. Powering down the Würzburg, the crew made a dash for the nearby shelters. They dived below ground, just as the guns opened up a murderous barrage on the in-bound British warplanes. The defenders had seen the raiders coming. They'd been tracked most of the way.

Frost's darkest worries appeared to be all too real.

Chapter 13

Thirty miles to the east of Bruneval, another group of figures scanned the skies for aircraft. Operation Juliet was back on, and 27 February was the night, or so Remy had been informed. At his Saint-Saëns landing ground, lying some twenty miles inland, the French agent waited with bated breath, especially after so many let-downs. The night was bitter. Calm, clear, but icy cold. He was chilled to the bone.

During the journey from Paris towards the coast they'd had a terrifyingly narrow escape. Having planned to take the bus, lugging three large suitcases bulging with German military documents, they'd loaded them into the rack atop the vehicle, when a Resistance driver had arrived with a van instead. Grumbling, Remy had helped manhandle the heavy cases down, unaware how this chance change of plan would save him. The bus was subsequently stopped by the Gestapo, all passengers – and their luggage – being thoroughly searched.

On such small twists of fate hinged capture or liberty, death or survival.

At the landing ground under a sky full of stars, Remy and his fellows worked quickly in the snow, driving in iron posts, each with a lamp attached to it and arranged in a triangle – the agreed marker for tonight's flight. They readied themselves to flash a recognition signal in Morse via torchlight, confirming that the pattern of lights had been set by friends.

The remote field lay a good mile from any road. It had taken half an hour to get there, trudging through ten inches of snow and laden down with 180 pounds of documents. Hard, sweaty, exhausting work. In an effort to ward off the chill, Remy was wrapped in layers – a woollen vest, woollen sweater, shirt, a second sweater, and over it all a trench coat. On his head he wore a beret, topped off with a thick mountain hood.

It was approaching midnight when a noise from the direction of the coast drew Remy's attention – the sound of a distant aircraft reverberating through the heavens, the throb of aero engines seeming to come and go on the still night air.

'Over there, towards Fécamp!' one of his fellows hissed. 'I can hear it! At least two of them, I tell you . . . No, they're gone now.'

Remy wondered if that had been his flight, and the pilot had somehow missed the landing zone. It wouldn't be the first time. Some minutes later he detected another engine noise, this one growing louder all the time – surely, an aircraft racing in towards them. Moments later there was a recognition flash from the cockpit, and the ghostly form of a Lysander dropped from the heavens, turned into the wind and touched down, coming to a rest lodged within the triangle of lights, its engine still running.

A figure jumped out. Remy had been told to expect an agent, codename Anatole. He was surprised to discover it was a woman. They shook hands briefly, the newcomer laughing with relief that she had made it. Remy gave her a rushed briefing on where she was lodging that night, before clambering up the Lysander's ladder, dragging the cases of precious documents after him. He threw himself inside, the pilot gunning the engine. They rumbled over frozen ruts and bumps for a few seconds, before getting airborne in a cloud of snow.

As Remy slid the Perspex canopy shut above him, the Lysander flitted north over white fields fringed with dark borders, and patches of black woodland. Suddenly they were speeding past an airfield, situated on the very coastline. Below, a white light darted across the runway from end to end – a German fighter, getting airborne. Remy tried to grope for the intercom to warn the pilot, but it was buried under the heavy cases. Unreachable.

'Hail Mary, full of grace . . .' he began to pray, as the Lysander sped over the cliff-tops and made a dash for the sea.

Remy's prayers appeared to have been answered. No hostile warplanes seemed to follow in their wake. Ahead lay an open run across the Channel, to the RAF base where they intended to make touchdown. At that moment, Remy would be able to deliver his precious cargo into the hands of those who could best use it. It constituted war-winning intelligence, of that he was certain. Action would be taken; raids planned; fleets of bombers sent out; men dispatched into harm's way.

Tonight it was Frost and his raiders who were about to leap into harm's way, a few miles along the coast that Remy had left behind him. In the lead Whitley, Charteris was poised to be the first man of the first stick to jump. 'Everything was very clear; you could see the coast, every house, tree and fence,' he noted. 'It was all black and white, clear cut in the moonlight . . .' The Cap d'Antifer lighthouse flashed past the Whitley's port side, the aircraft turning inland for the DZ. Angry bursts of tracer cut the night, and Charteris could feel Pickard flinging the aircraft from side to side, in an effort to evade the enemy fire.

His men kept asking how much longer before the jump – a sign of their nerves. Charteris didn't know, except that it was imminent. He had his eyes glued to the red light, waiting for it to switch to green. In those last few seconds he experienced an odd mixture of emotions. 'As you sit near the hole, it is a funny feeling; you watch the light, waiting for it to change . . . I felt as though I was acting in a play.'

In the aircraft's cockpit sat war reporter Puttnam with his bird's eye view. 'Now we were making our run-up, exactly the same as a run-up for dropping bombs – but at tens of feet from the ground, instead of thousands. A ravine, a little cove, the dropping place close to a house – 'Green!' In a flash the Jocks had dropped . . . Tug, tug, tug, we could feel them leave one by one . . .'

Charteris led his stick from the aircraft, plummeting into the void. Once he was through the slipstream, what struck him most was the peace and silence. 'It was a lovely drop, there was no wind and I came down like a feather . . . There was so little wind that the rigging lines wrapped themselves around me.' His boots thumped into undisturbed snow, and to left and right he could see further parachutes drifting towards earth.

After the first five men had jumped the containers were released, followed by the remainder. Now, to muster his force, break the cases open and arm themselves for war. Just a few hundred yards below the field in which they'd landed, a short stretch of heavily defended beach needed to be seized and cleared of the enemy. That was Charteris's mission and it was a vital one.

Above him, the aircraft rumbled onwards, Puttnam, the reporter, captivated by the scene. 'They dropped with perfect timing, without a second's delay . . . "Good luck, Jock!" we shouted, though we knew they could not hear . . . Another

Whitley came close behind us, also dropping its contingent . . . The operation went perfectly . . . We had done our job and had been told not to "hang around". We left the rest to the Army, to this gallant Airborne Brigade!'

Beneath the bombast, Puttnam had made an error in his reporting. All was far from 'perfect' with the drop, or that of the aircraft that came behind . . . as Charteris was just about to discover on the ground. It was easy enough to spot the containers, their lights glowing enticingly in the snow. In short order, they were broken open. As Charteris's stick was a fighting patrol, the contents were combat-heavy. No trolleys here; no robbing gear. It was all red lights, signifying weaponry, plus one glowing green, for signals kit; radios.

As his men armed themselves, Charteris took a moment to survey the scene. Something struck him as odd; unsettling. They had been dropped in a valley which looked almost exactly similar to the intended DZ. But as he studied the terrain, he realized that one thing was glaringly absent: there was no dark row of trees towards the lower end. The U-shaped depression also seemed too shallow – not at all what he had expected from the models they had studied.

For a moment he was utterly baffled. Had the modellers got it wrong, somehow? Had the trees never been there at all? The more he glanced about, the more he sensed that the terrain didn't match up with what he had been expecting. Finally, the horrible truth hit home: *they had been dropped in the wrong place.* But if that was the case, then where were they exactly? How far from the rest of the raiders, and more importantly, from their objective?

The realization was 'a very nasty moment', Charteris recalled. 'I felt very lost. There was no house [Château Gosset] and no wood visible.' The twenty-year-old lieutenant took a moment to calm and clear his thoughts. They'd been on the ground for maybe five minutes, and his men were converging on his position, awaiting orders. What he needed to determine was the direction they should move off in, to get to the beach, and how far it might be.

Charteris figured that in trying to evade the flak, the lead Whitleys had lost their way. But the next flight might be bang on target. Those aircraft hove into view, chased through the skies by bursts of enemy fire. Charteris watched them fly a low, purposeful trajectory directly over his position. From that alone he deduced that he and his men were on the right line, but still he was unsure 'whether we had been dropped too soon or too late'. Did the DZ lie further back along the bearing the aircraft had taken, or further onwards? No way of knowing.

On gut instinct, he decided to follow in the aircraft's wake, as if they had been dropped short. He gathered his men, explaining what he thought had happened. They were to move out at double time, following his lead. They took up a diamond formation, with Charteris at the tip of the spear, adopting a fast, loping pace. At such speed, over such terrain, he figured they'd cover a good six miles in an hour. But his 'secret worry was lest we should have to turn about'. That, he feared, would be a disaster for morale.

Charteris's orders were crystal clear, and they preyed on his mind. Having been dropped at 0015 hours, he had minutes to get his men into position to seize the beach and cliffs. 'At 0030 . . . move to attack L.M.G. posts in the valley, assault and take the pillbox, send one sec[tion] (2 L.M.Gs.) to hold the cliff to the South of the Beach . . . and send one sec to destroy the L.M.G. posts and pillboxes on the cliff to the north of the Beach.'

LMG stood for light machineguns – similar to the Brens he

and his men were now carrying as they struggled over the snowy landscape, each of which weighed over 20 pounds when loaded. In addition to those, they were laden down with Stens, grenades, ammo, medical kit, radios and personal supplies. Charteris sensed the mission hung in the balance, everything depending on how far he and his Seaforth Highlanders had been dropped from their objective . . . and how fast they could move under such punishing loads.

From his vantage point at the Whitley's hole, Frost was oblivious to such dramas. He could see everything the models had led him to expect, laid out like a toy-scape. Only the dusting of snow made it appear at all unfamiliar. Frost dropped his legs over the lip of the hole, readying himself to leap. His bladder felt full to bursting: too much tea and rum, he reflected, ruefully. Why hadn't they thought of that, back at the aerodrome, and rationed themselves on the liquids?

It was 0020 dead, and they'd been in the air for approaching two hours. He couldn't wait to get down. Strachan gave the cry: 'No. 1, Go!' A figure slipped from view. Frost jumped, his static line ripping out his parachute above him, and moments later he was floating through the air. Not a shot rang out in their direction. Not a figure could be seen moving below. No enemy forces gathered to ensnare them in fire. To all sides Frost could see terrain floating up towards him that was so intimately fixed in his mind.

He landed softly, plumping into a foot of snow. Oddly, his first thought was for his bladder. Having cut loose his 'chute, which he left where it had fallen – no time nor reason to bury them on this mission – he moved to one side and proceeded to relieve himself in the snow. Not the most tactical of manoeuvres, upon touching down in the thick of enemy territory, but a good first 'gesture of defiance', he told himself.

Above him, figures floated towards earth. One of them, Cox, was momentarily transfixed by the Whitley's fiery exhausts, seeming to glow red hot in the freezing air above him. Like many of the jumpers, he was amazed at how incredibly peaceful it all seemed. 'I landed with quite a gentle bump', he noted, rolling once in the snow to break his fall. 'The noise of the aircraft died away, and it was deathly quiet.' The thing that was most notice-able was 'the hush', which contrasted markedly with 'the horrible din inside the aircraft'.

Cox was struck by how lonely he felt, but then he heard 'rustling and saw something outlined against the snow'. Lights flickered on. Purple, for explosives and wrecking gear. That was just Cox's kind of kit, and it galvanized him into action. He struggled through the drifts, grabbed the pin and pulled it out, so extinguishing the lights, then proceeded to break open its contents. Another figure located another container, draped within its own parachute. Yellow lights – trolleys. Cox joined him, and together they clipped the two-wheeled contraption together, before piling onto it the contents from the first container. They were good to go.

Cox eyed the terrain, comparing it with the image he had seared into his mind, from studying the models. 'I could see the château in the moonlight and followed a path with my eyes to a clump of trees', his rendezvous point with Lieutenant Vernon and the sappers. It lay to the south of the chzteau, on the lip of the Bruneval gorge. There they were to lie low until the shock-troops called them in. He set off, heading over 'rough ground, the snow being somewhat of a hindrance', with one of Vernon's sappers helping drag the trolley.

More and more figures coalesced around Frost. CSM Strachan – last man out from the aircraft – was there, typically getting everything sorted. There was the odd burst of machinegun fire echoing in the distance, but to Frost it sounded as if it was directed at the fast-disappearing warplanes. Frost could barely believe that all could be going so well. It was the news from Lieutenant Ross, his calm and capable second-in-command, that burst his bubble.

Lieutenant Ross and his men had dropped just ahead of Frost, and it had taken a good few minutes for the parties to find each other. As he'd waited, Frost had watched the next flight of Whitleys disgorge their parachutists in a sizeable cloud. The night was so clear that he couldn't imagine the enemy hadn't seen British paratroopers in the moonlit skies. That meant he and his men had to move quickly, and strike while they still retained the element of surprise, which made Lieutenant Ross's news all the more alarming.

Apparently, Charteris was missing, together with his twenty men – those fierce Seaforth Highlanders whose job it was to clear and hold the beach. Not for the first time, Frost cursed inwardly the cumbersome plan of attack that had been foisted upon him. This was exactly the kind of thing he had feared. It didn't much matter whether they'd been shot down, or failed to find the drop zone: no one knew what had happened, except that Charteris and his men were nowhere to be found.

The situation was exacerbated by the lack of communications. Some radios had been lost during the drop. Those sets they did have didn't appear to be working properly. Either way, Frost had no way of communicating with his scattered Company. He resorted to the only course of action he could think of: he ordered

Ross to wait for as long as possible at the DZ, in case Charteris and his men turned up. If they didn't, he was to head for the beach and do his damnedest to clear it, with the two dozen men he could muster.

Frost's priority had to be to hit the radar site and steal the paraboloid. Without the radar, they had nothing. In a sense everything else – beach evacuation included – was a secondary concern. Fall-back plan sorted, Frost ordered the off. Moving at a gentle jog, the snow muting their footfalls, the raiders set out, a thin line of black figures silhouetted against moonlight. Behind them, former Marks & Spencer salesman, Lieutenant Timothy, led his men in the opposite direction, towards Bruneval village, intent on keeping the enemy garrison there tied down.

The last to drop, Timothy and his force of forty raiders had leapt from their aircraft at 0024 hours. They'd had their own trials and tribulations, including losing several of their radios. One man, Private Scott, had got bashed around the head by one of the containers, even as he'd drifted through the air beneath his 'chute. He'd landed feeling very shaken, and cursing the RAF dispatcher who'd released the container so quickly. His fighting knife had been torn away, his para-trousers ripped down the seam, and he'd have two black eyes come morning, but otherwise he figured he could fight. Another man had broken his ankle upon landing.

In another aircraft, there had been even greater dramas. 'X for X-ray' was the last Whitley in the flight of twelve, and the fifth man to jump had actually managed to get caught up in the hole. Having snagged his foot in the static line of the man coming after him, he'd tripped and fallen head first, finding himself suspended upside down, with two-thirds of his body hanging out of the aircraft. He was what was known as 'hung up' – a terrifying position for a parachutist to find himself in, especially when in the midst of a combat jump and under fire.

Those remaining had managed to drag him back inside, whereupon the pilot, with nerves of steel, had banked his aircraft around to attempt a second pass. He did just that, braving a storm of enemy fire, and all of the raiders – including the one who'd found himself so badly trapped – completed the jump. The last man touched down at 0030 hours. But amidst all the confusion, half a stick had been released above the wrong valley, landing where Junior Charteris and his men had done some fifteen minutes earlier.

Frost had approaching thirty of his raiders either released miles from the target, or injured in the jump. For now at least, over a quarter of his force was out of action, and not a shot had been fired in anger by his men. Worse still, the missing had been dropped on the wrong side of Bruneval village. To get to the DZ or the beach, they would have to fight their way through the German troops based there, or attempt to slip past them in the night. And as Frost had feared, the enemy weren't about to be caught napping.

A few miles offshore the Tormentor flotilla waited, the assault boats rocked by a gentle swell, the men still and quiet and wrapped up against the chill. With engines cut, all that could be heard was the eerie-sounding slap of sea against wooden hulls. As per their orders, they were observing strict radio silence, and were to communicate only in whispers. 'It is essential that all the boats should remain within easy hailing distance of one another . . .'

As they'd motored in towards the cliffs, 'several Whitley Aircraft were distinctly seen at a low altitude' amidst a 'certain amount of light A.A. tracer fire,' Commander Cook reported – the dozen warplanes heading in to make their drops. The flotilla of boats had come to a halt at 'Point W', the pre-arranged location at which they were to loiter – supposedly close enough to shore to ride to the raiders' rescue, but not so close as to be in danger of being spotted.

Then Commander Cook, fresh from playing his trump-card in Nelson's former cabin, got a stroke of unexpected luck. All of a sudden, the Cap d'Antifer lighthouse had emitted a few short flashes, enough to enable him to get an accurate fix on his exact location. Acting on gut instinct, Cook had decided to push a mile or so closer to the shore. It was only later that he would realize how fortuitous this decision would prove: on such seemingly small acts could turn the entire fate of a mission.

In the bows of one of the assault boats, Donald Preist – code-name Noah – hunched over his specialist receiver kit. For an age, or so it had seemed, his headphones had been playing the rhythmical beat of the paraboloid. All of a sudden it had stopped. No matter on what frequency he might try to search, the airwaves had fallen deathly silent. Preist could only hope that had to spell trouble for the Würzburg operators, and maybe success for the raiders.

Now and again there were sporadic indications of Jock Company – or possibly the enemy – in action ashore. 'Signs of activity, tracer, Very lights etc., were noticeable,' those riding in the boats noted. The Tormentor crews eyed the coast searchingly, wondering what on earth might be happening.

In fact, even as the first paratrooper's boots had thumped into the blanket of snow coating the clifftops, so the alarm had been raised among the German garrisons. Having tracked the Whitley's approach, the enemy had spotted parachutists filling the moonlit skies. The raiders could hardly have chosen a worse night on which to attack. As luck would have it, a unit of the 685th Infantry Regiment – the Wehrmacht forces garrisoning the area – were engaged in a night exercise. Those men, fully awake and battle-ready, were ordered to investigate, forming up in a convoy to make haste towards the radar installations.

At the paraboloid itself, the off-duty Luftwaffe guards had received a rude awakening. One, *Flieger* (aircraftman) Heller, had been sleeping soundly, despite the noise of warplanes overhead, his boots and tunic laid by his cot in the dugout. With all the air activity of recent weeks, he'd grown accustomed to such disturbances. But even as the twelve Whitleys had roared through the skies, so rough hands had shaken Heller awake, along with his fellows.

The sentry was new to his post, and confessed he'd not been able to raise the wider alarm, as he couldn't find the field telephone in the dark confines of the dugout. Pulling on boots and jackets, the figures made a dash for the *W-Gerät* (the W-apparatus; the Würzburg) which was their all-consuming responsibility, running into their *Unteroffizier* (the sergeant in charge of the station) as they did so. He'd grabbed their French-made M29 light machinegun – large quantities of such French weaponry had been captured and introduced to German service – even as two of his men made a dash across the snow to fetch reinforcements.

Meanwhile, the Luftwaffe troops based at the fortified farmstead of Le Presbytère had also had a rude awakening. Those working the night shift at the Cap d'Antifer lighthouse had called, warning that parachutists had been spotted. The Luftwaffe commander,

Oberleutnant Melches, reacted by sending out scouts, and within minutes those men reported that British paratroopers had been spotted. They appeared to have split into several groups, and to be advancing on the nearby chateau and the Würzburg station. Melches ordered his men to action stations, to repulse the British attackers.

In Bruneval village, the 685th Infantry Regiment garrison had also received a warning by telephone. *Oberfeldwebel* Huhn split his force into two patrols, one to move north through the gorge, securing that and the beach, while the other swept the high ground. At the beach itself, the *Feldwebel* – deputy platoon leader – in charge had darted out of the Stella Maris villa, even as the Whitleys had thundered overhead. Inside, the phone had started ringing. It was headquarters, warning that parachutists had filled the skies.

The *Feldwebel* had roused his men, mindful that their defences were set to repulse a sea-borne assault, not an attack from inland. Faced with such a threat, he ordered that one of the machineguns be shifted from its position covering the beach to behind the villa, to menace any advance from that direction. That done, he'd spotted shadowy figures moving on the high ground. He let rip with his machine pistol at what he was convinced was the British parachutists, before firing a white flare in an arc high above, to signal the alarm.

Fearful that the British were massing on the heights, he moved all but three of his men into the trenches set to the rear of the villa and issued grenades. He left Corporal Schmidt to man the telephone, and two to keep watch on the beach. Otherwise, all attention – all weaponry – was focused inland, on the gorge and the cliffs rising to either side. It was 0030 hours, and the German defences were set. Patrols were heading out and reinforcements had been called for. It was the last thing that the depleted force of British raiders needed.

By now, Frost and his men had covered the six hundred yards to the chateau and the radar pit, fanning out in stealthy silence. Amazingly, they'd yet to encounter any enemy, or been under fire. As Frost stole towards the door, so Lieutenant Peter Young led his section towards the paraboloid, moving at a low crouch through the snow. Young's job was to take his men 'direct to the set and defend it, while Flight Sergeant Cox and his Engineers took it to pieces'. But first, the German guards would have to be dealt with.

Young and his men were 'heavily laden with grenades and Sten Guns . . . and with each man carrying his prized fighting knife . . .' As he stalked the paraboloid's defenders, Young steeled himself to execute his orders: *No prisoners will be taken other than Offrs [officers] and technical personnel.* Despite this, excitement and enthusiasm were at 'fever pitch'. No one had wanted to miss out on this mission: 'Here, in the dreary, depressing days of early 1942 was actually a chance to hit back,' Young recalled.

Silently, footsteps muffled in shallow drifts, he slipped his men into their positions, 'picking our way through the knee-high barbed wire that surrounded the set'. There they halted, just a few dozen yards short of the target. Before them sat the prize – a dark, angular silhouette, ghostly-black against moonlit snows. It seemed utterly deserted, but appearances can be very deceptive. Young passed around a hushed order: his men were to remove the pins from their grenades, in preparation for an attack.

All of a sudden, the first enemy figures appeared. 'Groups of Germans wearing overcoats over pyjamas climbed up slowly from the dugouts,' Young observed. They stood, staring in his direction. He didn't doubt that he and his men had been seen. They must have been instantly noticeable against the snow. More enemy figures appeared, but still no one opened fire. As for Young, he had to wait for Frost's signal – the single blast on the whistle, as he led his men through the doorway of the nearby chateau.

Frost found himself on the front driveway of the Château Gosset, feeling almost as if he were in a dream. As he stole through the snow towards the grand, arched entranceway, so a second force was circling around, to come at the building from the rear terrace. He was this close to what they believed was the headquarters of the radar station's Luftwaffe garrison, yet still no sign of the enemy. It felt eerie. Unsettling. And Frost could sense watching eyes.

He crept ahead, closing on the four-storey building 'silently and stealthily', weapon at the ready. He reached the door. Even stranger: it was hanging open. No need to ring the bell, he told himself, wryly. But was it a trap? He felt for his whistle. It was 0040 hours, and they'd been on the ground for just twenty minutes. Frost brought the whistle to his lips and blew a 'single, long blast'.

Moments later he'd charged into the chateau's dark interior, six men on his heels, the rest of his force hitting it simultaneously from the rear. Without pausing to check, grenades were hurled through doorways and rooms swept with Sten fire. Even as he and his men attacked, Frost could hear wild yells issuing forth from the direction of the paraboloid, plus long bursts of fire from a machinegun. It didn't sound like a British weapon.

But he had other worries on his mind right now. The ground floor of the chateau seemed devoid of furniture. Deserted, almost.

Uninhabited. His men dashed from room to room, checking for any enemy presence. All of a sudden, bursts of fire echoed from a top-floor window. Figures stormed up the staircase, yelling obscenities and screaming 'Surrender!' Nagel was in the vanguard crying '*Hände hoch!*' But the fire from the upper storey continued unabated.

A German sentry had spotted the raiders going into action at the Würzburg, and he was raking Young and his section with fire. Within seconds Frost's men had kicked open the door to his room, cutting down the figure at the window with long bursts of Sten fire. The chateau was taken, but its storming had raised more questions than it answered. The place had proved empty of furnishings, maps, files or communications kit, and otherwise deserted. It was certainly no headquarters, that was for sure, which probably explained why it had been so lightly defended.

Frost would later learn that an RAF bomber had dropped a stick of incendiaries on the building, several months back, one of which had crashed through the roof and landed on a *Feldwebel's* bed. Following that, the German garrison had decided the chateau made too distinctive a target. They had moved permanently into the bunkers adjacent to the Würzburg.

Which was where Lieutenant Young and his men were in the midst of fierce and bloody action.

Chapter 14

Frost's whistle blast was the signal for all hell to be let loose. At the Würzburg station, *Flieger* Heller saw the *Unteroffizier* in charge unleash a long burst from the French light machinegun, rounds from the weapon skittering across the snow all around the figures gathered there. For a brief moment the Würzburg's defenders had mistaken the mystery force for their own troops, coming to reinforce their position. The volley of grenades that had been lobbed in their direction following the whistle blast had clarified things very swiftly.

Lieutenant Young had led the charge, the Jock Platoon raiders yelling out their Scottish battle cries as they dashed forwards, leaping the wire and hurling grenades into the nearest trenches and bunkers. 'We hunted them out of the cellars, trenches and rooms with hand grenades, automatic weapons, revolvers and knifes,' Young wrote in his war diary of this brutal stage of the battle. He had Sergeant Gregor McKenzie on his shoulder, a Black Watch veteran and his hard-as-nails NCO. Together they used bursts from their Stens to silence the *Unteroffizier's* gun, cutting him down in a bloody heap.

Grenade after grenade was hurled, the cliff-tops echoing with the sharp crack of explosions and the cries of the dying and wounded. Smoke drifted eerily over the scene. A German soldier was felled by a grenade, just as he was trying to detonate the demolition charges, which had been planted around the paraboloid in case of just such an emergency. In the citation for the medal McKenzie would win, he was praised for spearheading the attack, leading by example. 'He was personally responsible for killing several of the enemy and showed great gallantry under fire.'

Nagel, the SOE man and German interpreter on the mission, joined Young and McKenzie at the Würzburg. The raiders were 'absolutely fabulous' in action, he would remark, clearing the trenches at close quarters on all sides. The German troops had 'never seen such savages' as Jock Company, Nagel declared.

'In a few minutes we had captured the set and the defenders were dead,' wrote Young. Seeing the carnage unleashed by the paratroopers, the few German survivors had turned and fled. One of those was *Flieger* Heller, who made a dash towards the cliffs. But as Young moved through the trenches, finishing off the enemy, he spotted the distinctive figure trying to escape. Young gave chase. In his panic, Heller tumbled over the cliff-edge, but managed to cling onto a ledge just yards below. Young arrived, only to find Heller trying to climb back up again, while simultaneously raising his hands in surrender.

The sight of it was too much for the British lieutenant: he burst out laughing. 'I had never seen anything funnier than a German trying to scramble up the lip of a cliff with his hands up,' Young remarked. Perhaps it was because of that, or maybe he was just mindful of how they'd failed to take even the one prisoner – either way, Young decided to spare Heller's life. It was a rare act of mercy by the man spearheading the first bloody and brutal minutes of battle, and not all of Young's men would approve of the way he had finished off some of the enemy.

Having searched Heller, Young marched him back to the paraboloid, where he was confronted by one of his own men. Sergeant McKenzie seemed shocked at the wanton bloodshed, facing up to Lieutenant Young and accusing him of being a 'cruel bastard'. Before the matter could get any more heated, the commanding figure of Major Frost arrived. He reminded everyone of their orders: they were to 'take only the experts prisoner and to kill the remainder.' Doubtless, some of those that had been killed *were* German radar experts, so Sergeant McKenzie had a point, but there was little time to argue about it now.

Frost ordered a cordon of steel to be flung around the radar station. This was the objective of the raid – the prize - and it needed to be safeguarded at all costs. To that end, he called for most of those at the Château Gosset to move down to the Würzburg. But as figures began to dash the hundred yards across the snow separating the two sites, so a machinegun opened up from the direction of Le Presbytère, some 300 yards north-west of their position. Caught in the fire as he exited the chateau, one man stumbled. Operation Biting had just suffered its first casualty. Private H. McIntyre died where he fell.

There was no time to pause or mourn. Frost ordered Lieutenant Naumoff and his men to fan out on the far side of the radar pit, establishing a screen of Bren gunners to unleash a barrage of fire on Le Presbytère, so blocking any further incursions from that direction. If any German troops tried to creep closer, they were to be nailed by the shorter-range Stens.

One man who formed up that cordon was Private Scott – the unfortunate figure who'd got bashed around the head by a container, even as he'd made his jump. Seemingly fully recovered, he was placed on a Bren gun menacing the woodland. Shortly, he noticed 'six men in single file' advancing towards their position. 'There was no order to challenge them, so I fired a couple of short bursts and they went to ground.' It occurred to Scott that with enemy forces creeping closer, 'we would get something in our backs when we withdrew.'

His defences sorted, Frost turned his attention to their lone prisoner, *Flieger* Heller. He was worried at the speed and vigour of the German response, plus he had urgent questions to put to the man. It was now that Nagel, Frost's German interpreter, would prove his value many times over. Nagel stepped up to the prisoner, grabbed the swastika sewn onto his blue Luftwaffe coat and ripped it off in enraged disgust. Via Nagel, Frost demanded of the prisoner how many German troops were in the immediate vicinity, and especially at the beach.

Flieger Heller seemed to ponder this for a moment, before puffing himself up and answering, defiantly: 'A thousand.' Once Nagel had translated, Sergeant McKenzie figured the man had to be lying, and it would be a good idea if he told the truth. Accordingly, he 'hit the Hun a hell of a belt on the jaw', as Frost described it. Nagel grabbed the stunned figure by the lapels and dragged him upright, threatening to kill him if he didn't start talking. By now, all of Heller's bravado seemed to have gone. He was young and he was terrified. He started to shake with fear.

Trying to calm the man, Nagel promised to keep him alive, as long as he cooperated. There were no more than a hundred troops assigned to the radar's immediate defences, *Flieger* Heller admitted. That was what Frost had been led to believe. Now that Heller had been broken, he really started to talk, and his next words worried Frost greatly. He was Luftwaffe, he said, and he and his fellow radar operators had been woken sixty minutes ago with the warning that British parachutists had landed. Frost's instinct that they had been tracked and watched all the way had proven largely correct, which left him wondering when the first enemy reinforcements might put in an unwelcome appearance.

It was a chilling proposition. There were armoured cars and panzers in the area. Against those kinds of forces he and his men would have zero defences, for their heaviest weapons were the Brens. Did any of the local garrisons have mortars, Frost demanded of the prisoner. Those stationed at Le Presbytère did, Heller answered, but they were Luftwaffe as well, so not well versed in the use of such weaponry. Some small relief there, Frost told himself. Either way, there was little time to lose.

By now, the 685th infantry unit that had been carrying out their night exercise had reached Le Presbytère. They brought with them two light machineguns, which they set up in the woods at the western corner of the fortified farmstead. Together, there were sixty troops positioned at Le Presbytère now – mixed Luftwaffe and infantry. Most were armed with Mauser rifles, which put the Würzburg station well within range.

'I was getting a little worried,' Frost would report of this moment, with typical understatement, 'for the German fire was increasing.' He called for Vernon and Cox, together with the sappers, to head over from the point where they had taken cover, just to the south of the radar.

In manhandling their trolley over some wire, Cox had managed to cut his hands. 'First blood to Jerry,' he'd muttered to himself grimly. From his vantage point at the lip of the gorge, he'd heard the sound of fighting echoing across from the chateau and the radar site. 'The rattle of machinegun fire and the shouts of the Germans and British were almost continuous,' he remarked. Having lain in waiting for a good twenty minutes, he was itching to get at the Würzburg.

It was 0100 when they heard the call, voices yelling for Vernon, Cox and their team to dash forward: 'Come on, the RE!' They darted across the snow, slipping inside the defensive cordon, where 'parachute troops had taken up a position around it and were kneeling down'. Cox found the Würzburg to be housed in a pit dug into the ground, surrounded by a sheltering wall of turf. Several dugouts branched off it: one for tools, one for electric power, and the third complete with cots for the off-duty radar crew.

As incoming fire pinged and snarled off the metal apparatus, voices kept yelling at Cox to 'Keep down!' But he was utterly transfixed by what they'd found here, and to be so close to it; to have it within their grasp. It was beautifully engineered. Grabbing his notepad, he began to scribble down his observations. 'Design very clean and straightforward . . . Like a searchlight on a rotatable platform, mounted on a flat, four wheeled truck. Truck has its wheels raised and is well sandbagged up to platform level. Paraboloid is ten feet diameter and hinged, so that radio beam can be swung freely up or down or sideways . . .'

The entire device could 'rotate through 360 degrees' and 'move with the touch of a finger'. It could be raised and lowered, 'radiating the beam from sea level to several thousand feet . . . Telefunken labels everywhere . . .' Telefunken was the German manufacturer. A cabin containing the display lay to one side. 'Tearing aside the rubber curtain that protected the units, we saw our prize, switched off but still warm.' Cox's notes became more particular now, as he studied the 'transmitter . . . the first stage of the receiver . . . metal-finned rectifier . . . the Pulse Gear . . . a 3-inch cathode ray tube . . . the intermediate amplifier . . .'

There was 'just enough light to work by, with moon reflected off snow,' but now and again Cox had to risk a quick flash by torchlight to check detail. All the while the incoming fire was intensifying. 'Zing! Zing! went two bullets by my ear,' Cox recalled. Having realised the set was still warm, he was more than a little intrigued. 'Hey, Peter!' he called to Nagel, having to yell to make himself heard above the deafening noise of battle. 'This thing's still hot. Ask Jerry if he was tracking our aircraft.'

Nagel put the question to Heller, their by-now very helpful and cooperative prisoner. Heller confirmed that they had been. First the Freya had picked up the fleet of Whitleys at a distance, then the Würzburg at around twenty miles. As the warplanes had come in low and practically straight down their throats, the Würzburg operators had expected to get bombed, so they'd powered down the unit and taken to the shelters, their position being 'extremely exposed'.

Heller seemed convinced that the 'English killed and ate their prisoners,' Cox noted. Indeed, he appeared plagued by such irrational worries. That January, he had been on leave and he'd confided in his wife about the isolation of their top-secret radar station. It was so out on a limb that 'the English might easily make a raid and capture it,' he'd told her. Weeks later they'd done just that, and now Heller seemed worried about whether his wife was some kind of a traitor, passing intelligence to the British.

Cox didn't mind what fears might assail Heller, as long as they kept him in line. An experienced radar operator, his testimony would be crucial to helping them reconstruct the paraboloid back in Britain and to uncovering its secrets. As Cox finished making his notes, a sapper started smashing off the Würzburg's labels, using a hammer and cold chisel: they constituted vital pieces of intelligence for Jones and the boffins at TRE. But every sound ringing out from the paraboloid, or flash of light pulsing out across the snow, drew a storm of enemy fire in return.

'Heavy firing came from the farm [Le Presbytère],' Lieutenant Young remarked. 'Soon bullets were striking the set, but Vernon and Cox worked on undaunted.'

Lieutenant Vernon broke out his Leica and snapped off the first photographs, but the glare of the flash threw the paraboloid and the wreckers into sharp contrast, silhouetted by blinding flare against snow. It drew a vicious hail of fire. Figures to left and right unleashed a string of curses at Vernon, but the lieutenant had his orders. He snapped off another photo, with similar effect: bursts of fire tore furrows through the drifts to either side, rounds snarling and ricocheting off the paraboloid's steel structure. More angry yells and swearing from the paratroopers.

Finally, Frost intervened, suggesting that it wasn't worth getting his entire force killed for a few lousy photos. Indeed, it was high time to start the looting proper. Grabbing their SOE-supplied burglary bags, the team got to work. Cox didn't want to leave anything, deciding 'to take all I could in the time allotted'. He and Vernon got busy unscrewing the Pulse Gear and Amplifier, which came away with ease. 'Everything was solid and in good order,' Cox noted. The exception was the aerial, situated in the very centre of the dish, which proved to be jammed tight.

Those men detailed to remove it were horribly exposed to the enemy's fire. One, Sapper Stan Haliwell, vaulted onto the wall surrounding the Würzburg, brandishing a hacksaw as he prepared to slice off the aerial. From his vantage point he could just about lean into the dish and reach it. But his next thought was whether 'the power had been switched off, otherwise it might have been a shocking experience'.

He paused for a moment, as bullets cut through the air all around, wondering if the insulated handle of his hacksaw was enough to prevent electrocution. In that instant Lieutenant Vernon dared another flash, to get a photo of the aerial in situ, 'which risked a perfect hail of bullets'. There was some 'writing and signs' daubed in white paint on the inside of the dish. It looked like a diagram of a bomber, with dozens of markers against it, plus one of a ship, with a couple of marks against that too. They had all the appearances of 'kills' chalked up on the side of an aircraft.

With little time to vacillate, Sapper Haliwell 'took a chance and . . . started sawing'. The blade flew through the metal, which seemed to be some kind of softer alloy, slicing the device free in seconds. The sleek, black, T-shaped unit came away intact, the aerial itself being almost two-thirds the height of a man. Haliwell was ordered to 'guard it with his life'. Now the challenge was to get it down to the beach and spirited away to Britain, and to the boffins who so coveted it.

Busy in the Würzburg's innards, Cox found there were 'bullets flying much too close to be pleasant', but at least he was sheltered by 'the metal of the paraboloid itself'. The screws holding the transmitter in place seemed too deeply recessed to be reachable. He ran through Jones's shopping list of the pieces of the paraboloid he absolutely needed: '1. Aerial complete (this is probably in the centre of the paraboloid). 2. The aerial probably connects to "something". Bring me the "something"'.

Cox was convinced the transmitter was that something, and he was determined not to leave without it. He flashed a light around to check: no doubt about it, they would have to use brute force to rip it free. His momentary use of the light didn't prove very popular. 'Each time we flashed a light to see what we were doing, there were howls of protest from our fellow parachutists,' Cox would recall of this moment. 'I can . . . understand how they felt. We were busy, but they were just standing or kneeling there, being shot at.'

Calling for Vernon, the two men braced their feet against the structure, as another sapper wielded a crowbar. They 'gripped the handles and body of the transmitter, violently lifted it up and then down, until with a rending sound it came away . . .' They'd torn the transmitter free, together with the frame that held it. This was an immense stroke of good fortune, for the frame turned out to be a vital piece of the paraboloid's technology in itself. It constituted a remarkable switching device, allowing the Würzburg's signal to be beamed out and the echoes received back again, all via the same aerial – a crucial feature of the design.

It was 0115 by now, and Vernon, Cox and the sappers had managed their wrecking mission in record time. But Frost was getting anxious. 'The fire from the edge of "Le Presbytère" increased and it became extremely uncomfortable in our area,' he remarked. He gave the word: they needed to get moving. Using crowbars, the wreckers indulged in a last-minute free-for-all, ripping out whatever they could get their hands on.

Vernon risked a final dash below ground, to the bunker situated immediately beneath the paraboloid. He flashed his torch around, spying a bloodied corpse slumped in one corner. It looked as if the German had been shot while trying to dash out of the enclosed space. A horrible way to die. Off the bunker lay a small tunnel, leading to a pit lined with corrugated iron, in the very centre of which was a steel box. From above echoed the muffled thumps of gunfire, plus the yells of the paratroopers. No time to investigate further. What they couldn't steal away they were going to sabotage, anyway.

He hurried out again. 'We were under fire from the wood, and they seemed to be sniping at us,' Vernon remarked. It was high time to make themselves scarce. Together with Cox and the other sappers, he piled the radar loot high on the trolley – transmitter, receiver, aerial, small screen, pulse generator, frequency amplifier, dials and displays, plus several boxes housing complex electronic circuitry whose function wasn't immediately obvious.

Frost's anxiety reached fever pitch, as a paratrooper reported that lights had been spotted: vehicles were approaching Le Presbytère. Were they trucks bringing reinforcements, or the dreaded armour? There was no way of knowing. But the very fact that the Germans were driving into battle with their vehicles showing lights – i.e. not observing a blackout – reflected the urgency of their movements. Whoever or whatever those vehicles constituted, no one doubted that they were there with deadly intent.

More to the point, it was barely an hour since the first para-troopers had touched down, and already the enemy seemed to be mustering reinforcements and firepower. The response time of the German coastal units seemed to be far quicker than either the intelligence had suggested, or the mission planners had anticipated. Frost made his decision. He ordered an immediate withdrawal, with all forces heading for the beach.

He sent a runner to Lieutenant Naumoff, commanding the

cordon of men facing off against the forces at Le Presbytère. Naumoff was to fall back with Frost's men, leading the way to the beach. 'Don't forget the password – BITING!' Frost urged his runner. Naumoff was far from being a trigger-happy kind of fellow, but he'd been in the heat of combat for some time now. A mystery figure dashing up from behind might be in real danger of being shot, if he couldn't deliver the password.

Of course, Frost had no idea what might await them when they reached the beach. Had Lieutenant Charteris and his Seaforth Highlanders made an appearance? Or had Ross and his men been forced to attempt to clear it unaided? Was the route to the sea via the Bruneval gorge even clear? With no radio contact with any of his units, Frost was reduced to using his whistle and runners to communicate with his men. There was only one way to find out what had happened at the shoreline. He would have to go there and see for himself.

Two miles to the south of Frost's position, Junior Charteris was very much alive and fighting. At first he'd taken the most obvious course of action, pushing north towards the sound of battle. Shortly he'd spied 'the lighthouse on the Cap d'Antifer, and I knew where I was'. He'd been dropped near a small hamlet called L'Enfer, some three miles south of the radar stations. He figured he and his men had covered a third of the distance that separated them from the beach. They'd try to slip between Bruneval and the sea, making for that narrow neck of terrain to avoid the German troops stationed in the village. Or so he intended.

In fact, *Oberfeldwebel* Huhn had already dispatched his patrols, probing the terrain around Bruneval village in search of the British parachutists. It was one of those units that Charteris and his men were first to encounter. Quite without warning, a fierce burst of fire rang out from the night-dark landscape, bullets cutting the air. One of Charteris's men fell. Private Donald Sutherland had been hit multiple times in the shoulder. Charteris made a dash for the cover of some nearby woodland, crying for his men to follow.

Sutherland, though badly wounded, was urged to keep up. They could wait for no man. Though he tried to stagger onwards, Sutherland quickly fell behind. Having dragged the wounded man into some cover and given him morphine, Charteris pressed on. They couldn't afford to delay. 'I was sure . . . that speed was more important than silence,' he remarked, as he led his men crashing through the trees. Having been ambushed due south of Bruneval, he reasoned they had no choice but to detour inland, passing to the east of the village.

As they charged through the woods in a dogleg, Charteris heard a sudden scream of alarm. Glancing in that direction, he spied 'a Jerry about 4 or 5 yards from us'. The German had actually joined Charteris's patrol, keeping with it 'for some time', mistaking it for a group of fellow Germans. Having discovered his error, he'd let out the bloodcurdling scream. Charteris levelled his weapon and pulled the trigger. But in the rush of the moment, he'd forgotten to release one of its two safety catches, and it failed to fire. The German, eyes wide with terror, loosed off a shot with his rifle. It was almost point-blank range, but in his fear and shock he'd failed to take aim. The bullet whistled harmlessly into the trees.

Behind Charteris, Sergeant A. Gibbons, his second in command, levelled his Sten, murder in his eyes. The figure to whom the German had first attached himself was Private Tom Hill, who was loaded down with four pan-magazines of Bren ammunition. Realizing he was in danger of getting felled by Gibbons' Sten, Hill dropped to the floor. An instant later, Gibbons let rip with 'the whole of the Sten magazine', cutting the lone enemy figure down.

Charteris led his men onwards, hurrying through 'scrubby and difficult' terrain. They reached the eastern fringes of the village, but Charteris didn't pause. He plunged through seemingly deserted streets, making a 'lot of noise', but finally reaching the road that ran through the gorge direct to the sea. Placing a Bren gunner on the near side to provide cover, Charteris led the dash across open ground. From there, they'd climb before turning west, to take the beach from the high ground.

But as Charteris and his men began to dash across and scale the 400 feet of the valley's far side, a hidden enemy gunner opened fire. The raiders were caught on the hillside, with only scattered bushes for cover. Tracer rounds threw fiery arcs across the gorge, as Charteris's Bren-gunner, and the troops of *Oberfeldwebel* Huhn traded shots, the narrow defile echoing with fire. As machine-guns stitched rows of blasted holes in the snow, Charteris's group became scattered. By the time he'd reached the heights the young lieutenant had no more than ten men remaining.

The rear end of his patrol had cut loose in the gorge, but Charteris knew them to be 'stout fellows' who would march 'to the sounds of the guns'. Indeed, several of those men proceeded to enter 'the village of Bruneval and two of them killed three Germans with a knife,' Frost would report of their actions. 'In general, the paratroops were very keen on their knives, so much so that I saw several of them plunge them into dead Germans.' Such was the hunger to strike back at the enemy, at this early stage of the war, not to mention the raw and burning hatred.

From his clifftop position, Charteris could hear the noise of battle echoing all around now. Most worryingly, there was fierce firing from the direction of the sea, which had to mean their evacuation route was yet to be secured. In which case, he had to up his pace, for his men were needed at the beach, some 500 yards from their present location. Laden with their heavy weapons, Charteris 'pushed on with the remainder of the men, moving still at a fast lollop,' and despite the exhaustion that was beginning to take hold.

As Charteris and his men began to move, there was an ear-splitting roar: the demolition charges on what remained of the Würzburg had detonated, ripping through the dish and the cabin, hurling plumes of smoke and debris high into the air, mangled components landing with a sharp hiss in the snow to either side.

'That is one less Würzburg: the REs have blown it,' Cox remarked, simply. The aim of this was purely deception: there had been nothing much left to destroy. It was to hide the truth of their daring theft from the enemy. As for Frost and the rest of his raiders, they were hurrying for the beach, struggling to drag their heavy trolley-load of loot through thick snow.

Some 3,000 yards offshore, the Tormentor flotilla also found itself in some trouble. Dark and silent, the assault boats and MGBs should have been invisible, their silhouettes merging with the moonlit-grey smudge of the shoreline. It would take nothing less than an enemy vessel sailing into their midst for the flotilla to be spotted. But shortly before 0200 hours, that was precisely what appeared to be happening. The flotilla had closed to '1.8 miles from the beach,' when they sighted 'four enemy ships . . . approximately one mile to seaward.'

The German vessels were silhouetted against the moon's luminance. Commander Cook recognized the distinctive forms of 'two single funnel Destroyers, and two "E" or "R" boats.' The E-boat – German *Schnellboot* (fast boat) – was feared by Allied sailors. Streamlined, sleek, seaworthy and heavily armed – both with torpedo tubes and cannon – the E-boats could outgun and outrun anything in the British flotilla. The similarly sized R-boats – German *Raumboote* (minesweepers) – were also well-armed with cannon and depth charges. As for the two German destroyers, they would have the Tormentor flotilla at their absolute mercy.

In one of the MGBs, Lieutenant Bill Wescott – the early 'hush-hush' recruit into the Tormentor flotilla – was aghast at the proposed course of action his boat's commander suggested taking. 'Thank goodness I did not know our role when we set sail from Portsmouth,' he remarked. Wescott's MGB was to act as the decoy if any German ships spotted the Tormentor flotilla, 'to engage and draw them away from Bruneval beach!' It would be a suicide missions in all but name, as the MGB would be easy fodder for the German warships.

As the enemy vessels drew level with the British ones, the four warships reduced speed to a dead slow. After a few minutes in which the Tormentor crews could do little more than hold their breath and pray, the ships began to move again, but on a clearly altered course. Had they been alerted to the Tormentor flotilla's exact position? What else could explain their behaviour? One of those waiting on the assault boats, Sergeant Eric Gould, was 'scared to death' at the sight of the powerful warships, especially when he overheard a sailor's whispered remark: 'God, I hope they don't see us, or they'll blow us out of the water.'

Fortunately, the Tormentor flotilla was 'lying under the silhouette of the cliffs. All our engines were stopped, so no noise was heard'. Eventually, the German vessels steamed past, seeming not to have seen or heard anything untoward. In fact, the German ships were making for the port of Le Havre, a few miles further south of their position. They had slowed and altered course, awaiting the flash of a harbour light to guide them in.

Cook and his men would receive fulsome praise for remaining 'extremely cool in the presence of two enemy Destroyers and two "E" or "R" boats'. Indeed, Cook's earlier decision to move his flotilla closer inshore had been fortuitous in the extreme. Had he not done so, the German vessels would have steamed right into their midst. As a report subsequently pointed out, 'the dispersion point, three miles off shore, may have proved an unhappy one as it appeared to be directly on the enemy shipping route.'

Ashore, the selection of the evacuation beach also seemed to be proving a distinctly 'unhappy one', for the German defenders weren't about to give it up any time soon. Lieutenant Ross had lingered on the DZ for as long as he could countenance, but there had been zero sign of Junior Charteris and his men. In the assault plan, it was their job to spearhead the beach assault, while Ross and his gunners would remain at the mouth of the Bruneval gorge, providing cover. With no sign of Charteris or his men, Ross had no option but to clear that much-coveted stretch of shoreline himself.

He'd set off, leading his force along the heights in the direction of the sea. Moonlight glinted and glittered off the snow. It made them all so very visible. Ross felt horribly exposed. He found a patch of sparse woodland, which tumbled down into the depths of the gorge via a gully of sorts, providing a modicum of cover.

Sliding from tree to tree, he led the way downhill, making for the road below. But no sooner had they started the descent than a white flare erupted from the direction of the Stella Maris villa, throwing the entire gorge into stark relief. It was followed instantly by a long and savage burst of machinegun fire.

Ross dived into the snow, his men doing likewise, as they found themselves pinned under a murderous barrage. Risking getting his head blown off, he chanced a quick glance in the enemy's direction. The fire was coming from a series of defences set to the rear of Stella Maris – weapons pits, connected by trenches. He figured six or seven Mauser rifles were firing, plus the machinegun itself. All were in good cover with excellent fields of fire. Against that Ross boasted ten men, himself included, armed with two Bren guns and a handful of rifles – their only usable weapons at such range.

For long minutes the two sides traded fire, neither showing any sign of giving way. It had all the hallmarks of a stalemate. Ross and his men commanded the high ground, but the Germans had far better cover. Then one of his men, Sergeant Jimmy Sharp, began to half-crawl and half-slither down the slope, in what appeared to be a death-slide. Somehow 'dragging himself flat on the snow', that lone figure managed to reach the barbed wire barricade the enemy had thrown across the road. With unbelievable bravery, Sharp reached up and began to cut his way through.

Inside the Stella Maris villa the phone was ringing angrily. Initially, it was ignored, as men rushed to gather up ammo, grenades and more flare rounds to light up the battle scene. Eventually, Schmidt, the telephone orderly, grabbed it. On the line was Major Paschke, Commanding Officer of the 1st Battalion of the 685th Infantry, the unit tasked with the defence of this section of coastline. Paschke demanded to know what exactly was going on. Schmidt told him: they were under assault from British parachutists. Paschke demanded to speak to the *Feldwebel* in charge. Schmidt dashed outside to fetch him, but was immediately driven back in again.

The fire from the British was intensifying, accompanied by the deafening roar of grenades being thrown at close range.

Chapter 15

The snows at the lip of the gorge were now stained a violent red. Frost could barely believe it, but Gerry Strachan – bull-necked and tough, one of the foremost Ladies from Hell – had taken the full brunt of the burst. Seven rounds had torn into C Company's seemingly indestructible Company Sergeant Major, even as he'd led the trolley party towards the beach and its uncertain promise of safety.

It was the gunners positioned around Stella Maris villa who'd spotted Frost's party, sky-lined against the moonlight. Cox, too, had been caught in that first 'terrific hail of machinegun fire . . . little spurts of snow showed how near we were to getting a packet. I had the aerial in one hand, and that was struck by a bullet, and one of the sappers had a groove cut in his boot.' Rounds tore into the trolley too, piled high with its precious load.

Somehow, the looters had escaped that burst of fire unscathed . . . all barring Strachan, who'd been cut down as if by the Grim Reaper's scythe. Frost dragged his bloody form back from the brink, pulling him 'into some dead ground'. Crouching in what little cover he could find, he proceeded to try to save Strachan. He'd taken three rounds to the stomach, causing terrible injuries. Frost grabbed some field dressings, pressing them into Strachan's wounds in an effort to stop the bleeding, after which he administered a shot of morphine.

Each time any of his troops tried to move, 'the machine-gun opened up,' Frost reported. Much that the noise of battle might reverberate across the gorge, there was no safe way onwards dragging that unwieldy trolley, which was proving next to useless across such terrain. Perhaps they had been fools to ever think there would be. 'Obviously, something was seriously wrong with this part of the plan,' Frost concluded. As if to reinforce that impression, he heard a voice echo up from below.

It was Lieutenant Ross, yelling above the din of battle. 'Don't come down! The beach isn't taken yet!'

Moments later, a runner arrived from Lieutenant Timothy's party, bearing more bad news. On the heels of Frost's withdrawal, the Germans had advanced from Le Presbytère, and they'd already retaken the Château Gosset. Frost and his party were in danger of getting caught on the lip of the gorge along with their trolley-load of loot, trapped between the enemy forces below and those advancing from the rear.

Crouching low to avoid the fire, Frost issued an urgent set of orders. Cox and a few men were to stay there in cover and protect the booty come what may. Only once the enemy gunners had been silenced were they to attempt a descent. Lieutenant Young and Sergeant McKenzie were to take a few men forward, and go to Ross's aid. Frost, meanwhile, would lead an assault party back the way they had come, to drive off the enemy. Grabbing every man he could, including Lieutenant Vernon and several of his sappers, Frost hurried off, leading from the front as always – a long line of black figures disappearing into the snow.

At their vantage point, hunkered down with the trolley, Cox and those left with him were surrounded by discarded bags of wrecking gear. Lieutenant Vernon and his men had little further use for it, for they had the fight of their lives on their hands now. Cox felt very isolated. He could hear the battle for the beach raging below, 'punctuated by the explosions of grenades'. Minute by minute he lay there in the bullet-whipped snow, hardly daring to breathe. 'I could not join in the fight,' he remarked, 'because it was my job to look after the gear we had taken.' The wait seemed interminable, the inactivity sheer torture.

All of a sudden, a new sound reverberated across the headland. Incredibly stirring to Cox and his sappers, it must have struck the fear of God into the enemy. A crescendo of bloodcurdling yells rose above the battle noise: '*Caber Feigh! Caber Feigh! Caber Feigh!*' – Gaelic for 'The Antlers of the Deer'. Since time immemorial this had been the battle cry of the Seaforth Highlanders, whose distinctive cap badge displays a highland stag. Charteris and his men were making for the valley of death, leading a wild charge.

The battle for the Bruneval gorge assumed a ferocious, bloody intensity. Having joined Ross's force, Lieutenant Young and Sergeant McKenzie found themselves facing a resolute enemy 'fighting from secure pillboxes'. To make matters worse, 'flares and distress signals were going up from the German positions all around.' Above the deafening roar of battle, Young thought he could hear the 'ominous sounds of engines being started up and the menacing rattle of tank tracks', which made seizing the beach all the more vital.

Even as Ross, Young and McKenzie pressed home their attack down the throat of the gorge, so they heard 'heavy firing and cheering coming from the OTHER SIDE of the German positions. The two lost planeloads under Lieutenant Charteris . . . had arrived just at the crucial moment.'

Having dashed across the cliffs, Charteris led his men down a dry gully, arriving at the sea itself. 'I felt as naked as a baby,' he remarked, 'on the beach which I knew to be held by the enemy. I had thought for a month how to attack this house. I had examined all the photographs . . . but when I came to do so, the reality was quite different from the expectation.' He'd never once imagined assaulting the villa from the sea side, for obvious reasons.

Even so, the move proved a masterstroke. The garrison at Stella Maris was caught in a pincer movement – unintended, but highly effective all the same. The distraction caused by Charteris's frenzied charge along the beach, and their cries of *Caber Feigh!*, gave Ross and his men the opportunity they'd been waiting for. They rushed the wire barrier forming the road-block, forcing a way through. Seconds later, they were in among the German trenches to the rear of the villa, hurling grenades at close quarters.

By now, Charteris only had Sergeant Gibbons and two others of his men with him. Having been on the move and in combat for ninety minutes or more, they were close to exhaustion. But it did little to temper the ferocity of their assault. Showering the villa with volleys of grenades, they thundered across the road to storm it. Their grenades landed on the villa's wide balcony, which overlooked the sea, a whirlwind of shrapnel tearing through the windows.

Charteris and his men hurled more grenades into the basement, before storming through the villa's main doorway. 'We charged into the house shouting *"Hände hoch! Komm hier!"* . . . phrases we had learned for the occasion,' Charteris recalled. Inside one room, Corporal Georg Schmidt was still doggedly at his post, manning the telephone. On the far end, Major Paschke was trying to make himself heard, above the deafening noise of battle.

Hearing Charteris and his men entering the villa, Schmidt cut the call, extinguished the lights and darted into an inner room. Moments later figures burst in, spraying Sten rounds into the darkness. Schmidt could see them silhouetted in the doorway, but he could not bring himself to open fire. His small garrison had held out for ninety minutes, but it was now that Corporal Schmidt decided, sensibly, to surrender. Sergeant Jimmy Sharp – the man who had crawled alone to cut the wire – took him captive, explaining that shortly the German corporal would be making a journey by sea, '*nach England*'.

Charteris, meanwhile, hurried up onto the villa's flat roof. From behind the cover of the ornamental battlements, he spied the system of defences running uphill to its rear. He dashed back down again, and with Sergeant McKenzie at his side, lobbed a first grenade into the entrance to a trench, 'which began in a small yard cut out of the hillside behind the house'. Lieutenant Ross appeared, the two assault forces having linked up at last. Ross handed Charteris more grenades, after which the young lieutenant stole into the trench system, primed to clear what remained of its defenders.

A figure appeared with his hands raised in surrender. It was a young German, *Infanterist* (infantryman) Tewes, who was bleeding from a neck wound. He was taken captive. On the slope above, the final German position, a pillbox was stormed. Half a dozen of the raiders surrounded it, pouring fire into the slit windows, while two figures belly-crawled ever closer. Once they were within range, they posted grenades through the narrow openings.

The resulting blasts tore into its squat, slit-windowed interior.

Two German soldiers were felled by the explosions. The remainder broke and ran, making for the cover of the woodland lying a short distance inland. Charteris took charge of the pillbox now, siting a Bren gun there so as to menace the treeline, just in case the enemy had any ideas about trying to mount a counter-attack. That done, he organized the general defences, placing a cordon of men fifty yards inland to cover the gorge.

'I also posted men in the captured German slit trenches,' Charteris reported, 'and while doing this I remember wondering where the Navy was and looking out to sea. There was no sign of them and I began to think that we should not get back . . . By then, of course, the position was fairly serious because we were an hour behind schedule.'

It was 0230 by now, and Charteris was correct: things were running way behind time. Through no fault of their own they'd only just secured the beach, long after they were supposed to. More importantly, Frost and his raiders were scattered across the clifftops and still engaging with the enemy. Worse still, due to signals teams being dropped in the wrong place and kit malfunctions, neither Charteris nor Ross had a workable radio, which meant that they had no means to contact the Tormentor flotilla, to let them know the beach finally lay in friendly hands.

Commander Cook had been given a cut-off point at which he was to withdraw his boats, lest they get caught off the French coast come daybreak. 'If no signal to close the beach has been received by 0230,' and the cove appeared as it if might still lie in enemy hands, he was to 'order his force to return to England. The landing craft are not to wait . . . after 0315, as this is the latest time for beginning the return passage.' With every passing minute, that deadline was fast approaching.

Frost was painfully aware of how time was running out. He and his cobbled-together force had cleared the Château Gosset in a full-frontal charge, guns blazing. Under such a frenzied assault, the Luftwaffe troops had been driven off. That done, Frost was back at the clifftops, flashing out to sea with his torch, its lens covered by a blue filter. He was signalling the letter 'F for Freddy' in Morse – the agreed codeword using blue light, to signify that the beach was taken. Somewhat ominously, there was not a hint of any response from the moonlit waters.

At the lip of the gorge, Cox heard a cry echoing up from the depths below: the beach was taken! It was time to move. Under the influence of the morphine, the terribly wounded Strachan seemed capable of walking – just. Rambling and delirious, he was able to stumble forward. 'The slope was so steep that we abandoned the trolley,' Cox remarked, 'and the men carried the apparatus on their shoulders.' Like that, they dashed and skidded and lurched down the sharp incline.

Towards the bottom of the gorge a cry drew them up short: 'Halt! Who goes there?' Cox gave the password – BITING – and they were waved on.

They reached the road, turned right and made for the beach. The first sight that met Cox's eyes was Lieutenant Charteris, quartering a pillbox, warning that 'if there were any Germans left, to surrender at once.' Worryingly, there was no sign of any assault boats. The Tormentor flotilla was nowhere to be seen. Cox and his fellows took cover in the lee of the cliff, staring out to sea, wondering 'if we should be killed or taken prisoner.'

CSM Strachan began yelling orders. They made little sense. The men tried to ignore him, but Strachan was a man wholly unused to being sidelined, and especially since the morphine had been administered 'rather lavishly'. Heller, the prisoner seized at the Würzburg, was there too. At least he couldn't understand a word of the kind of nonsense that the semi-delirious Strachan was uttering. Few could, his speech was so slurred.

Lieutenant Timothy arrived on the beach. Seeing the shocking state of Strachan, the former Marks & Spencer salesman pulled out a cricket sweater from his pack. He'd worn it in the aircraft, as an extra layer. He offered it to the wounded Strachan. He was in need of its warmth on that icy, February beach,. As Strachan's blood seeped through the cricket-white, Lieutenant Timothy resigned himself to never getting it back again.

During the fierce battle for the gorge, Corporal Stewart, the Jock Company gambler, had taken a powerful blow to the head and was now one of the walking wounded. With blood seeping from under his jump helmet, he confessed that he feared that he was done for. 'I've had it,' he moaned, morosely. 'Here – take my wallet.' With that he stuffed it, thick with winnings, into the hands of the nearest man, Lance Corporal Freeman. Curious, Freeman inspected Stewart's injuries. 'Och, you've only got a scalp wound,' Freeman said, trying to reassure him. Stewart brightened, before demanding the return of his wallet in no uncertain terms.

In was 0235 hours by now. Offshore, a breeze began to blow, the resulting swell slapping against the pebbles. On that breeze rode a sea mist, ethereal at first, but thickening with every second. Visibility was dropping and the sea conditions were worsening, even as the men on that beach desperately needed those crewing the assault boats to ride to their rescue.

By now, a couple of signallers with working radios had made it to the beach. But try as they might, they could raise no response from the Tormentor flotilla. It was hugely frustrating. They were so near to pulling this off, and yet still so very far from safety. Lieutenant Ross ordered another piece of electronic gadgetry be activated. The raiders had been entrusted with a Rebecca-Eureka unit, a radio homing device deployed by SOE, one that was so secret it even had a built-in demolition charge, so it could be blown up if at risk of capture.

In theory, with the Rebecca unit beaming out a signal from the beach, the Eureka sited on one of the Tormentor craft should detect that signal and be able to home in upon it. In theory. In practice, Ross had little way of knowing if it was even working, let alone if anyone aboard Cook's flotilla had heard it, or was listening. Ross busied himself with a roll-call, trying to tally up if all men were accounted for. Along with the half-a-dozen wounded, they had two confirmed dead – Privates Scott and McIntyre – plus six missing.

Lieutenant Charteris tried to busy himself searching the prisoners, but he noticed that the sea looked 'very bright in the moonlight, and very, very empty'. It would be a dark irony if, having survived being dropped in the wrong place, and a running battle across miles of hostile terrain, the Navy failed to put in an appearance now. Frost arrived, having given up signalling with his torch from the cliffs. Upon learning of the sorry state of their radio communications, he ordered the first stage of the emergency procedure to be put into motion.

It was 0245, and they simply had to get the boats in. Any second now Frost expected to hear cries of alarm from the gorge, as enemy forces came rumbling around the far end. At Frost's signal, a green flare was fired from either end of the beach, the two lights arcing up into the heavens, to intersect directly above their position. Frost searched the horizon, eager for any sign that their signal had been seen, but there was nothing visible among the thickening mist.

Waiting under the cliff with their 'precious equipment', Cox and the sappers strained their ears for any signs of engines out to sea. 'Can you hear them?' he ventured. No one could. Cox was getting downhearted. Hope was ebbing away. One of his companions kept moaning that they were all going to get captured. Cox tried to argue that there was 'still plenty of time.' Trouble was, he didn't quite believe it himself any more.

Reluctantly, Frost ordered men from the beach to take up defensive positions on the heights above. Making a last stand on this cursed stretch of shoreline was the last thing that he wanted to do, but what other options were there? There was little need to direct the raiders to exactly where they needed to go. It was obvious. Cox noted how 'the fighting men could hear the sound of battle and started in a trot towards the same.' Like most, Lieutenant Young was aware of increased enemy fire as 'shells started whistling over'.

Frost's gaze wandered across the empty sea, alighting finally upon a small fishing boat. It was almost too insignificant to have warranted notice, but he figured that in extremis he could squeeze eight souls aboard, along with the trolley-load of loot. First places would go to the wounded, which left two others. One would be Cox for sure, the other very likely Vernon – the paraboloid's custodians. But did either have a modicum of seafaring experience? Frost just didn't know.

There was one last resort: the SOS signal. Frost figured he had nothing left to lose. He turned to his Very gunners and asked for 'Fireworks', the agreed codeword. The two figures dashed to either end of the beach, from where they unleashed a red flare, searing in an arced trajectory across the beach, their glowing flightpaths muted by the gathering mists. If seen, the SOS signal would signify – *grave danger; bring all craft in as quickly as possible*. But Frost was doubtful: visibility was no more than 800 yards by now.

Desperate eyes scanned the horizon, searching for the faintest sign of a response. There was none. As Frost well knew, there was an agreed codeword to be given over the radio if the Tormentor flotilla was unable to reach the beach. It was WILLOW. He fully expected to hear that now, over the airwaves - that was if his signallers could raise any kind of a contact. That would signify the very worst – that the raiders were now utterly on their own.

With 'a sinking heart' he called together his section commanders. Lieutenant Timothy had received reports from his outlying positions: headlamps had been spotted further inland, as convoys of vehicles converged on their position. Things were not looking good, to put it mildly. It could only be a matter of time now. Somehow, despite their fatigue, they had to organize the defence of an indefensible position.

Some 1,800 yards offshore, Commander Cook was plagued by anxiety. Wraiths of sea mist seemed to wrap themselves ever tighter around his assault boats, blinding them to the shore and muting all sound. Even so, Cook was well aware that the raiders had to be embroiled in the fight of their lives. Already he'd detected 'grenades, rifle and machinegun tracer bullets and occasional flares . . . in the vicinity of the valley'. But without a clear signal that the beach was theirs, it was impossible to determine what exactly he should do.

Repeatedly, his signallers had tried to make radio contact with the raiders, but no joy. Finally, Cook decided to chance his arm: 'although no reliable communications had been established, it was decided to close to the beach.' Slowly, engines running at minimum revs and muted, the flotilla of eight assault craft crept towards the mist-enshrouded shoreline, the gunners tense over their Bren guns and Boys anti-tank rifles, which were braced against sandbags set upon the gunwales.

Not a man among them spoke. The tension was almost unbearable.

At around 300 yards off-shore, Cook ordered the flotilla to a halt. Here they would loiter in silence, waiting for a sign. The first intimations of contact proved transitory. At 0230 hours a dim blue light was spotted blinking from the clifftops. But enshrouded in the shifting mists, Cook remained unsure what those 'faintest flashes' might signify. The torchlight was eclipsed by 'the brightness of the moon . . . coupled with machinegun flashes and pyrotechnics from the beach'.

Cook was left wondering whether those flashes constituted a friendly signal, or whether it was a ruse by the enemy to lure his flotilla closer into shore, within range of their guns. There was no way of knowing. But the next sign from the shore seemed wholly unambiguous: Cook's Eureka unit picked up its companion set, beaming a signal directly seaward. Now he had an exact fix on the beach, and a strong indication that it lay in friendly hands.

Moments later, a pair of green Very lights arced in a shallow inverted U-shape above where Cook now knew the beach had to lie. The meaning was crystal clear. Cook couldn't respond, for showing any lights might betray the presence of his flotilla. But he ordered the first two boats to head in 'immediately to embark troops', whereupon the next would follow. In two formations line astern the assault craft turned towards shore, taking 'soundings with poles' as they neared landfall.

Then, Cook's radio finally crackled into life. Contact had been made with a signaller ashore. He was calling for an emergency beaching. Cook gave the new order: all boats were to head for the beach as fast as possible, and those aboard should anticipate a hotly contested landing. Gunners hunched closer over their weapons, as engines roared and in line abreast the assault boats surged towards the shore, white water foaming at their blunt-nosed prows.

Riding in the lead craft was a distinctive figure: balding, scholarly, with thick, horn-rimmed glasses, the man codenamed Noah was itching to get sight of the fabled paraboloid. How much had Cox and his robbers managed to loot, he wondered; had they even managed to get their hands on the thing at all? Had they wrecked it, he fretted, or was it somehow miraculously intact? It seemed inconceivable that amidst all the din of battle, a sensitive set of electronic components – the enemy's top-secret radar unit – could have been spirited away safely. But Preist lived in hope.

As the boats emerged from the mist, a ragged cheer went up from the shore line. 'There they are! There they are!'

'The boats are here! The boats are coming in! God bless the ruddy Navy!'

Almost immediately, the flotilla came under a murderous hail of fire. German forces were swarming onto the clifftops, from where the open assault boats made easy targets, their dark shapes silhouetted against the moonlit sea. It was now that the vessel's gun-crews came into their own. The men of the South Wales Borderers and the Royal Fusiliers 'opened up a terrific and effective barrage on the enemy, who were pressing hard,' Cook reported.

He began yelling orders over a megaphone, to try to manage the chaotic landing, but his voice was drowned out by the roar of sixteen Brens and as many Boys rifles. Fire from the boats swept the cliff-tops, as heavily laden figures dashed towards the water's edge. But from the heights grey-uniformed figures lobbed down grenades, as machinegun fire swept down from several vantage points.

And so the savage battle for Bruneval beach was joined.

Chapter 16

On catching sight of the assault boats, men who had begun to lose heart felt their spirits soar. Charteris was elated. *By God, it's coming off,* he told himself joyfully. Having led the bloody attack on the radar station, Lieutenant Young could barely believe it when, 'materialising out of the darkness came the ugly shapes of our landing craft. Never had such ungainly vessels looked so beautiful.' He was doubly glad when the 'men of the Royal Fusiliers and South Wales Borderers . . . poured a hail of fire onto the cliff-top.'

Standing on that benighted stretch of pebbles, Frost faced a phalanx of assault boats whose gunwales seemed to be ablaze, Bren muzzles sparking fire. Spears of tracer scorched above his head, tearing into the enemy positions. But the Tormentor flotilla's onslaught would prove a double-edged sword. While it certainly put the enemy's heads down, 'the noise was indescribable,' Frost reported, 'and I could not make myself heard.' Chaos ensued.

The lead assault boat, ALC 134, was supposed to be reserved for the wounded, plus the looted kit. Cox, Vernon and the sappers waded into the icy swell, staggering under the weight of the radar components they carried. Cox himself was bearing the precious aerial, holding it above his head in an effort to keep the five-foot T-shaped device out of the water. Waist deep in the surf, he passed it into the eager hands of Preist, then clambered aboard. By the light of the moon the TRE scientist examined the sleek aerial, studying it in utter fascination.

So many men swarmed onto the vessel that shortly it became stuck fast. As figures jumped overboard to push and shove, so 'a machinegun opened up from the top of the cliff.' Bursts of fire tore into the water to either side of the boat, showing as angry splashes of white in the moonlight. 'We could see the tracer bullets,' Preist remarked. 'Obviously it was aimed at us. We were sitting ducks . . .' The ALC's gunners returned fire with interest, but the tide was falling now, and the greatest fear was a repeat of the disastrous dress-rehearsals, when the assault boats had become stranded on the Dorset coastline.

Ordering those in the water to heave for all they were worth, the ALC's skipper, Lieutenant Donald Quick, finally managed to free the craft. With its engines on full power he tried to pull away, but the boat was badly overloaded, some fifty raiders having crowded aboard. Lying low in the water, it was being swamped. Lieutenant Quick ordered all hands to bale, using whatever came to hand. Some of the Jock Company men were laden with the spoils of war: German rifles, bayonets, helmets. The latter were put to good use now, bailing out the ailing craft.

All the while, Preist, Cox and Vernon were desperately trying to prevent the delicate radar equipment from getting soaked in salty, gritty seawater. Having made just a few hundred yards, the overcrowded ALC's motor burned out, leaving the vessel wallowing on the swell and well within range of the enemy. It was now that an MGB roared to the rescue. Sailors threw a line over and took the stricken craft in tow.

Finally, ALC 134 seemed out of the worst, but not so her

sister ships. The skipper of ALC 125 decided to drop his kedge anchor – a light anchor commonly used by small craft to aid in steerage and to pull a vessel off a beach. But in the stiffening swell the anchor line failed, and the boat was about to broach, being driven broadside onto the rocks. The coxswain was forced to power away and to come around for another try, all the while under murderous fire.

Those raiders who'd suffered the worst injuries were being screamed at to keep moving. One ALC took several aboard, but pulled away too quickly and shipped water up to the men's knees. The boat's medical teams were frantically trying to inject morphine and to cope with sodden dressings and bandages, amidst icy, bullet-torn conditions. In all the chaos, one man tumbled into the freezing sea. He was hauled back aboard by the medics. Frozen stiff and in shock, he had to be 'dried and wrapped in blankets'. As for the badly wounded Strachan, he kept yelling out at the top of his lungs that he needed a drink.

Further down the shore, the skipper of ALC 135, Sub-Lieutenant Turner, was forced to leap into the water, using a rope to steady his craft. Even as bullets ripped into the swell to either side of him, Turner yelled for the raiders to wade out and jump aboard his vessel. Having loaded up fourteen sodden souls, he pulled off the beach, only to discover that one man had been left behind. Turner turned his assault boat around, dashed back in, and jumped into the sea once more to rescue that lone figure.

Frost and Charteris remained ashore, calling in the last of the rearguard. As men raced for the beach, there was a howling in the air above them and the first mortar crashed down, shards of blasted rock cutting across the scene. 'By this time the enemy's fire was all over the place,' Charteris reported. It was his men who'd been providing the final defensive perimeter. They fell back in haste, making for the one remaining assault craft.

'I and my Platoon were the last to board,' Charteris remarked. 'Major Frost was the last onto the boats.' Frost found himself having 'to wade out about five or ten yards' to make it. Once he was aboard, the assault boat pulled away, but it loitered just a little offshore 'to see if anyone was left on the beach'. When no one appeared, it turned for the open sea, harried by fire.

It was 0315 as that last boat drew away from the rocks. Even as it did, there was the snarl of heavy engines and the flash of headlamps, as a column of enemy vehicles nosed through Bruneval gorge. They would arrive at the beach, only to discover that their prey had slipped away. As a German military report would conclude: 'The Commandos [sic] embarked just as strong reinforcements reached Bruneval.' Light artillery and motorized infantry units had converged on the battle scene, followed shortly by a column of panzers. Against such armour or guns, Frost and his raiders would have been rendered all but defenceless.

As soon as the Tormentor flotilla was out of enemy range, ALC 134 was brought close to MGB 312. Preist leapt across from one ship to the other, telling 'the chaps on the ALC to hand the gear up'. He found himself 'leaning over the rail. When I went up, the ALC went down. It was tricky. I visualised with horror the consequences, after all the hard work . . . of dropping the stuff in the drink'. Once all the radar components had been transferred and Cox brought aboard, MGB 312 set a course for England at its top speed of twenty knots.

As the sleek vessel powered away from the French coast, pounding through the swell, Cox, no seaman, became distinctly queasy. Preist warned him this was no time to be seasick; not just yet anyway. First, he needed to come below decks, to relate to Preist all that he had learned at the site of the fabled radar. Preist, of course, had been dying to visit it. He'd not been able to. Securing Cox's eye-witness account while the memories were still fresh – that was the next best thing.

'It's a beautiful job,' Cox remarked, eyeing the pile of looted kit. Preist agreed. The German radar equipment was spectacular. 'The Jerries must have had RDF [radar] as long as us, or longer,' Cox added. Again, Preist agreed. Once they got to examine the loot, they'd know exactly how long the enemy had had it for, but he suspected 'the total will be in years, and nearer ten to one.' Then he warned Cox to 'keep it all under your hat, my friend.'

There were still some trying to argue the Germans didn't have radar, a coterie of senior British scientists foremost amongst them. As the young and brilliant R. V. Jones had discovered, hubris and complacency ran deep, engendering an emperor's-new-clothes scenario: much that the evidence might stack up to the contrary, the nay-sayers stubbornly refused to accept the enemy's mastery of radar. That the German technology was actually this advanced and so beautifully made – it was sure to cause a storm of controversy.

Even as Cox, Preist and the looted paraboloid powered away from the French coast, Frost received alarming news. Transferred to one of the MGBs, he learned that a radio signal had just been received from the beach. Two men were calling for help. They'd been among those dropped at the wrong location, near the small hamlet of L'Enfer. Fighting their way north, they'd become pinned under heavy fire, which had prevented them from getting to the beach. But they were there now, and desperate to be rescued.

In the chaos of the evacuation, it had proven impossible to count everyone in. Frost was hardly surprised that men had been forgotten. He argued that he should take one of the assault boats and return to look for them. Commander Cook, rightly, refused. He explained to Frost about the powerful fleet of German E-boats and destroyers lurking nearby. He could not risk a boatload of sailors and raiders alike. As it was, they had precious little time to put enough distance between themselves and the enemy, come daybreak.

Frost hated leaving a single man behind. But reluctantly, he had to accept the sense in Cook's words. In fact, in the confusion of the withdrawal it was actually six of the raiding party who had been unwittingly abandoned. One of them was seriously injured, and three of those left behind were the Company's DIY medics, those equipped with supplies of bandages and morphine. Typically, they had been reluctant to leave the side of a wounded comrade.

The more powerful MGBs took the assault boats in tow now. Frost's spirits received a boost when a signal was received from MGB 312, speeding across the Channel with the loot. Preist confirmed that they had 'managed to get practically everything that was wanted'. The key objective of the mission had been achieved.

Amazingly, the raiders had suffered only two killed in action, Privates McIntyre and Scott, though they had eight wounded on the boats, some of whom, like Strachan, were in a bad way. The priority now had to be to get those aboard the Tormentor flotilla safely out of enemy waters. But the wind had stiffened to a Force

5, slowing the boats to six or seven knots. In the heavy seas the open assault craft started shipping water, and tow ropes began to snap. Progress proved painfully slow, as they inched away from the shoreline.

On Bruneval beach, three figures had found uncertain refuge in a small sea cave. Privates Thomas and Willoughby, plus Lance-Corporal McCallum, were three of the six men left behind. They'd actually reached the beach just as the final assault craft had slipped away. No amount of shouting or waving had managed to call it back again, and neither had their radio signals. As German forces had surged out of the gorge, the men had slipped into the cavern's beckoning embrace – the only place of hiding they could find.

The enemy soldiers didn't tarry long. After a brief search they were gone. Thomas, Willoughby and McCallum ventured out, only to discover two more C Company men – Privates Embury and Cornell – hidden among the rocks. The fugitives huddled together, discussing in hushed tones what on earth they were to do. Fortunately, all had received a similar briefing on escape and evasion procedures. Two options seemed open to them. One, to linger on the coast and try to get away by boat. The other, the long journey overland to southern – Vichy – France, and from there to neutral Spain or Portugal.

All agreed they stood a greater chance if they divided forces. Embury and Cornell reckoned they were better off heading inland. The other three favoured a seaborne means of escape. With a final farewell, the two parties split up, stealing away into the uncertain night and to whatever the future might hold. Thomas, Willoughby and McCallum made their way south along the shoreline, until they came upon a larger cave. They crept inside, deciding to wait there until first light, and whatever promise of escape the dawn might bring.

Via the illumination from the moon Embury and Cornell managed to scale the cliffs, but it proved terrible going. Neither had a map, although one did have a compass sewn into the button of his coat. Using that, they pressed onwards for three miles, until they reached the outskirts of Le Tilleul village. Remembering their briefings about how Normandy farmers were generally inclined to help the British, they sneaked into a half-timbered barn. Come morning, they would seek assistance – food and sustenance, at the very least – from whoever the owner might turn out to be.

Le Tilleul lay no more than a mile from Le Presbytère, where the Luftwaffe garrison they had been fighting that night were quartered. Of course, the farmer might be pro-Nazi, in which case he had only a short distance to travel on foot or by bicycle to give them away. Or he might simply be fearful of reprisals: the Germans had made it clear that anyone caught helping the enemy faced '*puni de mort*' – death. But that was a risk they would have to take.

By the time the two fugitives had crawled into the barn, Colonel von Eisenhart-Rothe, overall commander of the 685th Infantry Regiment, had issued his orders. His men were to scour the beaches, cliffs, farmsteads and fields surrounding Bruneval, searching for any British survivors. In one stretch of dark woodland, Private Sutherland – the first of Junior Charteris's section to get shot – was lying low. Sutherland had suffered five bullet wounds: three to the shoulder, one to his elbow and one to the wrist. He'd been left with a supply of morphine, but even so he was weakened by blood loss and in great pain. He was the sixth man to be left behind by the departing raiders.

With dawn approaching, Sutherland staggered to a nearby farmhouse. Having knocked, Sutherland, who spoke little French, showed the owners his dog-tags, explaining that he was 'Tommy . . . Anglo'. The Delamères lived there. Seeing how badly injured the young British soldier was, they gave him hot coffee laced with Calvados, a locally distilled apple brandy. They knew the penalty for helping British soldiers, and Sutherland, weak with pain, was adamant that he should surrender. Only treatment in a hospital would save him.

Come dawn, Sutherland would be the first British parachutist taken captive by the enemy. Within days not one of those six British fugitives would still be at large. Though their escape attempts would prove extraordinarily spirited and brave, all would be in enemy hands.

As the sun lightened the grey-hued swell on that morning of 28 February, the Tormentor flotilla were but fifteen miles off the coast of France. Cook knew that at first light, an escort of RAF warplanes was supposed to take up position above them, but no aircraft appeared. He felt terribly exposed, his fleet horribly cumbersome and vulnerable. The flat-bottomed assault craft were hardly built for open, winter seas such as these, even under tow, and there remained sixty-five miles still to go.

Cook scanned the skies, worried that 'we were, at daylight, extremely close to occupied territory which had been so recently "stirred up". In fact, the absence of air-cover was no fault of the RAF's. They were awaiting the flotilla's exact position, so a flight of Spitfires could provide a protective screen in the skies overhead.

At around 0710 four aircraft hove into view; tiny black specks, low on the horizon. Cook remarked drily: 'You can imagine our relief when the first four Messerschmitts turned out to be Spitfires.'

Thereafter, 'Spitfires covered the party,' Cook reported, providing a 'lane of fighters' all the way back to England. Four *Chasseur*-class destroyers, flying the Free French flag, arrived, and they were joined by the British destroyers HMS *Blencathra* and HMS *Fernie*. After thirty minutes, a second shift of warplanes took over from the first, and it was now that the enemy decided to put in an appearance. A flight of ME109s dived from the clouds, but the British fighters drove them off.

At last, Cook felt his fleet was reasonably secure. By 0815 hours, he transmitted the following message to headquarters: 'Operation complete success. Six killed. Two prisoners (taken). Three (our troops) left ashore. Position . . . 50 deg 04' N 0 degs 10' W.'

Inevitably, there were errors in that signal: three German POWs had been taken, six raiders had been left ashore and only two had been killed. Even so, this was the first intimation that Frost and his Jock Company might have pulled it off. It was the catalyst for a flurry of activity. The War Office were told to issue the press communiqué, the one that had been prepared with painstaking care. By 0950, Churchill was informed that there was good news at last. Word of the mission's success was also passed to the various intelligence services that had been involved in its conception and planning.

The press statement was issued right away. It read: 'In a combined operation, joint Forces of the Royal Navy, Army and Royal Air Force successfully attacked an important Radiolocation Post on the North coast of France. Its destruction was carried out by Parachute troops who were dropped from bombers of the Royal Air Force. The operation was finished according to schedule, and the parachute troops ... are being brought back by the Royal Navy.'

Within hours, the story was making headlines on the BBC: 'British parachute troops have been in action in Northern France ...' The reporters also made the vital connection to the bigger picture: 'The enemy is now using radiolocation – the means of detecting an aircraft by means of ether waves – which was used so successfully by us in the Battle of Britain.' They were indeed.

All that day the story continued to make headlines, even as the Tormentor flotilla was making its triumphant entrance into Portsmouth harbour. Once the flotilla had docked, at around 1645, Cook sent a signal to Mountbatten, sounding a note of particular triumph: 'Your inspiring message received PM Friday 27th 1942 was much appreciated by all. Boche bitten!'

Come the evening Reuters reporter Humphreys had aired his eyewitness account, with Major Frost, Commander Cook and Charles Pickard of *Target for Tonight* fame all getting a subsequent mention by name. The front page of the *Evening Standard* was dominated by the story: 'Army, Navy & RAF Raid N. France In The Dark: British Paratroops Followed Up By Infantry Wreck the Nazi's Radio "Eyes" Across The Channel.'

One vital piece of detail was omitted from the press coverage, and would remain top secret – that the paraboloid, rather than simply having been blown up, had been comprehensively looted. 'The remainder of the station was destroyed,' wrote Mountbatten, in a SECRET report on the raid, 'so that the Germans would not know whether any part of it had been successfully removed.' Or so they hoped.

The German propaganda machine also whirred into action. At 1225 the German High Command had issued an official bulletin over the German radio network. 'Last night, British paratroopers landed on the North French coast and attacked a defence post. They had to retire across the sea two hours later owing to strong German counter-action.' Lord Haw-Haw, the Irish-American traitor and Nazi propagandist, whose real name was William Joyce, would also wade in, scathingly referring to Frost and his raiders as 'a bunch of redskins'.

The Wehrmacht placed their own spin on the story, downplaying the raid's intent and purpose. But in truth, Hitler was apoplectic. 'This was a grand plan,' Luftwaffe General Kurt Student, commander-in-chief of the *Fallschirmjäger* (German parachute forces) would remark of the raid. 'The successful execution by Major Frost sent a great shock through Hitler's headquarters.' The general was there when Hitler received the news, the Führer turning incandescent with rage.

Hitler had not been informed until hours after the raid: none of his staff had wanted to be the one to break the news. It was made all the worse in that there had been an audacious follow-up attack. The morning after the raid, a group of senior German officers had gathered at the blackened hole that had housed the Würzburg, but which now 'gaped wide and empty'. Without warning, a Hurricane had swooped from the clouds, the pilot letting rip with his four Hispano 20mm cannons, strafing the sombre gathering. His daring and opportunistic strike lent insult to injury, as far as Hitler was concerned.

In London, Churchill, by contrast, was positively buoyant.

He was revelling in the moment. *Finally, something to celebrate. Finally, proof that his concept of airborne operations did have merit.* He decided to summon Frost to a meeting, so he could hear all about it at first hand. Still hung over from a night's serious carousing aboard the *Prinz Albert*, the Operation Biting commander was just getting into a much-needed bath at Tilshead, when there was a hammering on the door.

'You have to get up to London!' a voice yelled. 'The Prime Minister wants to know all the details.' They were sending a staff car, the speaker added, and the driver knew exactly where to take him.

As Frost was spirited to London, so another of Biting's foremost champions was heading north. Cox, the reluctant parachutist, had been given two weeks' leave. He travelled back to Wisbech, having sent a message home: 'Kill the fatted calf.' The papers were full of stories of the raid by now, and it didn't take a genius to work out where Cox might have been and what he might have been doing these past few days. In Wisbech, Cox received a hero's welcome.

It was late evening by the time Frost's car deposited him at an address in Birdcage Walk, on the southern edge of St James's Park. A dark stairwell led down from street level to a subterranean labyrinth running beneath Whitehall – Churchill's hallowed War Rooms. Frost was led to one, on a table in the centre of which was their very own model of the Bruneval terrain and the target – the model they had so exhaustively studied prior to departure. It brought the memories flooding back again.

A figure entered. It was Clement Attlee, the leader of the Labour Party and deputy Prime Minister in Churchill's coalition government. Attlee eyed Frost curiously, asking him to relate what had happened on the raid. Though reluctant to perform twice – once now, and once in front of Churchill – Frost didn't exactly feel he could say no. He began telling the story. Shortly, Attlee interrupted him, asking how he could be so certain of all the detail. Frost told him that was because he had commanded the raid on the ground. Attlee seemed surprised that Frost had actually been there. Frost repeated that he had, and that he'd been summoned to London to brief Churchill in person.

'Good heavens,' Attlee exclaimed, in some confusion; maybe it was better if they waited until Churchill got there.

More men arrived, the Chiefs of Staff pre-eminent among the dozen or so political and military leaders. Mountbatten wandered in, and Frost was relieved to have some like-minded company at last, in the form of the Chief of Combined Operations. Then the man himself was there, smoking a cigar and resplendent in his siren suit, the one-piece garment invented so those woken by bombing raids could slip it over nightclothes and hurry to the shelters, combining ease of wear with a certain modesty.

Frost guessed he had to stand out in his Cameronian Major's uniform, with its utterly distinctive rifle green jacket and Douglas tartan trews, the traditional Highland Scots trousers trimmed with leather. Churchill made a beeline for him, fixing the young parachute major with a sparkling gaze, beneath bushy brows.

'Bravo, Frost, bravo,' he rumbled, in his signature soft-voiced growl. 'And now we must hear all about it.'

Frost proceeded to give a short account of this 'most exciting and unusual tale' – one that was of necessity brief, because in the past forty-eight hours Mountbatten seemed to have learned all there was to know about the raid, and to have gained a far better grasp of the story, or so it seemed to Frost. As he wasn't one to hanker after the limelight, he was happy to let the Chief of Combined Operations take the lead.

At one stage Churchill interrupted, to check with Frost about the accuracy of the intelligence he'd been given. Frost affirmed that it was faultless, even down to the name of the German sergeant who had commanded the enemy's strongpoint. At another point, Churchill demanded to know who had masterminded the intelligence side of the operation. It was Wing Commander the Marquis de Casa Maury, Frost told him, the man who was standing right beside them, having joined the gathering. In response, Churchill turned the most piercing look upon de Casa Maury, leaving none in any doubt as to the exacting scrutiny of that gaze.

When the account of Biting was finished, Churchill lit up the room with one of his rare, beatific smiles. *Good news. At last, some good news.* For a brief moment he appeared almost cherubic. Then, all serious again: 'What did we get out of all this?'

By way of response Sir Charles Portal, the Air Chief Marshal, entered into a long-winded technical explanation, but he was cut short, Churchill insisting he 'stop all that nonsense' and switch to 'language normal mortals can understand'. Quite unperturbed, Portal pointed out two immediate benefits arising from the mission. One, by studying the purloined kit, it raised the very real promise of Britain being able to improve her own radar. Two, after careful study it should be possible to jam the enemy's radar, so blinding their all-seeing eye.

Silent now, the Prime Minister seemed most impressed. Moved, almost. He approached the model of the target, eyeing it most thoughtfully. He reached out a hand, running his stubby fingers gently up the steepest of the chalk contours, like a caress. As he did, he half-spoke, half-murmured: 'This is the way they will come, if they come, up and over the cliffs, just where we least expect them.' By 'they' he meant the enemy, of course.

Then, taking a firmer grip on himself, he turned to face the gathering. 'Now, about these raids,' he growled, 'there must be more of them. Let there be no doubt about that.' After which, having made his prophetic pronouncement, Churchill was gone.

If Frost had ever doubted the true import of Operation Biting, he certainly didn't any more. Those two points raised by the Air Chief Marshal – defeating the enemy's radar; improving our own – could mean the difference between winning or losing the war. And there was more. Apart from the vital morale boost from the stories in the press, Operation Biting had achieved one further signal success: it would lay to rest the ghosts of Operation Colossus once and for all, being hailed as the Allies' 'first wholly successful airborne operation'. It was the pivot upon which the mindset of Britain's leaders would switch from defensive to offensive thinking. *About these raids, there must be more of them:* that had been Churchill's reaction, and it had been so utterly telling.

As far as Biting went Frost's job was done now, as was that of CSM Strachan, Junior Charteris, Lieutenant Timothy, Cox and all the others of his raider force. For them, it was mission accomplished. Only one of those deployed on Biting would be intimately involved in its aftermath – the man codenamed Noah, Donald Preist. As for the rest, they would go on to partake in other missions and new airborne adventures. Indeed, after a short spell of leave Frost would embark upon a tour of airborne forces – American, Canadian, Polish and others – spreading the parachutist's gospel, ensuring that airborne was firmly on the map and never to be wiped off again.

At one demo later that spring, Frost stood shoulder to shoulder with the King and Queen, who expressed themselves delighted with the proceedings. Airborne operations had won full royal assent, and 'the Prime Minister, who had initiated the formation of our Parachute troops, was encouraged to ensure we had the necessary support,' Frost remarked. Airborne forces would go on to play a pivotal role in D-Day, both as parachute and glider-born troops, dropped ahead of the main fleet to seize key strategic targets.

As just one indication of the iconic status airborne forces would attain, consider this signal from General 'Boy' Browning, dated 15 January 1943. 'All Para Units: General Alexander directs that 1 Para Brigade be info that they have been given the name by the Germans of "Red Devils". General Alexander congratulates the Brigade on achieving this high distinction.' Airborne forces were feared by the enemy, just as Churchill, Keyes, Browning, Mountbatten and Frost had intended.

As for the next chapters of the Operation Biting story, they would be written by the scientists and the spies.

Chapter 17

The day after that portentous War Rooms meeting, Churchill received his first written briefing on the scientific import of Biting, containing material that he was keen as mustard to get his hands on. It confirmed that '75% of all the equipment that it was possible to get' had indeed been captured. This, together with the testimony of *Flieger* Heller, the German radar operator and now POW, promised to enable a 'complete reconstruction of the equipment' so as to show what it was capable of and, crucially, how to defeat it.

In a flurry of further documents, Churchill would be furnished with in-depth intelligence analysis, technical plans of the Würzburg, schematics of the radar installations, plus labelled photos of the key purloined components – including the transmitter-receiver, frequency amplifiers and pulse generators. It represented an extraordinarily in-depth haul of scientific data for any individual to digest, and especially for a man who was the leader of a nation then embroiled in a struggle for survival that embraced practically the entire world.

Churchill would write of the Bruneval raid that Britain had seized 'a key piece of equipment in the German radar defences', which would 'greatly help our air offensive'. Others in high office would herald Operation Biting as being the 'most marvellous thing', which 'saved thousands of lives of Bomber Command crews'. But all of that lay sometime in the future. For now, the early studies of the Bruneval paraboloid proved that the nagging fears of Jones, Preist and the other enlightened experts seemed more than justified: not only did the Germans possess radar, they were ahead in the race to master the technology.

As the soldiers had been summoned to London, so were the scientists. Fresh from his heroics, Preist met with Air Chief Marshal Sir Charles Portal, who professed himself thrilled at the success of the mission. No price could be placed upon the propaganda value. 'All the war news has been bad,' Portal pointed out, 'but here is a great success.' The captured Würzburg was already in London, being subjected to intense scrutiny. Preist would admire 'the German craftsmanship and technology it revealed', while worrying how much the enemy 'were ahead of us'.

R. V. Jones – the scientist to the spies, and chief instigator of the raid – was electrified by the haul. It was little short of a miracle that so much priceless technology had been spirited away from the enemy in such short order and with the looters being under fire the entire way – from the radar site to the beach, and even as they withdrew on the boats. That nothing had been forgotten, shot up, abandoned, doused in water, blown up, dropped in the sea or recaptured was testament to the sheer grit and determination of those tasked with stealing it.

As he studied the components, Jones realized how finely engineered it was. Designed in modular units, it was a simple exercise to deal with any fault just by slotting in a replacement. The more he scrutinized the stolen Würzburg, the more he found that parts had been replaced, and that each new component came with a unique works number and date of manufacture. It was classic Teutonic record-keeping and scrupulous efficiency. From that,

Jones was able to work out which plants were making which equipment and the numbers being churned out, from which he was able to calculate the average rate of production of sets: it amounted to around one hundred per month, allowing for ample supplies of spares.

That number was vastly in excess of what anyone had anticipated. As the stolen set appeared to be of a 1939 design, that had to mean that *thousands* of such Würzburgs were in use by Nazi Germany – more than enough to ring the coast of occupied Europe. It also signified that at the outbreak of war, this had been the level of sophistication of the enemy's radar technology. Three years had passed since then. What advances had been made in the interim? Jones had received reports of a so-called '*Würzburg-Riese*' – giant – in operation, one that measured 25 feet across the dish, with a huge spinning antenna at its centre.

Jones knew that a Luftwaffe radar operator had been taken prisoner during the raid. Gathering up the pieces of the radar unit, he made his way across the city to the RAF prisoner interrogation cells at Cockfosters, in north London. At what had become known as the 'Cockfosters Camp', his old friend Squadron Leader Samuel Denys Felkin was busy questioning captured Luftwaffe personnel, most of whom were decidedly reluctant to offer up their secrets.

Felkin was a self-taught interrogator who had been serving as a pilot at the start of the war. He proved utterly brilliant at his work, introducing hidden microphones to capture POWs chatting to each other, and 'stool pigeons' – exiled Germans and Austrians, posing as fellow POWs to wheedle out their secrets. It was Felkin's work with Luftwaffe POWs that had helped alert Jones to the existence of the German beams, those used to guide their bombers onto target, and which had in turn led to the Battle of the Beams.

Over time, Felkin and Jones had become firm friends. Fortunately, the Operation Biting prisoner required little subterfuge to persuade him to talk. Indeed, *Flieger* Heller had proved positively loquacious, or so Jones had been told. What Jones wanted of the man was a sense of how the Würzburg was used in the thick of battle – something that might justify the scores of supposed 'kills' that had been daubed on the radar dish in white paint. At the Cockfosters Camp, he settled down to talk to the man, the pile of Würzburg components within easy reach.

Heller, it transpired, had been no ideal Luftwaffe recruit. Quite the contrary. Shortly after the outbreak of war, his wife had given birth to a baby girl, and Heller had requested compassionate leave to pay them a visit. It had been refused. He had decided to absent himself anyway, and was duly arrested by the German military police. Days later his daughter had tragically died, and by then Heller was facing a court martial. Sentenced to six months in a military prison, he'd been released after two for good behaviour, and posted to a Luftwaffe unit.

But Heller had soon absented himself again, and this time he received a year's sentence at the notorious military prison of Torgau Fort Zimmer, in north-east Germany, the hub of the Wehrmacht's penal system, where he worked as a prison labourer for much of the time. Towards the end of 1941 he was released and posted to the French coast, to serve on a Luftwaffe radar team, the hundred-strong 2nd *Zug* of the 23rd (*Schwere Flugmelde*) (*Ortsfest*) Regiment West Frankreich – in other words, the Bruneval aircraft reporting company. He'd spent nine weeks at the Würzburg site, learning the craft of the magical all-seeing eye, by the time the British raiders fell from the skies.

Having spent sixteen months of the last two years in various military prisons, and having been denied any time with his baby daughter, who had subsequently passed away, Heller didn't feel any great loyalties to his country or to his former employers. As Felkin noted, 'P/W [prisoner of war] is very willing to impart all he knows . . . His low morale is due in no small measure to the harsh treatment meted out to him during his period of service.'

Somewhat worryingly, Felkin had concluded of Heller that he was of 'limited intelligence', and had received little specialist training on the Würzburg. For Jones, it didn't particularly matter. Heller's practical, can-do attitude and know-how, coupled with his keenness to help and his seeming inability to concoct lies or falsehoods, would trump any supposed limitations in his intellectual abilities.

Jones and Heller sat on the floor of a room at the Cockfosters Camp, along with a translator. The British scientist watched in fascination as the German radar man proceeded to assemble the purloined kit, slotting together one unit after another until it was mostly complete, bar the radar dish itself. Heller had done so with real dexterity, but the Würzburg's components were ingeniously engineered and it was akin to clipping together something made of Meccano.

As he worked, Heller chatted away in German, a translator rendering an English interpretation. In a way, Felkin had been right: Heller was certainly no Einstein. But he was a member of a team of Luftwaffe operators who had manned a cutting-edge German radar unit, one that had accounted for fifty-eight 'kills' of Allied aircraft, according to the marks chalked on the paraboloid.

That had to count for something. At Jones's prompting, Heller explained how he and his teammates had notched up a 'kill' for any aircraft they had tracked, and onto which they had vectored searchlights, anti-aircraft fire or fighter planes with lethal consequences.

The Freya site would warn the Würzburg operators by telephone of any in-bound aircraft, after which Heller and his team would trace range, bearing and altitude, the details of which were passed to the regional plotting centre, using the unit's call-sign, 'W-110'. Despite their diminutive size, the radar stations sited at Bruneval had been able to detect aircraft at anything up to 150 kilometres, and to track them all the way. The fact that there were apparently two ship-kills daubed on the dish, reflected the fact that the Würzburg could be lowered to such an elevation as to pick out vessels at sea, Heller explained.

The operations of both the Freya and Würzburg systems, which worked in conjunction with one another, were some of the most closely policed secrets of the German Armed Forces. Security was utterly rigorous, especially concerning the Würzburg, which the Wehrmacht believed to be a 'masterly weapon of defence.' Crews from the two units weren't even allowed to visit each other, even though they worked just a few hundred yards apart. Though they hailed from the same unit and were relieved at the same times, they were 'strictly forbidden to talk to each other about their work'.

Ironically, thanks to Heller's talkative ways, Jones left Cockfosters having been treated to an insider's view of one of the Wehrmacht's most closely guarded secrets. Crucially, Heller had also 'thrown a great deal of light on the action of that portion of the apparatus which could not be brought back' – the main screen and the dish itself. Thanks to his testimony and practical demonstrations, coupled with his own studies of the Würzburg, Jones had gained unprecedented 'first-hand knowledge of the state of German radar technology'.

Heller and the other POWs taken on Operation Biting were in many ways the lucky ones. By May that year, the troops garrisoning the coastal defences at Bruneval seemingly got their comeuppance for failing to thwart Frost and his raiders. The men of the 685th Infantry Regiment were shipped from the fresh fields of Normandy to the blood-stained ground of the Eastern Front, where their ranks would be decimated. Very, very few of those based in and around Bruneval would survive the war. Corporal Schmidt, the telephone orderly, and Infantryman Tewes, both taken captive at the Stella Maris villa, were fortunate. They spent the rest of the war as POWs in England. So, too, did Heller, whose testimony had already yielded so much.

But there was more – much more – to come.

One week prior to Operation Biting, a new Commander-in-Chief had taken over at RAF Bomber Command. Ever a controversial figure, Air Marshal Arthur Travers 'Bomber' Harris had been instructed by Churchill to increase the reach and punch of RAF bombing missions. Harris invoked scripture when pledging that Nazi Germany, having pounded Britain in the Blitz, 'sowed the wind, and now they are going to reap the whirlwind'. On the night of 3/4 March 1942, three days after Frost's raiders had ripped out the heart of the Würzburg, Harris took full advantage of that fact, launching what was then the largest Allied bombing raid of the war.

Just to the west of Paris centre lay the suburb of Boulogne-Billancourt, location of a massive Renault factory, which was then manufacturing 18,000 trucks, plus other military vehicles, for the Wehrmacht each year. Come nightfall on 3 March, 235 bombers – 89 Wellingtons, 48 Hampdens, 29 Stirlings, 26 Manchesters, 23 Whitleys and 20 Halifaxes – were dispatched in three waves, charged with obliterating the factory. As it lay in a very built-up area, the bombers were to head in at low level guided by flares, so as to minimize civilian casualties.

En route, only a dozen aircraft lost their way. Of the 223 bombers that unleashed their payloads over the target, many from as little as 3,000 feet, all but one would make it back to their airbases in Britain. In a raid that lasted 110 minutes, only a single Wellington was shot down. The results on the ground were unprecedented. Over 400 tonnes of explosives were dropped over the target, large sections of the Renault plant being destroyed and vehicle production halted for many months.

Though there were, unavoidably, civilian casualties, the raid was hailed as a great success. It received a blaze of publicity, rather as the exploits of Frost and his raiders had done, just a few days earlier. As with Biting, some aspects of the Billancourt raid remained top secret, the chief of which was that the bomber stream had been routed over Bruneval, to take full advantage of the obliteration of its Würzburg radar. As the Operation Biting War Diary noted: 'The destruction of this radio-location station had the aim of making possible the British raid on the Renault factory, on the night of the 3rd to 4th March 1942.'

To those in the know, the Paris raid proved an absolute revelation. It had shown how, if the enemy's radar was blinded, then concentrated streams of Allied bombers would get through to their targets, with few losses and scoring spectacular results. There could be no more telling demonstration of the need to blind the enemy's all-seeing eye, which gave enormous impetus to those now studying the purloined Würzburg in an effort to work out exactly how they might poke the enemy's eye out. This was what everyone hungered for now.

Even as the RAF's bombing fleet had returned to its bases, so Jones had sent Churchill his initial findings on the Würzburg. Crucially he concluded his 4 March four-page report by suggesting that a key weak point had been identified. Because the paraboloid was tuneable over a large range of frequencies, that made it very hard to 'jam' using traditional methods, but Jones pointed out that 'dropping suitable reflectors, such as sheets of tinfoil, will be highly successful' in blinding the Würzburg. He signed off by reminding Churchill that this was a suggestion that 'the present Prime Minister' had first made 'in 1937'.

Indeed it was. In December 1937, at Lindemann's urging, Churchill had taken up the somewhat *Boy's-Own* idea, 'to scatter from the air packets of tin-foil strips', which would be 'cut to a special length so as to simulate a bomber on the enemy's radar screens'. The simple aerial release of hundreds of such strips should create a host of false echoes, so hiding any Allied aircraft. The concept had been codenamed WINDOW, for the simple reason that it had no hidden, giveaway meaning. WINDOW was ruled top-secret, especially since the British military-scientific establishment largely believed that only it had radar, which meant that it had everything to lose if the enemy found out about the tinfoil-strips deception.

WINDOW, the idea that Churchill had championed, had been swept under the proverbial carpet. But now that Operation Biting had proven the capabilities of German radar, perhaps it needed revisiting. Jones certainly thought so. So, too, did the boffins at

TRE. After a swift London scrutiny, the Würzburg components were loaded up and trucked down to TRE's Swanage laboratories. There, the radar was reassembled, plugged in, powered up and brought back to life – so the boffins could get a handle on just what it could do. Jones was so excited at the Frankenstein-like resurrection of the Würzburg, that he was cautioned twice for speeding when driving from London to Dorset to check on the progress.

TRE's in-depth analysis revealed the high-tech wizardry of the Würzburg, and a host of new technologies. The aerial consisted of a 'centre-fed half-wave dipole' with 'supporting structure, which houses a balance-to-unbalance transformer. A very efficient method is used for common transmitting and receiving . . .' The 'transmitter consists of a single-valve grid modulated Colpitts oscillator, using a Telefunken LS180 valve (a hitherto unknown model).' The radar's 'mixer employs a double diode (Telefunken LG2, hitherto unknown) . . . housed in a cast light-alloy box.'

To a layman, much of the technical detail appeared mind-boggling. 'The local oscillator which is a highly-stable one of unique construction using metal-coated ceramic material for the tuned circuits, consists of a tuned-plate tuned-grid push-pull triode oscillator, probably on 200 cms, driving a simple triode frequency quadrupler . . . The output is injected equally onto the anodes of the diode mixer capacitatively by means of a prong.' But beneath the scientific mumbo-jumbo, the high regard of the TRE boffins for the purloined German equipment shone through.

As they were at pains to point out, the 'engineering design and construction are outstanding', stressing how 'one of the greatest contributions of the Bruneval raid was the practical demon-stration of the quality of German RDF production.' As the unit had been designed in 1939, they concluded of Britain's capabilities, 'we could not even have matched the performance of the German equipment.' In some ways the Würzburg seemed over-engineered, or perhaps it had functions that could not yet be guessed at: 'the most remarkable feature of this unit is its very high frequency stability, which is much higher than needed for its present purpose.'

Crucially, the TRE scientists determined that the Germans now had a type A, C and D Würzburg, and possibly also a type B. Type B, they postulated, might well be 'the giant (24-foot diameter) Würzburg, which first appeared on a flak tower in Berlin.' In an intelligence coup, a grainy photo of a *Würzburg-Riese* had been smuggled out of Germany and delivered into British hands. As to types C and D, they remained a mystery. The Germans graded their anti-aircraft fire into three levels: *Vernichtungsfeuer* (annihilating fire); *Stoerungsfeuer* (harassing fire), and *Sporrfeuer* (barrage fire). At least one Würzburg could deliver the most devastating kind: *Vernichtungsfeuer* (annihilating fire). But which one?

Noting how 'the success of the raid seems remarkable', TRE 'searched for any weak points which would permit an easy method of jamming'. Their studies of the reincarnated Würzburg suggested that Jones and Churchill were right: the simple tin-foil deception – WINDOW – was the only viable option. Secret trials were planned, to try out for real the scattering of airborne clouds of tin-foil. They were to be executed over the North Sea, where few watching eyes might bear witness, and where the clouds of WINDOW should be lost for ever in the grey swell, never to come to the attention of Britain's enemies.

TRE suggested that 'a maximum density of 10 echoes per

square mile should be aimed at,' using WINDOW, 'to conceal the normal aircraft echo.' They should seek to carry out 'tests on the reactions of operators on the ground to a WINDOW attack' – in other words, ascertaining how radar operators responded to their screens being scrambled by scores of false echoes. All of this would help determine WINDOW's efficacy and how the enemy might react. TRE also started work on a Würzburg clone, which would become known as 'the German radar', one that would ape the original unit's capabilities. But all of that was still to come.

By 6 March 1942, Churchill put forward Jones – the scientist to the spies – for a 'high honour in the next list . . . a CB.' CB stands for a 'Companion of the Most Honourable Order of the Bath', an ancient chivalric order given to honour those who had contributed greatly to Britain's cause.

A host of further honours were showered on the Biting raiders. Frost was awarded a Military Cross (MC), the citation praising his 'outstanding leadership and determination. The success of the operation was largely due to the ability and conduct of Major Frost.' Lieutenant Charteris was also awarded an MC, being praised for 'the utmost determination and initiative' with which he 'led his men across unknown country to the beach', assisting at the 'vital moment in overcoming the defences, thus ensuring evacuation'.

The Military Medal (MM) was given to Flight Sergeant Cox, whose citation concluded that 'the success of the operation on the technical side depended largely' on his actions, during which he was 'continually under enemy fire'. Sergeant McKenzie – who'd helped spearhead the assault on the radar pit – was also awarded an MM, winning praise for being 'personally responsible for killing several of the enemy'. Sergeant Grieve, of the Seaforth Highlanders – one of Charteris's men –was also given the MM, in recognition for finding his way 'to the objective through strange country', and for 'conspicuous gallantry in the face of enemy fire'.

There was a similarly impressive haul on the Navy side. Commander Cook was given a Distinguished Service Cross (DSC), Cook's citation praising his 'cool and resolute leadership, combined with the skill and daring in landing the beach parties and re-embarking all troops under fire'. There were also DSCs for Lieutenant Quick, who skippered the lead assault craft, and Lieutenant Coles, who resurrected the ailing engine of one of the ALCs. Two Distinguished Service Medals (DSMs) were awarded to the naval personnel, and a host of Mentions in Dispatches (MIDs), including one for Lieutenant Young, who along with McKenzie had led the assault to vanquish the Würzburg's defenders.

Wing Commander Pickard was also granted a bar to his Distinguished Service Order (DSO), and there would be a French Croix de Guerre with Palm awarded to CSM Strachan, who would in time make a miraculous recovery from his wounds, returning to serve in airborne forces for the remainder of the war.

One of the Biting raiders could not be considered for a decoration, because he had subsequently fallen into enemy hands. A month after Biting, Peter Nagel, the SOE agent and German Jew on the mission, had deployed on Operation Chariot, the Commando raid on the dry-dock in the French port of Saint-Nazaire. Nagel was sent on the mission at Mountbatten's express orders, for 'he knew how to deal with the Germans.' Wounded by a grenade blast to his arms, back and legs, Nagel had been captured, and just a few minutes before HMS *Campbeltown*, a navy warship packed with explosives and rammed into the dock-gates, had blown up.

Fortunately, Nagel had adopted the cover name of 'Private Walker' for the raid, Walker being a real British soldier who had 'disappeared from the Army between the wars'. His German captors, though initially suspicious of Nagel's 'non-English' accent, failed to break his cover, and 'Private Walker' won the right to be treated as a bona-fide prisoner of war. Nagel would never stop trying to escape or causing trouble to the enemy, not until the camp he was then in – Moosburg, near Munich - was liberated at the end of the war.

By anyone's reckoning, the Bruneval raiders had secured an extraordinary haul of medals. It served to underline what a signal success Operation Biting was seen as being. At that time, in the spring of 1942, the power of the Nazi war-machine was at its zenith, their reach almost unlimited. Biting was a timely poke in the eye.

The Germans reacted to having their eye taken out with typical efficiency. In the immediate aftermath of the raid they dynamited the Château Gosset, levelling it to the ground, arguing that it had served as a distinctive landmark to guide the raiders onto their target. They also began a programme to massively strengthen the defences at all such radar sites, which meant that hundreds of coastal installations were fitted with thick coils of barbed wire. Unbeknown to them, this would backfire spectacularly.

In what became known as Nazi Germany's 'wiring panic', such efforts only served to identify the sites to the ever-alert photo reconnaissance squadrons. From the air, the new barbed wire left an indelible signature. Where the razor-sharp coils were strung around such stations, so the grass grew unchecked, distinctive dark rings appearing around Nazi Germany's top-secret radar facilities. For the photo interpreters at Danesfield House, this proved wonderfully revelatory. Shortly, scores of such sites had been identified and mapped.

The German military and its paramilitary enforcers – the *Geheime Staatspolizei* (Gestapo*)* and *Sicherheitsdienst* (SD), the Nazi party's security service – launched a search for those who had helped Frost and his raiders on the ground. They did so without let-up or mercy. A French couple that had aided some of the raiders left behind were caught, tried and sentenced to death, being sent first to the concentration camps. And sadly, those in France whose mission had been so secret and so fraught with danger, and whose intelligence had proven so incisive for Operation Biting, were about to pay the ultimate price for their bravery and fortitude.

Remy's Confrérie Notre-Dame was about to reap the whirlwind.

Chapter 18

Having flown out of France on the night of the raid, in the SOE's Lysander, Remy was in London when news of Biting's success broke. It was brought to him in a very special way. One of his SOE handlers arrived on the Saturday, the day after the raid, brandishing the early edition of the *Evening Standard*, with the bold front-page headlines: 'British Paratroopers ... Wreck the Nazis' Radio "Eye" Across The Channel.' Remy read it all with a growing sense of joy and of pride: *at last. At last they had managed to hit back.*

His handler explained how the intelligence provided by the Confrérie Notre-Dame had proven invaluable, enabling them 'to work it all out down to the smallest possible detail'. It was the very best of news. 'Such words make wonderful hearing to an intelligence agent,' Remy remarked. But the real credit, of course, lay with Pol and Charlemagne, the two men who had masterminded the recce of the Bruneval defences with such remarkable bluff and front. Remy asked for a message to be dispatched, congratulating them on their incredible work. Short and succinct, it was sent right away.

Remy's handler then turned to the suitcases of documents he had just delivered. They included files stolen from the German U-boat base at Lorient, on the western coast of France. How Remy had managed to get his hands on them beggared belief.

The Keroman Submarine Base had been built on the orders of Grand-admiral Karl Dönitz, and consisted of three gigantic reinforced concrete structures capable of sheltering thirty-five U-boats. Whether they were vulnerable to Allied bombing had been hotly debated: those documents should prove it either way. They were priceless.

In London, Remy lunched with General de Gaulle. The General expressed himself pleased as punch with the success of the Bruneval raid, and the role that Remy and his network had played. The potency and spirit, not to mention the immense value, of the French Resistance had been proven at last. Then, after a moment's hesitation, De Gaulle demanded of Remy if he really did intend to return to France and to his work there.

'You're not going back?'

'Oh yes, General,' Remy replied, simply.

'You'll get caught, you know.'

'I sincerely hope not.'

'Oh yes you will. People always get caught in that kind of work.'

De Gaulle seemed saddened; fatalistic almost. Remy was annoyed. There was so much to be done. Why was the general trying to dissuade him? The one thing that was foremost in his mind right then was devising a better means of getting intelligence to London than via the radio, or the Lysander. Both means were unreliable and prone to interception by the enemy. Instead, they must pioneer a sea-borne route. They would purchase an unremarkable but seaworthy fishing boat, and find a discreet and loyal crew.

At night, the trawler would sail into the Channel, to rendezvous with a similar-seeming British boat. Secret recognition signals would be employed. Buoys would be moored in certain pre-arranged spots, so a 'dead-drop' method could be employed, the two crews never needing to see each other, let alone meet. Instead, a waterproof tin trunk would be lashed to the buoy, loaded with the precious dispatches and documents, for the British 'trawler' to collect later. An explosive device would be fitted to the trunk, in case any unwanted visitors tried to interfere with its contents.

It was an ingenious idea. Plans were set in motion. That done, Remy prepared for his return to France. But the day before his scheduled departure, he received terrible news. A message had come in from Bob, his radio operator in Paris. 'Phoebus, L'Enfant, Mars, Chopin, ABC and almost all radio operators arrested . . .' It was calamitous news. De Gaulle's words – *You'll get caught, you know* – seemed hauntingly prescient. In the backlash following Operation Biting, the Confrérie Notre-Dame had been penetrated and busted wide open.

Remy was asked if he still intended to return to France. Of course, he confirmed. He duly took to the skies in the SOE's lone, unarmed Lysander. On one occasion, a Lysander had shaken off four enemy fighters, hedge-hopping, weaving in and out of church steeples and trees, in an effort lose them. It had finally done so and safely returned to Britain. But many a flight had not been so fortunate. The pilot had to navigate his way by the faintest of indications – a railway, the line of a canal, a river glistening silver in the moonlight. Then he had to find a small field somewhere in rural France, from where a triangle of lights would be blinking at him, beaming out a message of resistance and of hope . . . or, of course, of entrapment.

That night the Lysander made it, depositing Remy on a landing ground not so far from Saumur, a historic town in north-western

France. From there, Remy made his cautious way back to Paris. From those of his network still at large he learned what had transpired. One of his veteran radio operators, Phoebus, had been on the air, when a *Funkabwehr* detector van had nailed him. He had been seized complete with his radio set, codebooks and, worse, a notebook listing members of the Confrérie Notre-Dame, together with address details.

Worse still, Pol – Roger Dumont, the mastermind of the Bruneval intelligence-gathering operation – had just been arrested. Remy rushed to Pol's Paris apartment. It was full of sensitive material, including messages written by Remy himself. They left Pol's place loaded down with suitcases full of incriminating documents, plus Pol's typewriters. But tragically, it was Remy's triumphant message from London that had been the cause of Pol's undoing.

Remy's signal had read: 'Congratulations success Bruneval which has resulted destruction important German installation while taking and killing numerous Boches . . .' The message had been intercepted, and the Germans had managed to break the code. They had used it to discover Pol's real identity, and his arrest had followed. A year later, Roger Dumont would be executed at Fort Mont-Valérien, in Paris, an ancient fortress used to incarcerate condemned members of the Resistance. Over one thousand would perish there during the war.

By late March 1942 one of Remy's most trusted agents was as good as dead, sucked into the dark maw of the Gestapo. On the eve of his execution, he would write a letter to his family: 'All that I have done I have done as a Frenchman. I regret nothing.' Pol was but one of several dozen of the Confrérie Notre-Dame so taken, and the hunt was very much still on. Bob, Remy's radio operator, would perish a year later from torture, having been likewise ensnared by the *Funkabwehr*. For Bruneval, for the purloined Würzburg, the Confrérie Notre-Dame had paid a heavy price ... which made it all the more vital that the intelligence that it had yielded be acted upon to the utmost, lest they would have died in vain.

But before that could happen, the enemy were determined to launch a counter-strike, and TRE itself was to be the target. In early April 1942, ENIGMA intercepts uncovered a surprise plot: it seemed as if the Germans, enraged by Biting and its aftermath, intended to do pretty much the same. If the British could steal their radar, then what better way to retaliate than to purloin the choicest British technology – for make no mistake, the Germans were little fooled by the deception that Biting was all about sabotage, as opposed to robbery.

In a German military report issued shortly after the raid, they were clear that the 'British commandos' had 'dismantled parts of the set and also took photographs'. The bags of SOE robbery gear abandoned at the scene also provided strong evidence as to the raiders' true intentions. Biting had been all about theft of the German military's most sensitive technology, and so a plan was put together to do something remarkably similar, with TRE on the Dorset clifftops as the target. A German parachute battalion was moved to Normandy, setting camp more or less directly opposite the radar towers and research laboratories of TRE.

Its presence provoked near-panic in Britain. Having been warned that 'trainloads' of German airborne troops were preparing to attack, A. P. Rowe, TRE's director, described the news as 'a bombshell'. Churchill demanded immediate action. On 8 April the Chiefs of Staff proposed that, 'in the interim period, before the very secret equipment could be moved elsewhere, an additional battalion should be sent to the Swanage area, with the specific duty of protecting the two establishments.' That same day, Churchill demanded: 'When will it be there?'

Several hundred troops were dispatched to Dorset, to safeguard the laboratories and those who worked in them. They blocked the coastal roads and planted demolition charges within TRE's most secret equipment. If the Germans launched a retaliatory raid, they might even steal back again the reincarnated Würzburg, plus they could capture dozens of Britain's top experts. After all, TRE was no Bruneval radar station. It was the nerve centre of Britain's radar – and related – research and warfare.

Those based there spent their time discussing 'whether we should die to the last scientist, or run', Rowe reported. They began to play a bizarre game of cat and mouse. By day, they beavered away in their laboratories. By night, they drove out of TRE to remote and secret locations, taking with them their key technologies to hide from any smash-and-grab raid by the enemy. On his visits to TRE, Jones 'said nothing about the possibility of a reprisal', but 'our conspicuously worn pistols and steel hats testified to our apprehension.'

The game of hide-and-seek being played by the scientists was clearly no solution. At Churchill's urging, a Captain Spencer Freeman, CBE, who was attached to the Ministry of Aircraft Production, set about finding an alternative location for TRE. In his Hillman Minx, a four-door family saloon car, Captain Freeman quartered southern England and the Midlands, seeking an alternative. Eventually, he set upon the manicured grounds of Malvern College, the famous public school set against the backdrop of the Malvern Hills, in Worcestershire.

The school's motto *Sapiens qui prospicit* (Wise is the person who looks ahead) seemed particularly appropriate for a facility such as TRE. The College had the added advantage that it sat at the kind of elevation required by scientists to observe aircraft involved in experiments at a distance. There was also an airfield nearby, at the village of Defford, which was already in use by the RAF. The challenge was requisitioning Malvern College itself, which had long educated the scions of the rich and famous. But Freeman had backing from the very top, and no one was about to stand in his way.

On 15 May 1942 hundreds of TRE personnel began the move north to Malvern, 'in cars mostly so old that it seemed impossible that they could reach their destination', remarked Rowe. This being a thoroughly British undertaking, orders were issued concerning tea to be provided to the scientists at their new lodgings, and bearing in mind that strict rationing was in place: '1. Milk – 25 cups to one pint. 2. Tea – 20 cups to one pound.'

While Rowe didn't downplay the gargantuan challenges of such a move, he stressed the need for all to put a very British brave face on things. In his 18 May 'Order No. 1', Rowe declared: 'To move the whole of T.R.E. in a hurry is a tremendous task . . . We are all going to have some initial discomfort; a real effort is being made to solve the inevitable living problems and it is asked that temporary difficulties be accepted cheerfully. Exaggerated stories of discomfort or the spreading of despondency should be rewarded with a kick in the pants.'

Rowe declared a 'Zero hour . . . the time at which . . . all normal work on the Establishment will cease . . . Zero hour is 9 a.m. on Saturday, 23rd May.' At that point all the staff would concentrate on the move, the safeguarding of sensitive equipment and papers being of paramount importance. Rowe stressed the need to ensure 'the security of secret equipment on its arrival at its appropriate building', and that 'no secret or confidential papers whatever (registered or unregistered) should be put in Pickford vans.' The Pickford removals company had a foremost role in shuttling TRE across country, while trying to ensure its lorries did not 'run across' too many of Malvern College's 'well-kept' lawns.

By 30 May 1942, the move was complete: 1,500 TRE personnel had been shipped to Malvern and accommodated there; new laboratories had been built within the grounds of the College. 'All the staff have beds and feeding arrangements are satisfactory,' a 30 May report concluded. 'High priority work is already at 70% efficiency . . .' That very day Churchill was informed of the move's success, which signified that Britain's war-winning scientists had been put out of reach of the enemy. It had taken just two weeks – an incredible achievement, by anyone's reckoning.

Great things would be accomplished at TRE Malvern, and it would play a pivotal role in securing victory in Europe. TRE would enable the massed fleets of Bomber Command to smash the German industrial heartland of the Ruhr, so relieving pressure on the Eastern Front, and from TRE Malvern would be masterminded the deployment of the 'ghost fleets', which helped enable the triumph of the D-Day landings. But all of that lay in the future.

For now, having completed their move, the TRE scientists felt unduly exercised by one signal failure of Allied high command, as they saw it. The Würzburg having been pilfered, brought back to life, studied and understood, why wasn't the means to blind it being employed? WINDOW was the answer, but WINDOW was not being used.

It was a woman at TRE, Mrs Joan Curran, a talented scientist and mathematician, who'd mastered the technology, discovering how best rectangular strips of tinfoil cut to a certain length might make the most effective reflectors. At the American radar laboratories – the Rad Lab, in Boston, Massachusetts – further research was carried out on WINDOW, which the Americans would rename 'Chaff'. Their version utilized strips only a twentieth of an inch wide and one hundredth of an inch thick. They would prove highly effective at blinding Würzburgs.

All the tests indicated that WINDOW had so much promise, so why wasn't it being utilized? The German air defences were fearsome, bomber losses crippling. By June of that year, Jones and his team at the Secret Intelligence Service had worked out in detail how the German air defences operated. At first they'd nicknamed them 'The Main Belt', but they soon came up with a better name – 'The Kammhuber Line'. The concept of lines – the Siegfried in Germany, the Maginot in France, the Gothic in Italy – tended to work with the military mindset, being known and familiar. The name stuck.

It was coined after Major General Josef Kammhuber, who had developed defences stretching from Denmark in the north, through Holland, Belgium and north-eastern France – so menacing the route Allied bombers had to fly, to attack all-important targets inside the Reich. Fittingly, the Kammhuber Line was known in Germany as the *Himmelbett* – four-poster bed – line. It consisted of a series of 'boxes', each with a front of around 20 kilometres and a height extending to the ceiling of Allied bombing formations. Each box was the dedicated hunting ground for one

German night fighter. Within each, a Freya unit first detected the incoming bombers, whereupon a pair of Würzburgs would vector the night fighter directly onto target.

The Würzburg's plots were sent to a Command Room, where lights were shone onto a specially designed platform, called a Seeburg Table. A red light represented the Allied bomber, a blue the German fighter, the controllers using them to talk the Luftwaffe pilot onto his target. The Kammhuber Line proved remarkably effective, Allied bomber losses mounting steadily. But as one German fighter only was assigned to each box, Bomber Command developed the concept of the bomber 'stream' – saturating an individual box with hundreds of aircraft, to punch through, overwhelming it with sheer numbers.

The 'stream' concept brought only temporary respite. Kammhuber responded by feeding scores of fighters, like shoals of piranha, in among the massed ranks of Lancasters and Stirlings. Losses became unsustainable, and the arguments for using WINDOW were boosted, Jones being its foremost advocate. Who could argue against it, especially as the TRE boffins figured that 90 per cent of all Allied bomber losses could be laid at the door of the Würzburgs.

Sadly, others demurred. They argued that if WINDOW was used over Germany, the tinfoil strips would be discovered and the cat would be out of the bag. The Germans would realize what exactly had blinded their radar, copy it, and blind Britain's all-seeing eye in return. Jones ridiculed the idea. With the level of sophistication revealed by the stolen Würzburg, it was inconceivable that the enemy hadn't also rumbled the tinfoil-strip deception. Indeed, they had. The German military's own version was codenamed DUPPEL. It was seen as being so secret and so sensitive that even the Wehrmacht was shy of using it. Basically, neither side wanted to be the first to show its hand.

Jones and the TRE scientists kept lobbying for WINDOW to be used. In a June 1942 report, they stressed how crucial it was 'to provide our bomber offensive with valuable protection'. The boffins decided to stick their neck out still further, complaining that it was 'very disturbing' that the use of WINDOW was not being pressed for as 'the highest priority'. While recognizing that the 'political controversy . . . is not essentially our concern . . . it is our concern to ensure all the facts are available to those who will make the final decision'.

TRE was keen to start churning out the bales of WINDOW, but throughout that summer none was deployed. This was largely because the tests on British vulnerability to such deception had reached 'ominous' conclusions. If any release of WINDOW to blind the enemy was reciprocated, Britain's radar defences would likewise be rendered blind. The naysayers argued for a stay of execution, during which they would attempt to insulate British radar from WINDOW's feared predations. Much against Jones's and TRE's wishes, they got it.

Months passed, with no WINDOW being used. Jones argued that he had little doubt that deploying WINDOW would save 'hundreds of aircraft and thousands of lives', while boosting the accuracy of Allied bombing. It was only when Bomber Command losses reached potentially catastrophic proportions that the logjam was seen to break. With four variants of Würzburg vectoring night fighters onto Allied aircraft, plus the 20,000 flak guns and 7,000 searchlights in use in Nazi Germany, the Allied bomber streams were getting torn apart.

By the spring of 1943, those who argued for WINDOW had

gained the upper hand. The final decision was taken at the very highest level. On 22 June Jones was asked to give evidence to a top-level committee. He argued he was in no doubt that 'the Germans knew of WINDOW', so the arguments against its use were nullified. One of his greatest detractors remained Robert Watson-Watt, the self-proclaimed 'father of radar'. Watson-Watt argued that using WINDOW risked neutering Britain's air defences, laying the nation wide open to attack. He was over-ruled, and it was agreed that WINDOW would get the green light.

At dusk on 24 July 1943, 779 British heavy bombers clawed their way into the skies over East Anglia, setting a course over the North Sea. Their destination was Hamburg, and at the end of their pre-take-off briefings, a special announcement from Bomber Harris had been made. 'Tonight, you are going to use "WINDOW". It consists of packets of metal strips which produce almost the same reaction on RDF [radar] as do your aircraft. The German defences will become confused . . .' Harris's statement explained how WINDOW's use had been delayed, so Britain's radar defences could be rendered immune to such attacks.

The German radar teams were primed to expect a bombing raid. From intercepts of Bomber Command's 'radio chatter', the Germans knew that something special was in the offing. As the waves of bombers took to the skies, German long-range radar detected the head of a massive stream of aircraft. It was making for the north coast of Germany, to make landfall at around the location of Hamburg.

But shortly, the bombers began releasing their bales of tinfoil strips, one bundle per minute from each aircraft. Flying at 19,000 feet, those bundles had a very long time to disperse and for the tin-foil clouds to drift to earth. The reaction from the German radar stations was one of utter panic. 'They are multiplying! The British are reproducing themselves!'

So secret was the Germans' own version of WINDOW that the codeword, DUPPEL, was not allowed to be mentioned even in the highest-level meetings. Accordingly, their radar operators had not the slightest idea that such a technology might exist. Hamburg was then the most intensively defended city in the world. It boasted fifty-four Würzburg-controlled flak stations, twenty-two Würzburg-controlled searchlight batteries, plus twenty Würzburg-controlled 'boxes', complete with their night-fighter squadrons. That night, all would be rendered blind.

The intense blue searchlights, which normally waited erect above the city, before rushing to pounce, spider-like, on their targets, roved around the skies in demented confusion. The flak-gunners, devoid of intelligible instructions, were reduced to firing into the air above the city more or less at random, in the vague hope of hitting something. The night-fighter pilots waited in their aircraft for directions, but nothing was forthcoming. No radar operator was able to make sense of the chaotic, scrambled displays on their Würzburg screens. One German commander reported 'trying to intercept 700 separate bombers, without being able to locate one'. His recollection was typical.

Hitler was awakened uncharacteristically early the following morning, to be given the sombre news: Hamburg, with its all-important shipyards, U-boat pens and oil refineries, had been heavily bombed. More to the point, the Allies had deployed a new weapon in their arsenal of air-warfare: their own equivalent of DUPPEL, by which Hamburg's air-defences had been rendered impotent. Hitler's response was to order a massive acceleration of the V – *Vergeltungswaffen* (Vengeance) – weapons programme, and especially the V2. It would come too late to make any difference in the war, and in any case it would monopolize scarce resources that were needed elsewhere.

Once the WINDOW gloves were off they remained off. Hamburg was hit four times between 24 July and 3 August. Each subsequent attack employed the same simple deception, each with similar results. In each of the night raids, 40–50 tonnes of WINDOW were released at altitude, from a bomber stream lasting little short of an hour. The results were 'even better than could be hoped', Jones's team concluded. Churchill echoed such sentiments, adding that WINDOW had 'surpassed expectations'.

Of course, Operation Gomorrah, as the raids on Hamburg were codenamed, would prove controversial. The widespread use of incendiary bombs rendered the city into an inferno. Fire storms raged, with hurricane-force winds blasting human beings around like chaff, flinging them up in furnace-like eruptions of smoke and flame. Over 40,000 civilians died and almost as many were injured, much of the city being reduced to a smoking ruin. But likewise, the long delay in the use of WINDOW proved controversial. During the long months that Britain had vacillated, some 11,000 Allied bomber crew could have been saved from death or captivity and 1,600 warplanes saved, had WINDOW been used.

Either way, the Germans were unable effectively to counter the use of the tin-foil strips. WINDOW had changed the nature of air warfare overnight, and from July 1943 onwards it was regularly used as the Allied bombing campaign ramped up over Germany. Its impact upon Germany's air defences was 'monstrous', every single radar apparatus being foiled by an invention that was as 'primitive' as it was 'effective', according to one Luftwaffe luminary. Albert Speer, Nazi Germany's Minister for Armaments and War Production, concurred. He was horrified by the attacks on Hamburg: 'six more cities like this and we have lost the war,' he warned.

But more cities were not hit, at least not right away. The Allies had far more pressing priorities. Days after Operation Gomorrah, Bomber Command was instructed to strike a top-secret target – a supposed radar factory. It was said to be so important that the bombers would be sent back again and again until it was destroyed. The aircrews did not relish the proposition. The target lay deep inside the Nazi homeland. The summer nights were short and losses were expected to be high. But aided by WINDOW, the bomber stream struck home. The target, at Peenemünde, on Germany's Baltic coast, was very badly damaged.

Peenemünde *Heeresversuchsanstalt* (Army Research Centre) was actually the top-secret German rocket development centre, where the V1s and V2s, among other weapons, were perfected. The early August air raids, codenamed Operation Hydra, deliberately targeted the sleeping and living quarters, in the hope of killing as many scientists as possible. After that, secondary targets were the factory workshops and the experimental stations themselves. As a result of the air raids, Peenemünde was evacuated and the programme taken over by the SS, all facilities being moved underground.

In the summer of 1943 WINDOW had finally been allowed to prove its worth. The blinding of the Würzburgs was a major milestone on the road to victory. As with other significant turning points – Stalingrad; defeating the U-boat stranglehold over Britain; winning the race for the nuclear bomb – it didn't result in the immediate collapse of Nazi Germany, but it did represent another nail in the coffin for Hitler's Reich. The use of WINDOW had secured for the Allies a degree of freedom of the skies over Germany. When the Germans did resort to using DUPPEL, in January 1944, Britain's radar defences had been rendered largely immune to its effects.

By the time WINDOW was in regular use, an even more decisive application of the technology was in the offing. While the Germans' 'wiring panic' had revealed the location of its radar stations and many had been bombed, others had been left unharmed. Those stations were in areas where the Allies wanted the enemy to detect threats that didn't in truth exist, and to act upon that intelligence accordingly. The boffins at TRE argued that if a mass-drop of WINDOW could blind the Würzburgs over Hamburg, surely a subtler, more intelligent use of the technology could achieve far greater deceptions. Surely, entire invasion fleets and their flights of fighter escorts could be created, where none existed. At TRE, they proved this was possible, and they did so in advance of D-Day.

Unsurprisingly, the preparations for D-Day – the largest seaborne operation in history – were utterly exhaustive. The landing beaches had to be tested, so as to be sure they could take the weight of landing craft, trucks and armour. To do so, one of the most secretive units of the war, the Combined Operations Pilotage Parties (COPP), was formed. Made up of 200 men, mostly Royal Navy and Royal Engineers, COPP operators used mini-subs to creep close to the beaches, releasing divers and canoeists to carry out ultra-secret reconnaissance under cover of darkness. They were to win ninety medals during the war.

The men emerged from the sea, silent and unseen, to gather

samples of shingle and sand. They placed guidance beacons in places of hiding. They measured gradients, to see if amphibious vehicles could climb them. But they were also privy to the most sensitive intelligence of the war: the potential location of the planned landings. Jim Booth, a COPP operator who won a Croix de Guerre and two MIDs, remarked: 'We had to survive unde-tected for five days, on baked beans and soup in a confined space,' as their mini-sub, or X-Craft, lay on the bottom off Gold beach, at La Rivière. 'We did have suicide pills but we used to joke about it. No one was going to use them.'

If the D-Day fleet failed to materialize – and it was at the mercy of the weather – Booth and his fellows had orders to 'take the X-Craft to deep water – we were all Commando-trained in Scotland – and to scuttle the craft, swim ashore and join the Free French'. On their sector of Gold, if the troops tried to put ashore too far east, they would hit rocks and never get onto the beach. That would have spelled disaster. Booth's role was 'to mark the eastern extremity with lights and flags, to prevent this from happening'.

On the very morning of the landings on 6 June 1944, Booth and crew had sat off the coast at periscope depth, watching German soldiers play football on the beach. The Allied ships were only hours away, but the enemy, it seemed, had not the faintest idea that the invasion fleet was coming. That alone was testament to the power of the D-Day deception that had been put in place, to obfuscate where the landings would occur. The challenge for TRE had been to persuade the enemy that the Allies were going to put ashore on different stretches of coastline to those actually intended.

To this end, TRE had masterminded Operations Glimmer

and Taxable. In the former, the RAF's 218 Squadron released WINDOW in such patterns as to simulate a huge convoy of ships heading for the French coast. Stirling bombers dropped clouds of tin-foil strips at predetermined intervals, the Glimmer decoy fleet appearing to be making for the beaches at the Pas de Calais, where Hitler was convinced that the landings would occur. Meanwhile, the Navy was also busy on the water, with motor launches towing barrage balloons covered in tin-foil reflectors, simulating large warships steaming for the same stretch of French coastline.

In Operation Taxable, the RAF's 617 Squadron – of Dambusters fame – flew repeated circuits over the Channel, releasing WINDOW to mimic a ghost-fleet heading towards the French coast east of Normandy, at a steady eight knots. As Churchill famously espoused, 'In wartime, truth is so precious she should always be attended by a bodyguard of lies.' It was never truer than in relation to Operation Overlord – the D-Day landings. For Jones, masterminding such ingenious deceptions was one of the most satisfying episodes of the Radar War, one that his tiny unit had been 'looking forward to' for some years.

Crucially, it was Operation Biting and the theft of the Würzburg that had enabled the creation of the ghost fleets and the ghost squadrons underpinning the D-Day deception, per-haps the most sophisticated fakery ever devised by humankind. A non-existent procession of landing craft, destroyers, cruisers, battleships and squadrons of fighter escorts had been created in two places – the Pas de Calais and the Seine Peninsula – where none in truth existed, while the real invasion fleet steamed unnoticed towards the Normandy beaches. D-Day losses were less than a quarter of what Allied commanders had feared, largely due to the deceptions masterminded by Jones and by the teams based at TRE.

In 1935 Churchill, a long-time scientific visionary, had foreseen the wartime legacy of radar. In a speech made to the House of Commons he envisaged 'the methods which can be invented or adopted or discovered to enable the Earth to control the Air, to enable defence from the ground to exercise control – indeed dominance – upon aeroplanes high above its surface . . .' He foresaw how 'patience, perseverance, and above all the spur of necessity under war conditions, made men's brains act with greater vigour, and science responded to the demands.'

In late August 1945, with the war all but over and the world contemplating the recent use of the atom bombs against Japan, a press conference was held in London to reveal the vital role that radar had played. At it, Sir Stafford Cripps, the Labour politician and Minister for Aircraft Production, spoke alongside Air Chief Marshal Arthur Tedder, latterly Deputy Supreme Commander at Supreme Headquarters Allied Expeditionary Force (SHAEF), under General Eisenhower. Their words reflected how Churchill's 1935 predictions had become a wartime reality.

Proceedings opened with Mr E. Williams, the then Minister for Information, praising 'the least spectacular qualities that made Mr Winston Churchill the greatest war leader of our time – the selection of men of great capacity for jobs in which they could work harmoniously together as between our Allies and amongst themselves.' Many of those 'men of great capacity' were present that day, for a raft of senior scientists were in attendance.

Sir Stafford Cripps next took the floor, his sentiments regarding radar demanding instant attention.

'The whole world has recently been talking very much about the atom bomb and the dramatic part it has played in so suddenly bringing an offer of surrender from Japan. But today, by agreement with our American allies, we are going to reveal for the first time the story of an invention, Radar, which has played a greater part in the whole war than the atom bomb itself . . . Radar, more than any other scientific factor, has contributed to the final victory over Germany.'

In essence Cripps was right: the atom bomb had helped end the war, but it had played little role in the six years spent fighting and winning it.

Of course, in the summer of 1945 these were particularly new and arresting claims – radar remained a closely guarded secret – and Cripps underscored his opening remarks with emotive detail.

'The invention, with its almost limitless applications . . . was born simultaneously with the accession to power of Hitler in Germany, at the precise moment, in other words, when the shadow of that wicked man first began to fall over Europe. How radar was discovered and . . . the great contribution it made, first to our salvation in this country and then to the complete defeat of the enemy . . . has so far remained a secret. The time has now come when we can disclose the veritable marvels which were worked . . .'

Cripps went on to laud radar's role in the Battle of Britain, and the scientists who mastered the technology.

'Had these men not been working on this invention long before war broke out, it is doubtful – indeed, I think it might be said to be very doubtful – whether we in this island would have been able to hold the fort in those critical years of our lonely struggle in 1940 and 1941, when Germany threw the whole weight of her air armada against us . . . The first big operational test of Radar, and the glorious proof of its success, came in the Battle of Britain, which I am sure history will surely record as one of the decisive battles of the world. For had we lost it, who can say how different might have been the outcome of the war?'

Cripps and Tedder went on to chronicle the string of achievements of radar thereafter, culminating in what the latter described as the vital battle – 'the bomber offensive'. Tedder explained how radar 'first made possible the concentration of large squadrons of bombers over the right spot and at the right time . . . That, of course, was a vital factor in the final campaign in Northern Europe. Extreme accuracy and extreme concentration were absolutely essential at that time.' Both men paid tribute to the scientists, highlighting that 'the debt which we, and I venture the whole civilised world, owe to these men is one which we can never repay.'

Once they were done speaking, it was opened up for questions. After several, one of the reporters asked: 'Can anything be said about the anti-Radar devices used by either side? I am thinking of the metallic strips which were dropped by enemy aircraft and also used by our own planes.' The response was curt and succinct. That line of enquiry was rapidly silenced, for that was a subject 'we would sooner not have much publicity about.' While the Radar story was finally being told, WINDOW remained top secret, as did the long and dramatic story leading up to its use, one in which Operation Biting had played the key role.

Op Biting had been a small-scale raid in February 1942, involving just 120 men on the ground, but it was one with long-lived and fateful consequences. It had spawned an in-depth understanding of the enemy's key radar technologies, and how they could be blinded and defeated, and then so much more. It involved many more than Frost's raiders, although they had formed the tip of the spear. So many factors had proven pivotal: the men of Operation Colossus, who pioneered the first airborne operations; the daring and dash of the photo reconnaissance pilots; the inspired genius of the photo interpretations teams; the bravery and spirit of Remy and his Confrérie Notre-Dame; the single-minded conviction of Churchill, that Britain needed to strike back even in her darkest hour; the unorthodox thinking of Jones and his team – the scientists to the spies; plus the skills of the boffins at TRE, who brought the captured Würzburg back to life and forced it to divulge its secrets.

Donald Preist, the scientist-adventurer codenamed Noah, summed up the achievements of the Operation Biting team thus: 'When I think of the many ways we could have lost the War to the Germans, some involving technical matters, and when I think of all the sources of information available to a potential enemy ... I can only conclude that one thing is certain: THE PRICE OF LIBERTY IS ETERNAL VIGILANCE.' That was Operation Biting's precious, vital legacy.

Epilogue

Since the war, several observers have criticized the way in which the Operation Colossus raiders were abandoned, while simultaneously hailing the success of the raid. In his 1974 book on the Bruneval Raid, George Millar, DSO, MC, veteran of both regular forces and SOE, and post-war author, wrote of the SAS originals: 'They were an unusually impressive batch of soldiers. Their mission to blow up an aqueduct in southern Italy had been hastily conceived. They had accomplished it with ingenuity, courage and humanity . . .'

In the Imperial War Museum's publication, *Airborne Forces of the Second World War, 1939–45* – widely recognized as a highly authoritative history – Lt-Col. T. B. Otway concludes of the actions of the 11 Special Air Service raiders: 'The demolitions were effective, the pier collapsed, the waterway was broken in two where it had been supported by the pier and water flooded down the ravine. The operation was successful . . . It provided useful experience for parachute raids in the future and showed the wide flexibility and range inherent in airborne troops – and their ever-present threat to the enemy.'

Raymond Foxall, like Millar a Second World War veteran who turned author after the war, wrote of Colossus in the early 1980s, describing it as 'a little-known epic . . . that ranks among the most daring of the war.' He pointed out that 'the paratroopers fulfilled their orders. They blew away a section of the aqueduct, diverting the water supply for a month – the time it took the Italians to repair it.'

In the days immediately following Operation Colossus, all of the raiders were taken captive. Fortunato Picchi, as described earlier, was outed as an Italian national and shot. Of the others, two would escape to Britain, and more would escape into the Italian mountains. Anthony Deane-Drummond was the first escapee, making it into neutral Switzerland and from there to Gibraltar, where he caught a troopship to Britain. In March 1943 he sailed for North Africa, with 2nd Parachute Brigade. In 1944 he took part in the Arnhem raid – operation Market Garden – and was taken prisoner by the Germans. Deane-Drummond escaped again, rejoined the advancing British Army and fought until the end of the war.

After the war, he rose to the rank of major-general and commanded the SAS Regiment in the late 1950s, in both Malaya (now Malaysia) and Oman. For the latter deployment, and especially the SAS's daring assault on the Jebel Akhdar, in January 1959, he was awarded the DSO, ending up with a CB, DSO, MC and bar. He also went on to win the British Gliding Championships. The capabilities of the SAS demonstrated in those two very contrasting theatres of war – one tropical jungle, the other sun-blasted desert and mountains – led to the decision not to disband the SAS, which had been the intention once these 'emergencies' had been dealt with. The SAS had already been disbanded once, immediately post-war (although in its post-war war-crimes hunting team, it had lived on secretly until 1948; see my own book, *The Nazi Hunters*). After the SAS's decisive Malaya and Oman exploits, a second disbandment was ruled out of the question.

Corporal Alfred Parker – one of the Operation Colossus sappers – also managed to escape from captivity twice. The first time, he was recaptured in Italy and held by the Germans. He escaped again and made his way back to British lines, hitching a ride to North Africa in a US Air Force Douglas C47 Dakota aircraft.

Many of those held captive in Italy managed to break out of the POW camps, once the Italians signed the Armistice with the Allies in September 1943. After a gruelling thirty-one-day march, Sergeants Percy Clements and Arthur Lawley managed to cross the lines, making it back to British forces. Lawley – Deane-Drummond's second-in-command – went on to become a company sergeant major in the Airborne Division, taking part in the D-Day landings, receiving a certificate signed by Field Marshal Montgomery for 'outstanding good service and devotion to duty'. Sergeant Clements became a full lieutenant in the Parachute Regiment, going on to win an MC on operations in the Ardennes region of France.

As German forces took over those positions vacated by Italian troops, Hitler vowing to hold Italy at all costs, many of the X Troop escapees were recaptured and shipped north to POW camps in Germany. But Lieutenant George Paterson – 'the Big Canadian' – managed to leap from a train and escape from his guards, after which he linked up with Italian partisans in the mountains. Paterson became a legendary guerrilla commander, organizing hit-and-run and sabotage attacks against German and Fascist Italian forces, eventually being recruited by SOE. Dispatched by SOE to link up with a new Italian partisan force, Paterson was eventually recaptured by the Germans and imprisoned, before being rescued by the Italian resistance.

Another of the X Troopers, Lance-Corporal Harry Boulter

– the man who had broken his ankle upon landing at the Tragino aqueduct – also joined forces with the Italian resistance. Boulter fought with them for nine months, before being recaptured by German troops and imprisoned in Nazi Germany.

Lance-Corporal Robert 'Bob' Watson – the former bricklayer who'd helped Deane-Drummond blow up the road bridge adjacent to the Tragino Aqueduct – became another serial escapee, being recaptured several times. He finally reached neutral Switzerland on July 15 1944, and was awarded an MM for his efforts, having jumped from a train while en route to Germany.

Major 'Tag' Pritchard, DSO, MBE, was liberated from a POW camp when overrun by British forces, and was promoted after his return to Britain, serving at Sandhurst. But he contracted TB and had to retire from the military. He moved to London, and after a less than successful first marriage, he married again and lived happily until his death in 1982. Captain Gerald Daly, the RE sapper force commander on Colossus, remained in the military and attained the rank of lieutenant-colonel. Captain Christopher Lea managed to study for a law degree, even while held captive by the enemy. He was promoted to major after the war, but he left the Army to practise law, becoming a judge.

The mysterious Flight Lieutenant Ralph Lucky was promoted after repatriation from the POW camps, and commanded an RAF transit camp in Malta after the war. Trooper Alan Ross, the youngest of the X Troopers, was commissioned into the Territorial Army after the war.

The originator of Operation Colossus, Oxford don and classicist, Professor Colin Hardie, returned to Magdalen College after the war and remained there as an academic until his retirement in 1973. He retired to Wrackham Cottage, near Pulborough, Sussex, with his wife, and passed away in 1988. He was remembered as a 'staunch and true friend to learning and to those values it should nourish'. Few knew of the secret role he had played during the war. The outfit he had served during the war years, Churchill's SOE, was summarily disbanded in 1946.

Of those six men captured during Operation Biting, all would be sent to Lamsdorf POW camp in Poland, also known as Stalag VIIIB. They would spend the rest of the war there, being repatriated to Britain when Lamsdorf was liberated by Allied troops. Two, Privates George Cornell and Frank Embury, had almost managed to slip the drag-net set up by German forces, following Operation Biting. With the aid of a brave French couple, Maurice Lajoye and Mademoiselle Régnier, they had reached the border of the occupied zone of France, on the far side of which freedom beckoned. But Cornell and Embury were stopped by a suspicious German guard, and eventually their cover fell apart. Their two French resistance helpers were also captured, and sent to the concentration camps, Lajoye to Buchenwald and Régnier to Ravensbrück. They survived the war and eventually returned to France.

In October 1942 Flight Officer Tony Hill – the man who had secured the low-level dicing photos of the Würzburg – led a reconnaissance mission over another target in France, one that he felt it too dangerous for other pilots to risk. Sadly, Hill was shot down while executing his low-level pass, and although he survived the resulting crash he had broken his back. The French resistance were asked to break him free from the hospital where he was being treated and an aircraft was readied to spirit him back to Britain. He died before the attempt could be made.

In October 1942 the Parachute Brigade was despatched to North Africa, with Frost in command of the 2nd Battalion. Frost and his men jumped behind the lines from American Douglas C47 Dakota aircraft (a great improvement on the Whitleys). Dropped to raid Oudna airfield in Tunisia, Frost and his men became largely forgotten and abandoned, as Allied commanders focused on repelling a new German offensive. Running out of ammunition, with faulty radios and harassed by enemy warplanes, panzers and armoured cars, Frost and his men had to abandon their wounded and escape and evade over sixty miles of hostile terrain. By sheer grit and determination they pulled through, but 260 men had been lost – killed, captured or wounded.

Many of the Biting veterans were among those captured or killed. Major Philip Teichman, who'd briefly commanded Frost's company while he was earning his wings, was among the dead. So too was Lieutenant Euan 'Junior' Charteris, one of the real heroes of the raid on Bruneval. Charteris lost his life while leading an advance party to try to scout out a route back to Allied lines. He had reached his twenty-first birthday but sadly would not make his twenty-second. Frost was furious. In contrast to Operation Biting, which had been meticulously planned, the Oudna mission was rushed and lacking in intelligence; he and his men had been cut loose. He would later describe it as 'perhaps the most disgracefully mounted operation of the war'.

Frost and his men remained in North Africa, taking more than three thousand prisoners as the fighting progressed. Many confessed to how terrified they were, upon realizing they faced British Paras – it was in this campaign that German forces had nicknamed them *Die Roten Teufel* – the Red Devils. In the fighting, Lieutenant John Timothy – the former Marks & Spencer salesman – captured a German machinegun nest more-or-less singlehandedly, killing six enemy soldiers, and earning for himself an MC. He'd earn a bar to that MC in Italy in 1943, undertaking a search and rescue mission for escaped Allied POWs.

Lieutenant John Ross, Frost's second-in-command on Biting, would earn a DSO during the North Africa operations, and Sergeant Gregor McKenzie won the DCM in action there, to add to the MC he'd won at Bruneval.

After a series of fearsome Italian missions, 2 Para withdrew from Italy in late 1943, Lieutenant Ross having been captured by the enemy. The unit was next to see action in September 1944 in Operation Market Garden, in which Frost's 2 Para were given one of the toughest jobs of all, to capture and hold the furthest road bridge in Arnhem. Surrounded and outnumbered by German troops, Frost and his men held on to the bridge as they ran short of ammo, food and water. When an SS commander invited Frost to surrender, his response was: 'Tell them to go to hell.' Shortly after, Frost was wounded badly, and with hundreds of other casualties he was taken captive. His men fought on for another twenty-four hours, before being overrun by German forces.

John Timothy, then a major in command of his own company, was also engaged in the Arnhem operations. When his company was reduced to only six fighting men, he led an assault against an enemy strongpoint, winning his third MC in fifteen months. Finally taken captive, Timothy escaped towards the end of the war and linked up with advancing American troops.

Sergeant-Major Gerry Strachan was another Operation Biting veteran to fight at Arnhem, having been awarded a Croix de Guerre with Palm in January 1944 for his role in that operation. He too was taken captive during the Arnhem fighting, and, like Frost, would remain in captivity until the POW camp was liberated by Allied forces in March 1945. Sadly, Strachan never fully recovered from the terrible injuries he'd suffered at Bruneval: he died in 1948, aged forty-one.

Privates Thomas and Willoughby, plus Lance-Corporal McCallum – the three Operation Biting raiders left behind on the beach who'd taken shelter in caves – were duly captured, and spent the remainder of the war as POWs. They survived the war and were returned to Britain upon liberation of the camps.

In September 1942 RAN Commander Cook – the commander of the Tormentor flotilla – took up a new post, this time in his native Australia, where he had been asked to help establish an Australian Combined Operations Training Centre. He went on to establish the amphibious Training Centre at Port Stevens, just to the north of Sydney, which he named HMAS Assault.

Sir Henry Nigel Norman was appointed the Air Commander for the North Africa landings, but was tragically killed on 19 May 1943, when the aircraft he was flying in crash-landed shortly after take-off from the UK. Wing Commander Charles Pickard was the first RAF officer to be awarded the DSO and two bars during the war. Sadly, he was killed leading Operation Jericho, the 18 February 1943 low-level raid by Mosquito aircraft on the Amiens prison, in France, a mission launched at the request of the French resistance. His navigator, Flight Lieutenant Bill Broadley, DSO, DFC, DFM, was also killed. Broadley had been Pickard's navigator on the Operation Biting raid. The French government called for Pickard to receive a posthumous Victoria Cross for the raid.

R. V. Jones, the scientist to the spies, became a key V1 and V2 expert towards the end of the war, and later went on to take the Chair of Natural Philosophy at the University of Aberdeen. Churchill would herald Jones as being one of the 'heroes of World

War II'. In 1952, at Churchill's request, Jones became Director of Scientific Intelligence at the Ministry of Defence, but returned to the University of Aberdeen thereafter, until his retirement in 1981. In addition to numerous international awards bestowed upon Jones, he won the inaugural R.V. Jones Intelligence Award, founded by the US Central Intelligence Agency (CIA). A full description of his work during the war is contained in his excellent book, *Most Secret War* (see Bibliography).

After Operation Biting, Flight Sergeant Charles Cox returned to his regular duties as a radar technician. Post-war Cox set up a TV and wireless business, on Little Church Street, in his native Wisbech. Major John Timothy, MC and two bars, decided to return to his former career, rising through the ranks of Marks and Spencer to become the manager of their Wakefield store. Following his capture in Italy, John Ross spent the war busy with various escape committees, for which he would be awarded an MBE. He became a successful solicitor after the war in his native Scotland.

Peter Nagel – 'Private Newman' on Operation Biting – survived incarceration in various POW camps, following his capture on Operation Chariot. He tried various escape attempts, once by tunnel, and was sent to Lamsdorf POW camp, Poland – Stalag VIIIB. He managed to escape from there and reach as far as Klagenfurt, Austria, before being recaptured and returned to Lamsdorf. In spring 1945 Nagel was liberated by American forces, returning to the UK and his father's Leicester textile business, which he took over in 1950. On the fortieth anniversary of Operation Biting, he received a *Diplôme d'Honneur*, signed by the Queen and President François Mitterrand.

After the war, Nagel married a former WAAF, Muriel Phyllis

Owen, and their daughter, Jane Sabina, was born in 1949. By then Nagel was a naturalized British citizen. One evening, after staying late at work at his textile business, Nagel was set upon by a gang of muggers. Shocked by his swift, commando-style response, they soon ran away. Nagel died in 1983, aged only sixty-seven, from skin cancer. His daughter, Jane, inherited the statue that his 2 Para comrades had given to him. It is inscribed: 'Presented to Peter Nagel, from His Comrades of the 2nd Battalion The Parachute Regiment. A Brave Man and a Good Friend.'

After the war, Frost alone of the Biting raiders remained in the Army long-term, building upon the legendary reputation he'd earned during the war. He achieved the rank of Lieutenant-General and commanded the 52nd (Lowland) Division. After retirement in 1968 to a farm in West Sussex, Frost led numerous reunions for both Bruneval and Arnhem. Every year Dutch children lay flowers on the graves of the British and Commonwealth soldiers who fell during the battles around Arnhem. At Bruneval, two roads in the vicinity have been named Rue John Frost, and in 1977 the new road bridge across the Lower Rhine at Arnhem was renamed John Frostbrug, the John Frost Bridge.

In 1947 General Charles de Gaulle unveiled a monument to Operation Biting, at the pillbox above the site of the Stella Maris villa, just behind the beach itself. Some 20,000 former members of the French resistance attended the ceremony, as did a guard of honour from the Parachute Regiment.

In 1953 the source of the Oslo Report – the document from which R. V. Jones and others had gleaned so much insight into the enemy's extraordinary scientific and technological advancements during the war – was found to be the German physicist and fervent anti-Nazi, Hans Ferdinand Meyer. Meyer admitted it privately to R. V. Jones, prompting Jones to revisit the case of the Oslo Report. He concluded that it constituted 'the best single report received from any source during the whole war'. Noting how much Britain was in Meyer's debt, Jones proposed that the British government should 'recompense the source in some measure for the service which he rendered to us'.

However, Meyer, fearing reprisals against him and his family if his authorship of the report became publicly known, asked Jones only to reveal it after his death and that of his wife. Jones respected the German physicist's wishes, not revealing his identity until 1989. As a result, Meyer received no accolade or recognition for what he had achieved, risked – and suffered – during the war.

I have had some files opened via Freedom of Information or other requests, to assist with the writing of this book. One file remains closed and will not be released by the MOD. It concerns the episode within which the *Graf Spee* was scuttled and her radar unit photographed, documented and its remains salvaged and spirited to the UK. I can only imagine that file concerns activities of MI6 (the Secret Intelligence Service) either regarding the *Graf Spee* or other matters, that HMG feels should not come to light at the present time. One wonders what they may be, such that eighty years after the events portrayed they are still judged to be of such sensitivity.

The whereabouts of the purloined Würzburg remain a mystery to this day. The Radar Establishment at Malvern – the successor to TRE – has been unable to trace it, and neither could the Imperial War Museum, the Royal Signals or a number of other venerable military institutions.

Acknowledgements

In researching this book I was able to meet, speak to and receive assistance from many individuals who were exceptionally generous with their time. My special thanks and gratitude are extended to all, and my apologies to those that I may have inadvertently forgotten to mention.

Among others, I'd like to thank those individuals depicted in these pages, and their family members, who helped me, with great generosity, to tell their stories. Many thanks to Jim Booth, Second World War veteran and COPP operator, for sharing your compelling reminiscences of proving the D-Day beaches. Thanks to Alan Smith, for sharing your memories and recollections of growing up in and around the radar towers and laboratories of TRE in Dorset. Thanks to Malcolm Buckley, for your recollections and the photos and documents regarding your father, Edwin William Buckley, and his service with Airborne Division in the Second World War. Thanks to Chris Rooney, for sharing your father's wartime SAS recollections and memories, plus those images you generously provided to me. Thanks to John and Peter Jefferies, for allowing me to quote from the recollections of your father, David Cross Jefferies, of parachute jumps during the war. Especial thanks to Nicole Pickard, Wing Commander Charles Pickard's granddaughter, for the correspondence and the kind permission to use photos of her grandfather in this book. I'm very grateful to Mike Packwood, grandson of Lance-Corporal Robert Watson, for reaching out to me about the role he played in Operation Colossus, and for sharing recollections and memories, plus the photos used in this book.

My very special thanks are also extended to Jack Mann, veteran of the SBS, SAS and LRDG, for reading an early draft of this book and for your invaluable insights and recollections from the war years, plus the documents and photographs you were, once again, happy to share with me. These proved invaluable, as did your insight and perceptive comments.

Very special thanks to Dr Phil Judkins, Chairman of the UK's Defence Electronic History Society and of Purbeck Radar Museum Trust, for your guiding hand and excellent feedback at all stages of the research and writing process, which proved invaluable. Enormous thanks to Mike Burstow, and all at MRATHS, including and not limited to Hugh Williams, Martin Hutchinson, Ron Henry, Mike Dean, Lew and Sue Amphlett and Tony & Viv Waller. The tour of the MRATHS archive in Malvern, plus of Malvern and its historic places of interest relating to the Radar Wars, was illuminating and a real highlight. Thank you also to those from MRATHS who invited me into your homes and extended warm hospitality during my visit. The MRATHS charity is profiled in the closing pages herein. I'd also like to thank QinetiQ Plc, who host the MRATHS archive, for granting me access to view and peruse it at my leisure, at their Malvern headquarters.

I extend my very heartfelt thanks to TRE veteran Laurie Hinton and his wife, Ann, for inviting me into your home so I could hear your story, which was hugely appreciated. Again, I'm hugely grateful to John and Barbara Hooper, both of whom are TRE veterans from the Second World War, who shared with me your recollections of serving there during the war years. It was both a pleasure and an honour to listen to your stories. I'm grateful also to Evelyn Warton, who served with the WRNS during the war and taught pilots to better 'see in the dark', among other things – a story related at great length in her captivating memoir, *Brave Faces*, written under the pen name, Mary Arden. It was a privilege meeting you and listening to your stories. Both Eve, and her son Jamie Robertson, also assisted me greatly with relating the story of George Paterson, the man tasked to blow up the Tragino Aqueduct and a close friend of their family and godfather to one of Eve's sons.

I'm also immensely grateful to the late Max Arthur, a fellow author whose assistance proved invaluable. Thanks to fellow author and military historian Neil Thornton also, for invaluable help, guidance and contacts. My immense gratitude to Martin Sugarman, who proved enormously helpful in my research into Peter Nagel's war years. Thanks also to Ian Virgo, whose local historical research on the Dorset radar connection and all things TRE proved invaluable. Immense gratitude also to Frank and Suzie Parr, whose support of the Artist Rifle's Clubhouse, helping safeguard its venerable two-hundred-year history and unique archival record, has proven so invaluable.

Thanks especially to Ben Waddams, for your superb depiction of the scene from Operation Colossus, when the parachutists dropped into enemy territory on Britain's first ever airborne operation. A wildlife artist by profession, Ben was first inspired to paint the exploits of elite forces during the Second World War, when listening to my writing on audio books in his artist's studio. We have used Ben's wonderful paintings, inspired by my work, to help raise thousands of pounds for charities connected to my writing, and his painting of Operation Colossus graces the rear cover of this book.

In no particular order I also wish to thank the following, who assisted in many ways: research, proofreading, subject matter expertise, contacts, referrals. Tean Roberts, for your hard work and diligence, as always. Simon Fowler, for your expertise and inspiration, gleaned from the various archives. Paul and Anne Sherratt, for your incisive comments and guidance. Thanks especially to my good friend (and sensei) Sally Allcard for translations from the French and the German, which proved invaluable.

Thanks in particular to Nick Caplin, Renata Gomes and Catherine Goodier, at Blind Veterans UK, for all your help and assistance. I'd like to thank John Jones, of Hunters Gin, a foremost supporter of Blind Veterans UK (BVUK), a wonderful veterans charity whose archive proved instructive in the writing of this book (a charity profiled in the closing pages herein). I'd like to thank Bob and Jackie Skillicorn of The Bookshop Liskeard, for your inspired and enthusiastic support of authors and the book trade, and for your hosting the Cornwall launch of this book, a generous and much-appreciated gesture.

Thanks to Phil Williams, for research into historical aspects of this story. Thanks also to Asher Pirt, Dennis Worden, Christina and Ken Penman, Paul Hazzard, Rupert Paul Utley and Jeff Allum, for the various ways in which you helped enable this book to come to fruition.

The staff at several archives and museums also deserve special mention, including those at the British National Archives; the Imperial War Museum; the Churchill Archive Centre at Churchill College, Cambridge; and MRATHS. Some files from the National

Archives were made available to me as a result of Freedom of Information requests, and I am grateful to the individuals at the Archives who made the decision that those files should be opened. I'm also grateful to the Army Personnel Centre, Support Division, Historical Disclosures, for making the military records of Major John Dutton Frost available to me.

My gratitude also to my literary agent, Gordon Wise, of Curtis Brown, for helping bring this project to fruition, and to all at my publishers, Quercus, for same, including, but not limited to: Charlotte Fry, Ben Brock and Fiona Murphy. My editor, Richard Milner, deserves very special mention, as always. Many thanks also to Wendy McCurdy, at my American publisher, Kensington, and to all of her team, and to George Lucas, the agent who represented this book in the USA.

I am also indebted to those authors who have previously written about some of the topics dealt with in this book and whose work has helped inform my writing. I have included a full bibliography, but in alphabetical order the key texts are: *The Radar Army*, Reg Batt; *The Rise of the Boffins*, Ronald W. Clark; *Seven Assignments*, Brigadier Dudley Clarke; *Arrows of Fortune*, Anthony Deane-Drummond; *Return Ticket*, Anthony Deane-Drummond; *Night Raid*, Taylor Downing; *The Guinea-Pigs*, Raymond Foxall; *A Drop Too Many*, Major General John Frost; *Prelude to Glory*, Maurice Newnham; *The Bruneval Raid*, George Millar; *The Red Beret*, Hilary St George Saunders.

Thanks are due also to Eva and the ever-patient David, Damien Jr and Sianna, for not resenting Dad spending too much of his time locked away . . . again . . . writing . . . again.

Bibliography

Archives, Museums, Research Organizations

The National Archives, Kew, are a rich repository of documents underlying the stories depicted in these pages, including files related to the Special Operations Executive; the Army, Royal Navy and Royal Air Force; official War Office and Cabinet papers, plus records of the Chiefs of Staff meetings and Churchill's correspondence concerning same.

The National Army Museum's Special Forces Collection is an important resource of images, records and memorabilia from the war years, including from the operations described in these pages.

The Imperial War Museum also has a vast collection of documents, including those held at the IWM's London site, namely unpublished records and reports from those whose stories are told in this book, and photographs and film footage related to the operations portrayed. At the IWM Duxford, the Airborne Assault Archive also contains key documents and images related to the missions depicted in these pages.

The Malvern Radar and Technological Historical Society (MRATHS) archive, at Malvern, is a unique and comprehensive record of the activities of the Telecommunications Research Establishment (TRE) during and after the war, and includes some of the original hardware (technology) saved from countless experiments and scientific developments.

The UK's Defence Electronic History Society (DEHS) constitutes a wealth of information regarding the development of radar, and related technologies, during the Second World War.

The Purbeck Radar Museum Trust (PRMT) constitutes a rich resource of information for those interested in the activities of TRE at Worth Matravers during the war.

The Penley Radar Archives are an invaluable source of academic reports and studies on aspects of radar and related technologies developed at TRE.

The Medmenham Collection is a remarkable archive recording the activities at Danesfield House of RAF Medmenham personnel and those who served there during the Second World War.

The Churchill Archives Centre, at Churchill College, Cambridge, contains useful papers pertaining to Churchill's role in the development of special forces, and also the private papers of R. V. Jones.

Unpublished Sources

National Archives, DEFE 2-1523 PLANNING

National Archives, DEFE 2-153 PLANNING

National Archives, DEFE 2-152 FINAL REPORT 'Colossus'.

National Archives, AIR 7450 Early Plans, 'Magdalen College Oxford . . .'

National Archives, CAB 106-6 Witness

National Archives, AIR 7450 Early Plans, 'Water Project – Southern Italy'

National Archives, REM 3-100 WSC

National Archives, AIR 7450 Early Plans, 'Plan Factors'

National Archives, CAB 79/9 COS Meetings

National Archives, AIR 7450 Early Plans, 'Receipt for Photos . . .'

National Archives, AIR 20/1631 Bruneval: Raid on German RDF

National Archives, AVIA 7/7159 TRE REPORTS

National Archives, AIR 39/1 Raid on radio location Post at Bruneval (PICS)

National Archives, ADM 281/84 Graf Spee

National Archives, AIR 40/2572 'Oslo Report'

National Archives, HU 15-14 Soviet Intercepts

National Archives, AIR 40: 3048 1940 Report

National Archives, AIR 90/3047

National Archives, AVIA 7/7159 TRE REPORTS

National Archives, DEFE 2-100 REPORT

National Archives, DEFE 2-101 Appendices

National Archives, AWARDS RN 1-12316

National Archives, CAB 79/81

National Archives, CAB 79/17

National Archives, AIR 8/867

National Archives, AIR 39/43 Op Biting PLANNING

National Archives, DEFE 2-102 Planning

National Archives, WO 106-4132 REPORT

National Archives, PREM 3/73

National Archives, AIR 16/755 Fighter Command

National Archives, TRE 11-219

National Archives, AIR 32/8 Op Orders/Training for Op Biting

National Archives, WO 373/93

National Archives, PREM 3-100 WSC

National Archives, TRE No. JIM/62

National Archives, AIR 14/3583 'Knickebein'

National Archives, AIR 20/1626 'Knickebein'

National Archives, HW 5/5 (Knickebein) usage

National Archives, WO 208/3507 Extracts from interrogation reports

National Archives, WO 208/3506 Extracts from interrogation reports

National Archives, AIR 40/3046 Report No. 6

National Archives, AIR 20/1623 The Crooked Leg: report on 'Knickebein'

National Archives, HW 15/43/93 London; 1 NOBILITY reports German use of KNICKEBEIN

National Archives, HW 5/179 'BROWN' reports

National Archives, ADM 1/12316 Honours and Award (85)

National Archives, ADM 1/14233 Honours and Award (47)

National Archives, AIR 14/3296 TRE progress report

National Archives, AIR 2/7689 Various

National Archives, AIR 20/1546 German RDF captured at Bruneval

National Archives, AIR 20/8953 Radar and Radio Counter-measures (Code 61)

National Archives, NCUACS 95.8.00/B. 150 'The Intelligence Aspect of the Bruneval Raid'

National Archives, NCUACS 95.8.00/B. 31, B. 32 Report No. 15, Intelligence Aspect of the Bruneval Raid

National Archives, NCUACS 95.8.00/J. 126 First Draft

National Archives, NCUACS 95.8.00/J. 165 Second Draft

OG/CC/2260A 'I am hoping that midday . . .'

DEHS 'CHESS', 'Electronic Warfare and Strategic Bomber Offensives in Europe, an Attempt at Balance', Dr Phil Judkins and Arthur Bauer

DEHS, e-DEFENCE, No. 68, Part 1: March 2018, BRUNEVAL RAID 1942, AS SEEN BY C. W. H. COX, MM, RAF

'The Worth of Worth, Britain's Silicon Valley', Dr Phil Judkins, University of Leeds and Buckingham, Centre for Security and Intelligence Studies; Chairman, Purbeck Radar Museum Trust

MRATHS – WWII radar map, showing radar curtain strung around French coast

MRATHS – Early Enemy Radar

MRATHS – The Bruneval Raid, Operation Biting, Highly Secret TRE Technical Report on German Radar dated 8th May 1942

MRATHS – Bruneval, Don Preist

MRATHS – Bruneval Revisited, Nov '97, Don Preist

MRATHS – No. 11 Group Appendices, 27-2-43-28-2-43

MRATHS – 'The Second World War 1939–1945, Royal Air Force, Signals', Volume VII, Radio Counter-Measures

MRATHS – TRE Report 5-16A-EGA Investigation Flight No 1 1941May14 FGA-JWC

MRATHS – TRE Report 5-17 Investigations Flight No 2 1941Jun07

MRATHS – TRE Report 5-24 Investigation of Enemy RDF Coverage between Calais and Borkum D1100 1941Jul08

MRATHS – TRE Report 5-32 Investigation of night fighter intercepts 19Aug41

MRATHS – TRE Report 5-35 RAF-JWC 21Sep1941

MRATHS – TRE Report 5-47 Calibration of AB2 Receiver etc at 50cm 1941 undated

MRATHS – TRE Report 6-18-EGA Air Investigation ~1941

MRATHS – TRE Report 5-M-62 dated 21 June 1942, Case for Counter Activity to Enemy RDF

MRATHS – TRE Report 5-M-62 dated 5 July 1942, A summary of the case for significant increase in RCM effort

MRATHS – AP Rowe's admin order no 1, Move of TRE from Swanage to Malvern

Purbeck Radar Museum Trust, 'Secret War in Purbeck', Jonathan Penley & Dr Bill Penley

Purbeck Radar Museum Trust, Min-Biographies of Scientists – Donald Preist, A. P. 'Jimmy' Rowe

Penley Radar Archives, Radar Countermeasures, Sir Robert Cockburn

Penley Radar Archives, RDF at the Bawdsey and Bruneval raid, Mr. Don Preist

Penley Radar Archives, HQ – Directorate of Communications Development in London, Mr W. G. Allen

Penley Radar Archives, Original Theoretical Work on Wave-Guides, Dr W. D. Allen

Ian Virgo, 'Dorset & The Development of Radar' (unpublished paper)

Ian Virgo, 'Dorset's Radar War on the U-boat' (unpublished paper)

Mars & Minerva, The Journal of the Special Air Service, Vol. 13, No. 2, December 2018

Army Personnel Centre, Support Division, Historical Disclosures, D/ACP/HD/43847 John Dutton Frost

Published Books

Reg Batt, *The Radar Army: Winning the War of the Airwaves*, Robert Hale, 1991

Anthony Cave Brown, *Bodyguard of Lies*, W.H. Allen, 1976

Niall Cherry, *Striking Back: Britain's Airborne and Commando Raids 1940–42*, Helion & Company, 2009

Ronald W. Clark, *The Rise of the Boffins*, Phoenix House, 1962

Brigadier Dudley Clarke, *Seven Assignments*, Jonathan Cape, 1948

Anthony Deane-Drummond, *Arrows of Fortune*, Leo Cooper, 1992

Anthony Deane-Drummond, *Return Ticket*, Collins, 1953

Douglas Dodds-Parker, *Setting Europe Ablaze*, Springwood, 1983

Taylor Downing, *Night Raid: The True Story of the First Victorious British Para Raid of WWII*, Little, Brown, 2013

Taylor Downing, *Spies in the Sky: The Secret Battle for Aerial Intelligence during World War II*, Little, Brown, 2011

Ken Ford, *The Bruneval Raid: Operation Biting 1942*, Osprey Publishing, 2010

Raymond Foxall, *The Guinea-Pigs: Britain's First Parachute Raid*, Robert Hale, 1983

Major-General John Frost, *A Drop Too Many*, Buchan & Enright, 1982

James Goodchild, *A Most Enigmatic War: R. V. Jones and the Genesis of British Scientific Intelligence 1939–45*, Helion & Company, 2009

R. Hanbury-Brown, *Boffin: A Personal Story of the Early Days of Radar, Radio Astronomy and Quantum Optics*, Adam Hilger, 1991

Thaddeus Holt, *The Deceivers: Allied Military Deception in the Second World War*, Weidenfeld & Nicolson, 2004

R. V. Jones, *Most Secret War: British Scientific Intelligence 1939–1945*, Hamish Hamilton, 1978

Colin Latham and Anne Stobbs, *Radar: A Wartime Miracle*, Sutton Publishing, 1996

Brian Lett, *SOE's Mastermind*, Pen & Sword, 2011

George Millar, *The Bruneval Raid: Flashpoint of the Radar War*, Bodley Head, 1974

Alan Millet and Nicolas Bucourt, *Raid de Bruneval et de La Poterie-Cap-d'Antifer*, Heimdal, 2012

Maurice Newnham, *Prelude to Glory: The Story of the Creation of Britain's Parachute Army*, Sampson Low, Marston & Co., 1948

Paul Oldfield, *Bruneval*, Pen & Sword, 2013

Lt-Col. T. B. Otway, *Airborne Forces of the Second World War 1939–45* (1951), Naval & Military Press, 2019

Alfred Price, *Instruments of Darkness: The History of Electronic Warfare, 1939–1945*, William Kimber, 1967

David Pritchard, *The Radar War: Germany's Pioneering Achievement 1904–45*, HarperCollins, 1989

Remy, *Memoirs of a Secret Agent of Free France*, McGraw-Hill, 1948

Andrew Roberts, *Churchill: Walking With Destiny*, Allen Lane, 2018

A. P. Rowe, *One Story of Radar: An Account of the Work of the Telecommunications Research Establishment* (1948), Cambridge University Press

Hilary St George Saunders, *The Red Beret*, Beacon Odhams, 1958

Hilary St George Saunders, *The Green Beret: The Story of the Commandos 1940–1945*, Michael Joseph, 1950

Tom Shachtman, *Laboratory Warriors: How Allied Science and Technology Tipped the Balance in World War II*, Harper Perennial, 2003

Tony Spooner, *Warburton's War: The Life of Wing Commander Adrian Warburton, DSO, DFC*, William Kimber, 1987

Rick Stroud, *The Phantom Army of Alamein: How Operation Bertram and the Camouflage Unit Hoodwinked Rommel*, Bloomsbury, 2012

Martin Sugarman, *Fighting Back: British Jewry's Military Contribution in the Second World War*, Valentine Mitchell & Co., 2010

Peter Wilkinson and Joan Bright Astley, *Gubbins & SOE*, Leo Cooper, 1993

Index

Ringway demonstration
(1941), 147–9
Singapore, fall of (1942), 178
SOE, founding of (1940), 14,
38
Special Service, founding of
(1940), 26–7, 28, 30
TRE, threat to and moving of,
333–4, 336
War Rooms, 179, 309–12, 314
WINDOW plan, 322, 324, 342
Clarke, Dudley Wrangel, xxiii–
xxiv, 24–36, 103, 174
Clements, Percy, 70, 96, 353
Cockburn, Robert, 133
Cockfosters Camp, 316–20
Coles, Lieutenant, 326
Cologne, Germany, 114
Colpitts oscillator, 323
Colt automatic handguns, 5
Combined Operations
Keyes' resignation (1941),
139–40
Operation Biting (1942), 175,
204, 207, 209, 215, 310–11
Operation Colossus (1941),
12, 17, 42, 99–100, 103
Pilotage Parties (COPP),
344–5
Tilshead airbase, 215
'Come Sit By My Side If You
Love Me', 240–41
Commandos, 27–30
Companion of the Most
Honourable order of the
Bath, 325
concentration camps, 143, 167,
196, 328, 355
Confrérie Notre-Dame, 189–201,
218, 220, 227, 328, 329–33,
350
Cook, Frederick Norton
planning of Operation Biting,
173–7
training at Loch Fyne, 204,
207
rehearsal on Solent, 226
observation of beach shelf,
231–2
crossing of Channel, 233, 258
encounter with German
vessels, 279–80
C Company reaches beach;
SOS signal received, 288,
291, 294–5

extraction of C Company, 296
distress signal from stranded
troops, 302
arrival of RAF air-cover,
305–6
sends signal to Mountbatten,
307
Reuters report on operation,
307
awarded DSC, 326
return to Australia, 358
Cornell, George, 303, 354–5
Cotton, F. Sidney, 113–15, 117
Coventry, West Midlands, 135
Cox, Charles William 'Bill', 359
recruitment, 212–18
takes leave, 222–3
briefed by Preist and Jones,
223–5
rehearsal on Solent, 226
weather delays operation, 230
launch of operation, 236
flight across Channel, 239–40
jump into Bruneval, 253
stealing of Würzburg, 261
called to Château Gosset, 268
inspects Würzburg, 269–71
dismantling and removal of
Würzburg components,
272–3, 274
demolition of Würzburg
installation, 278
Germans re-take Château
Gosset, 284
guards Würzburg loot, 284–5
escape to beach, 289
wait for Tormentor flotilla, 292
arrival of Tormentor flotilla,
295
extraction by Tormentor
flotilla, 297–8, 300–301
return to Wisbech, 309, 312
awarded Military Medal, 325
Crash Boats, 29, 30–31
Crete, 140
Cripps, Stafford, 347–9
Croix de Guerre, 191, 326, 345
Curlew, HMS, 173, 177
Curran, Joan, 337
Curzon Cinema, 141
Czechoslovakia, 75

D-Day (1944), xxi–ii, 175, 313,
336, 345–7, 353
Dalton, Hugh, 38

Daly, Gerald Francis, 62, 71–2,
81–2, 89, 95–6, 354
Dambusters, 346
Danesfield House,
Buckinghamshire, 106, 109,
119, 171, 216–17, 328
Darwin, bombing of (1942), 223
Deane-Drummond, Anthony,
18–20, 74
preparations in Malta, 18–20,
22, 49, 50, 51
drop into Calitri, 52, 53,
55–62, 66
guards track to aqueduct, 72
detains station master, 76
identifies bridge as second
target, 76
demolition of bridge, 78–80
march to rendezvous point,
89–90, 95
escapes POW camp, 146, 352
Death Ray, 123
Deben river, 125
Defford, Worcestershire, 335
Denmark, 136–7, 337
Dennis, Sergeant, 8
Devon, England, 212
Dezimeter Telegraphie (DF), xx
dicing missions, 111–12, 116,
117, 119, 355
Dill, John, 26–7
Diplôme d'Honneur, 359
Distinguished Conduct Medal
(DCM), 357
Distinguished Flying Cross
(DFC), 3, 47, 112, 171
Distinguished Service Cross
(DSC), 326
Distinguished Service Medals
(DSMs), 326
Distinguished Service Order
(DSO), 3, 144, 145, 150,
170, 171, 326, 356
Dönitz, Karl, 330
Dorset, England, 120, 133, 135,
179, 221–2, 226, 298, 323,
333–4, 363, 365
Douglas C47 Dakota aircraft,
353
Dover, Kent, 207, 219
Dowding, Hugh 'Stuffy', 125
Drake, 163–4, 168, 227
Du Maurier, Daphne, 150
Dumont, Roger 'Pol', 194–201,
329, 332

382

Malvern Radar and Technology
History Society (MRATHS),
xxi–xxii, 361
Manchester bombers, 321
Marks & Spencer, 167, 241, 256,
290, 356, 359
Marlborough College, 19
Martin Model 167 medium
bomber, 46
Maryland bombers, 46–7, 96–7,
113
Mauser rifles, 268, 281
McCallum, Lance-Corporal, 303,
357
McIntyre, H., 266, 291, 302
McKenzie, Gregor, 264–7, 284,
285, 287, 325, 326, 357
Meccano, 318
Medmenham, Buckinghamshire,
105–13, 118, 119, 122, 139,
216
Melches, Hans, 201, 260
Mentions in Dispatches (MIDs),
326, 345
Messagero, Il, 145
Messerschmitt, 116, 306
Meyer, Hans Ferdinand, 131, 360
MI5, 137
MI6, 361
MI9, 34
Middleton-Stewart, Major, 145
*Milan Journal of Civil
Engineering*, 39–40, 43
Milch, Erhard, 126
Military Cross, 128, 325, 353,
357
Military Medal, 325–6
Military Office 9 (MO9), 27–30
Millar, George, 351
Ministry of Aircraft Production,
334
Ministry of Economic Warfare,
42
Mitterrand, François, 359
Monkton Coombe, Somerset,
160
Monte Vulture, Italy, 21, 49, 56,
61, 81, 96
Montevideo, Uruguay, 127–9
Montgomery, Bernard Law, 353
moon window, 36–7, 42, 156,
216, 230–31
Moosburg, Germany, 327
Morse code, 64, 209, 248, 289
Mosquito aircraft, 358

Most Secret War (Jones), 359
Motor Gun Boats (MGBs), 156,
233, 278–9, 298, 300, 301,
302
Mountbatten, Louis, 140–41
takes command of Combined
Operations, 140
planning of Operation Biting,
140–41, 153, 157
rehearsal on Solent, 175
War Cabinet approves
Operation Biting, 177–8
address on *Prinz Albert*,
210–11
interviews Nagel, 211, 242
weather delays operation, 229
launch of Operation Biting,
232, 235
receives signal from Cook,
307
Frost's debriefing, 310
Operation Chariot, 326
Mussolini, Benito, 52, 54, 84, 87,
193

Nagel, Jane Sabina, 359–60
Nagel, Morny, 209
Nagel, Muriel Phyllis, 359
Nagel, Peter, 208–11, 229, 235,
242, 263, 265, 267, 270,
326–7, 359–60
Naples, Italy, 146
Nastri, Nicol, 73–5
Naumoff, Peter, 167, 227, 274–5
Nazi Hunters, The (Lewis), 352
necklace charges, 77
Nelson, 163–4, 227
Nelson, Horatio, 13, 231, 258
Netherlands, 75, 337, 352
New Orleans, Louisiana, 174
Niven, David, 27–8
Noah, *see* Preist, Donald
Nobby, HMS, 174
Norman, Henry Nigel St Valery,
358
Operation Biting (1942), 140,
141, 148–9, 153–4, 170,
172, 222, 231, 235
Operation Colossus (1941),
33, 63, 87, 97, 98
Operation Torch (1942), 358
Normandie, 126
Norse mythology, 134
North Africa, 21, 29, 177, 203,
352, 353

Oudna airfield raid (1942),
355–6
Operation Abeam (1940),
34–5
Operation Squatter (1941), 36
Norway, 8, 28, 75, 127, 129, 203,
219
Norwegian campaign (1940), 99,
171
nuclear weapons, 343, 347, 348

oblique aerial photography,
111–12, 120, 136
observation balloons, 159–62,
215
Ofanto river, 58, 72
Olaf V, King of Norway, 8–9
Olympic Games, 150
Omaha Beach, xxii, 175
Oman, 352
Operation Abeam (1940), 34–5
Operation Biting (1942), xxi,
xxii, 152–313, 350, 351,
354–5
training at Salisbury Plain,
158–78
dummy drops, 172
Norman and Pickard's recce
mission, 172
recruitment of HMS
Tormentor, 175–7
War Cabinet approval, 177
recruitment of Preist, 183–8
Confrérie Notre-Dame recce
mission, 189–201
training at Loch Fyne, 202–3,
204–12, 221
recruitment of Nagel, 208–11
Mountbatten's address on
Prinz Albert, 210–11
recruitment of Cox, 212–18
training at Salisbury Plain,
215–18
news of Channel Dash,
218–20
publicity plans made, 220–21
rehearsals at Lulworth, 221–2
briefing of Cox and Vernon,
223–5
rehearsal on Solent, 226–7
final briefing, 227–8
weather delays operation,
229–30
Cook's observation of beach
shelf, 231–2

Malvern Radar and Technology History Society (MRATHS)

MRATHS celebrates the extraordinary history during World War II and since of scientific research in Malvern, UK. Founded in 2012, our aim is to ensure that this history is nationally known and celebrated.

In 1942 the TRE boffins from the South Coast were evacuated with 30 days' notice to Malvern, Worcestershire. The impact they had on the outcome of WWII, the Cold War and civil technology was huge. They helped defeat the German U-Boats in the Battle of the Atlantic and save the country from starvation. Their radars and ground-based navigation systems dramatically improved the bombing accuracy of our heavy bombers. They made D-Day a success by using radio decoys to deceive the enemy about our landing sites and to protect the troops from enemy aircraft using radar ships anchored off shore.

In the Cold War they led the technical modernization of our air defence systems, which is where civil air traffic control originated, and invented new communications systems including the world's first geo-synchronous communication satellite.

The long list of technology from Malvern surprises many: the first idea of an integrated circuit; the signal processors found in TVs and mobile phones; PIR (heat) detectors; heat cameras that allow firefighters to see in the dark and through smoke; LCD displays used in colour TVs, laptops, e-Book readers and small appliances such as clocks; X-ray detectors leading to the development of hospital CT scanners for accurate diagnosis; radars for weather forecasting; and radio astronomy.

MRATHS, with the support of QinetiQ, saved the historic archive which tells these stories.

Using this unique set of documents and objects, we tell the stories to the public of Malvern's science heritage and the people behind it through exhibitions and talks. We visit schools and support science teachers by telling students about inventions from Malvern and doing experiments with heat cameras and radars. We collect memories of employees and their families which bring a rich understanding to the origins of world-changing inventions.

MRATHS is a charity, and is presently raising funds to open a Science History Centre in Malvern, both to house our unique collection of artefacts and to open to the public as an interactive centre to tell the stories about the people and the science behind the many world-changing ideas. The vision for this centre is: 'To inspire the next generation of scientists and engineers by telling the extraordinary story of Malvern's scientific heritage.'

Please visit www.mraths.org.uk to find out more about us and learn how you can help us achieve our ambition.

Blind Veterans UK

Blind Veterans UK helps ex-Servicemen and women of every generation rebuild their lives after sight loss. It has provided rehabilitation, training, practical advice and emotional support to over 35,000 veterans since being formed in 1915.

The charity now supports more veterans than ever before, ranging from those who served in the Second World War and on National Service and have lost their sight through age-related conditions to those injured in Iraq, Afghanistan and other military conflicts. Blind Veterans UK has training and rehabilitation centres in Brighton and Llandudno that provide training, respite and residential care as well as recreational facilities and also provides services and support across the UK via a network of community teams.

It was established by Sir Arthur Pearson, founder of the *Daily Express* in response to blinded soldiers returning from the Front during the First World War. Having lost his own sight through glaucoma, Pearson was determined that they should have the training and rehabilitation to allow them to live independent and productive lives.

The same work continues today, and while originally formed to help those who lost their sight on active service, it is now open to veterans no matter what the cause of their sight loss, or the length of their service. To find out more about the work it does visit blindveterans.org.uk